The Stretchford Chronicles

The Stretchford Chronicles

25 Years of Peter Simple

*Extracts from the Way of the World
column of The Daily Telegraph*

Selected by Michael Wharton

Illustrated by ffolkes

M

Prefatory Note

The "Way of the World" Column first appeared on October 18, 1955, over the pseudonym "Yorick". But as other journalistic "Yoricks" made their existence known, this pseudonym soon had to be dropped in favour of "Peter Simple", which has been used ever since.

Since the Column began (it now runs to more than 4 million words), nine volumes of selections from it have been published at intervals, the last one, "Peter Simple's Way of the World", including material up to the summer of 1977.

This book is a selection (or distillation) of what I hope are the best and most representative items in these collections, together with additional items covering the period from 1977 to 1980.

The items—whether declamatory, satirical, fantastic, nostalgic or nonsensical—appear in roughly chronological order, year by year, without further arrangement.

Michael Wharton

Copyright © The Daily Telegraph 1980

ISBN 0 333 32381 5

First published 1980 by the Daily Telegraph Ltd
Reprinted 1981

First published 1981 by
PAPERMAC
A division of Macmillan Publishers Limited
London and Basingstoke

Associated companies in Auckland, Dallas, Delhi, Dublin, Hong Kong, Johannesburg, Lagos, Manzini, Melbourne, Nairobi, New York, Singapore, Tokyo, Washington and Zaria

Designed by Robert Wheeler

Printed in Great Britain by
Redwood Burn Limited
Trowbridge

Contents

Introduction

Monday morning—I write this on a particularly foul one in midsummer—is proverbially the low-water-mark of the week. For me and countless others it takes a further downward shove from being a Peter-Simple-less day as well. But then, Tuesday to Friday, breakfast-time becomes tolerable. I used to turn to the 'Way of the World' column before anything else in the three newspapers I took; now, with so little in other places worth more than a glance, I save it up for a heartener before I go about my business. Between works of literary criticism and books about drink, five volumes of selections from the column occupy an honoured place on my study shelves. With them I keep myself topped up, as it were, when the master is on one of his annoyingly frequent and prolonged holidays, or take an extra dose in the evening to hold back the onset of gloomy rage at the state of the nation.

I am not exaggerating what in some ways resembles a clinical dependence on a newspaper column. Whence comes this strange fascination? Well, for a start, we are shown into a recognisable world that is as rich and as original as almost any novelist's. All in all it is a pretty odd world, but even at its wildest it keeps offering sudden reflections of the one we inhabit. Peter Simple transforms hideous reality into something bearable. By his laughter and scorn, the dominant vices and follies of our age are made to look pathetically shabby. For the moment, it seems as if They can never win. The ability to produce that feeling is bound to exert a special appeal.

There is also the attraction of eloquent and versatile hatred. The roll-call merely starts with leftists and progressives of every shade; it goes on to anti-smokers, architects, planners, bureaucratic despoilers of the countryside (and ecologists too), birth-controllers and abortionists, pornographers, vivisectionists, multi-racialists, sociologists, actors and actresses, practitioners of experimental art, liberationists (of course), fluoridators, psychologists and D. H. Lawrence. But the main enemy, the ultimate heresiarch, is the adherent of what has been called scientism, the man who believes that, given the necessary research and the necessary experiments, every problem in the universe will eventually be solved. Woe to such unthinking optimism!

So far one can readily and gleefully follow. But it very soon emerges that a great deal of what has been built into the face of Britain (I can almost hear a roar of horror at that last phrase) is no less to be reprobated: cars and motorways, power-pylons and power-stations, aeroplanes and airports, anything and everything to do with television. Now words may in the end turn a leftist from his errant path; they will never move a single square yard of concrete. Granted, but in Peter Simple's own words, 'What decent man ever refused to fight for a good cause because he knew it was a lost one?'

This is more than Luddism. We are likely to notice, next to a paragraph defending a threatened grouse-moor or part of the Lake District, a stern reminder that the present régimes in South Africa or Chile, however repressive, are immeasurably less so than what in each case is likely to supplant them. Here we have a personage of stout principle, one who swims against the stream much more persistently than some who have built a reputation on seeming to do so. But he never does it out of perversity and he never loses the ability to laugh at himself.

Perhaps I have suggested that the spirit of Peter Simple is a purely destructive one. Readers of the column will know better. Some of the most effective pieces are unfashionably direct assertions of positive belief; the one that discusses the picketing of York Minster, for example, shows a combination of gravity and directness generally missing from English prose for a century or more, since the days when responsible people were not afraid of words like 'good' and 'evil'.

But let us not forget that we are talking about some of the funniest writing of our time. Just to mention any of those recurring institutions or characters will set the initiated grinning: *Doreen Bronte: The Formative Years,* by Julian Birdbath, St Bogwena's Hospital—Nurse Grimgerda Craggs in attendance, Clare Howitzer and her terrifying postbag from the lovelorn, the Stretchford Municipal Symphony Orchestra (cond. Sir Jim Gastropodi), Det-Sgt—or is it PC?—E.S. (?) Mackenzie of fluctuating age, star of Nerdley Special Branch . . . ('O' level question on the works of Peter Simple: Say why you would locate a given person or thing in Stretchford rather than in Nerdley and vice versa.)

Some such pieces are so hilarious that their far from hilarious moral or political content is almost overpowered. Now and then absurdity is exalted into a kind of poetry. I shall never forget the scene where Ron Fussell, the brilliant GPI Television producer, discusses his controversial film about Mozart—'as he spoke he danced brilliantly up and down, occasionally hacking at the furniture with an axe or setting his desk on fire in a frenzy of compassionate hatred.' This is new ground; I know of nothing like it anywhere.

This book is a treasure-house of truth, fantasy and wit. It commemorates twenty-five years of extraordinary and very gifted work, and will I hope be as shiningly successful as it deserves to be.

Kingsley Amis

THE FIFTIES

1955-57

True blue

A hundred years ago died Colonel Charles Waldo Sibthrop, Lincolnshire landowner and for nearly 30 years M.P. for Lincoln. His centenary has passed with little fuss—no statue unveiled at Lincoln, no centenary edition of his speeches; no mass rallies or memorial pilgrimages to his tomb. Yet in his way Sibthorp deserves all these things.

He was a diehard Conservative with more than the courage of his convictions. Like many people at the time, he heartily detested what was then—and, in some circles, still is called Progress; unlike many people, however, he took every opportunity of saying so, in the most forthright manner.

He attacked indefatigably industrialism, the factory system, railways and Free Trade. He attacked the principle of centralisation and of State interference with people and property—in short, all those measures by which in the 1839s and '40s the foundations of our Welfare State were being laid.

He was an eccentric man, of course. He wore old-fashioned clothes of tawdry magnificence; he had the reputation of a great gambler, wine-bibber and libertine.

He hated foreigners, Catholics, the Prince Consort and the Crystal Palace. His Parliamentary manners were often deplorable —though it is true that his habit of crowing like a cock when bored by Manchester radicals might well be equally effective to-day.

To his contemporaries he was a figure of fun, but, as things have turned out, he is not quite so ridiculous to-day. By the time his second centenary comes round he may well be even less ridiculous.

If by that time there is any space on this planet not wanted for military installations, laboratories, rocket-launching sites and police barracks, the people of 2055 (if there are any) may think of putting up a statue to the Colonel at last.

If people had only listened to him at the time . . .

Babes in the bath

You may see Socialism as a great road, stretching to infinity across a barren, waterless waste. Along it trudge half the peoples of the world, bowed, manacled, parched, exhausted. By the verges lie the gaunt wrecks of crashed and burnt-out nations; and skeletons picked clean by vultures and bleached by a pitiless sun.

Appalled by the prospect before them, certain Socialists, fainter in heart or stronger in head than the rest, have hesitated, halted or even turned back. These are now rebuked by Prof. G. D. H. Cole, who still steps stoutly ahead, undeterred, undeterrable, invincibly blind and cheerful.

Be of good courage, he bids his wavering comrades. "Much has been done badly amiss in the Soviet Union," he concedes, but the Soviet worker enjoys "in most matters . . . an immensely enlarged freedom." To throw away Socialism because it can be "perverted" to serve totalitarian ends is "to throw out the baby with the dirty bath-water."

This is familiar and most manifest nonsense. What has gone "amiss" in Socialist countries is no mere chance disfigurement, like a false moustache scrawled by a madman on a masterpiece. It is Socialism itself, taken to its logical conclusion.

The death of freedom, the enslavement of the masses, the withering of art and culture, the restless, ruthless hunt for scapegoats, the aggressive *folie de grandeur* of Socialist dictators —these are no mere "perversions" of Socialism. They are Socialism unperverted, an integral and predictable part of any truly Socialist system.

We are not faced here with so much dirty bath-water surrounding a perfectly healthy, wholesome Socialist baby. The dirty bathwater *is* Socialism, and the baby was drowned in it at birth.

Dylan as I knew him

By Ronald Dace

"Lend me another ninepence and make it up to seven-and-six—lovely, pocket-splitting, beer-belching, girl-giggling seven-and-six." Dylan didn't seem to be addressing anyone in particular, but I am proud to say I was the first to get my hand to my pocket.

I shall never forget that first meeting in the "Bag of Nails" in

1937. Dylan Thomas was in tremendous form, as he drank pint after pint and told us wonderful, revolting stories of Welsh life, full of lechery and vomit.

By the end of the evening I had managed to lend him £12 15s. 3d., had suggested he should take my girl-friend to Brighton for the week-end, and had had one-and-a-half pints of beer (I counted them carefully) spilled over my new tweed suit.

I still have that sacred beer-stained suit. I have treasured it, unworn and uncleaned, ever since.

During the wonderful weeks that followed I haunted the "Bag of Nails." Every now and then, to my disgust, Dylan would disappear and write poetry. I grudged every moment of the time when he wasn't borrowing my money, taking my girl-friends away from me, or pouring beer or worse down my neck.

I don't want to boast. But I honestly believe I had more of these attentions from him than anybody.

Vividly I remember the last time I met the Swansea genius. "Look what the great, black, yellow-blinking, whisker-twitching nightmare-tomcat has brought in," yelled Dylan as I entered the pub one evening. He promptly spilled a glass of light ale down my neck.

"Go on, Dylan," I murmured. I was loving every minute.

"All right, I will. Why don't you go and take a seagull-screaming, tram-ticket-swallowing, split-and-bandaged coffin-black running jump at yourself, and leave me alone?"

These words of purest poetry, the last Dylan ever spoke to me, are graven on my heart for ever. That is why I have been talking, thinking and writing about him ever since.

Sophistry

"We do not talk about the tastes of the mob; we talk about what ordinary people like. What some regard as the herd, we regard as the human family."

These noble words were spoken by Sir Robert Fraser, Director-General of the I.T.A. The Greeks called this sort of statement "making the worse cause appear the better"—in other words, Sophistry.

You know that people are being fed, day in and day out, on a diet of paper and shadows, a thin and wretched soup of clichés and stereotypes, boiled up from the sweepings of the human mind. So you tell them it is wholesome, nourishing food, plain perhaps, but to the taste of all ordinary people.

You know that people are being taught to live in a half-dead world where advertisements have taken the place of art and entertainment; that they are being encouraged to hate and despise taste and intelligence, the love of beauty and the sense of order.

So you tell them they are the human family, ordinary decent low-brow people, laughing to scorn, with great roars of wholesome laughter from their warm, loving human hearts, the desiccated highbrow, with his dead books and paintings, for ever lecturing them in high-pitched tones about the values and standards of civilisation.

Honest prejudice

Should women be allowed to conduct church services and preach? How Dr. Johnson would have rolled and roared at the prospect!

Yet the Archdeacon of Portsmouth was not alone in Convocation in urging it on; he slighted opposition to it as "partly emotional."

So it is, no doubt; but not the more to be despised for that. Bogus reasoning nowadays bombards us all with the most absurd propositions: that all races are equal, that women can do anything men do and vice versa, and so forth. Manifest nonsense, of course; yet reasoning of this kind speaks with such a loud voice, and buttresses its arguments with such an imposing array of facts and statistics, that even clergymen (who should know better) are rattled.

The ideal answer to faulty reasoning is correct reasoning. But how many of us have the equipment handy?

It is just here that emotion, which includes prejudice and a sense of the ridiculous, comes to our aid.

Faulty reasoning builds its gimcrack palaces; a gust of laughter will blow them flat. Faulty reasoning undermines all we hold dear: prejudice will halt it.

"Prejudice," wrote Taine, "is a sort of reason operating unconsciously. It has claims as well as reason, but it is unable to advance them. . . . It issues from a long accumulation of experiences."

Don't worry when you have nothing to set against a stream of what passes for reasoning except prejudice and a conviction that it is all twaddle. Stand firm—and win!

Dreams

"No one must dream of going back to the world of counts, bankers and capitalists." Thus sternly one of Hungary's non-Communist leaders during the country's brief and tragic false dawn.

Well, dreams are free; and, were I a Hungarian, I would dream of little else.

When the haughty count's game-preserves were inviolate, I would muse, my own little plot was respected. When the banker was free to make his pile, I and mine had enough to eat. When the capitalist rode safely through Budapest, supercilious in his Mercedes, I too could venture forth without fear.

Proud, cruel and grasping these men may all have been, and little loved in consequence. But how could I forget that when they went my country's happiness went with them?

Whitehall cavalry

The equality between police and citizen, Mr. Mikardo tells us, is destroyed when the policeman is put on a horse. This is a psychological error, the sage continues: "Crowds are like individuals, even like Prime Ministers—they are most likely to lose their heads when they are scared."

What Mr. Mikardo really wants, of course, is mobs on horseback and police on foot. This, however, might scare the police and cause *them* to lose their heads.

Even if police and mob are both mounted, or both on foot, the exact equality desired by Mr. Mikardo still eludes us. The police are still pre-eminent in height, strength, dignity of appearance and, above all, in the power to arrest those who displease them.

All this must be changed. Policemen must in future be small, weedy, furtive men, dressed in ill-fitting and unobtrusive rags and with a damp cigarette-end drooping permanently from the lower lip.

The power of arrest must be either abolished or made universal. Not till a mob has actually arrested a policeman for creating a disturbance can Mr. Mikardo's sword sleep in his hand.

Flat-earthers

Among the objectives of our landing at Suez is a desire "to make plans for the economic development of the area [the Middle East], to redress some of the great inequalities of wealth which now pervade it." This I learn from Mr. Selwyn Lloyd who ought—I suppose—to know.

It is certainly an inspiring thought for our troops that immediately in their train follows a support corps of planners, statisticians, Socialists, applied economists, sociology dons, income-tax inspectors, accountants and groundnutters of every description.

Less inspiring, perhaps, for the poor Egyptians.

What naïve crowds were those at Port Fuad, which goggled peacefully as the paratroops floated down upon them. If they had known what was yet to come, they would have fought like wildcats.

A new poet

The Burst Hot Water Bottle.
    By Eric Lard. Introduction by Colin and Angus Wilson. (Foot and Mouth Press, 8s 6d.)

There are a number of angry young men about nowadays, and once the commercial possibilities of professional anger are widely realised I imagine there will be many more. These people are angry because they have no money, because they aren't enjoying themselves, because the world is in a mess and they can't do anything about it.

Here is a new poet, Eric Lard, who seems to be angrier than any of the others so far. He is angry not only for the reasons mentioned above, but for a new reason—he is angry because the others thought of it first.

Eric Lard's command of language is slight, his imagination feeble. But he is extremely angry. In poem after poem he lashes out, yelling and screaming with fury.

In the long title-poem of this volume, "The Burst Hot Water Bottle," he uses commonplace domestic imagery to produce a cumulative effect of frustration, so that the final lines, where he is left staring at the ruins of the hot water bottle he has deliberately burst, provide a memorable image of a whole world in ruins.

Apart from being angry, Eric Lard has other claims to distinction. He was born in Birmingham in 1934, was evacuated to St. Helens during the war and later went to Reading University. He has never been abroad, is unmarried, and has an intense dislike of good-looking women, wine, flowers, music, art and the countryside.

His favourite dish is dried egg omelette with tinned mashed potatoes. He works in the registered letter department of a Croydon sub-post office. He is not interested in politics but thinks England is finished. He is still wearing the same clothes he wore when he was evacuated in 1939 and, in spite of success, says he intends to go on wearing them.

It is worth noting that the introduction by Colin and Angus Wilson also appears in a new anthology, "The Oxford Book of Introductions," edited, with introduction, by Angus Wilson. It is being dramatised for the Third Programme.

Send for Nidgett

The key post of labour relations chief for the National Coal Board is now vacant. No doubt Lord Mills will be considering the claims of one obvious candidate for the job—General Sir Frederick Nidgett, known throughout the Royal Army Tailoring Corps as "Tiger" Nidgett.

General Nidgett was G.O.C. London and North Eastern Command from 1939 to 1945. Since then he has given ungrudging service in many departments of the national life.

To mention only a few of his assignments—he has been a Governor of the B.B.C., a director of a great industrial molybdenum combine, Director of Retrospective Planning to the Control Commission in Germany, and the Chairman of the 1948 Working Party on the Pottery Gnomes Industry. He has been Chairman of the Chicory Marketing Board (£8,000 a year), President of the Commission of Inquiry into railway refreshment facilities (£11,000 a year) and Vice-Chancellor of Retford University (£900 a year).

When I called on the Nidgetts at their Surrey home, I found Lady Nidgett busy packing. The General's pink boyish face creased in a smile and his pale blue eyes twinkled.

"Yes," he said, "it looks as if it's going to be up-sticks-and-away for us once again. Of course, it's early days yet, and the whole thing's a bit cloak-and-dagger. But, after all, there are quite a number of jobs I haven't had yet. As far as I can remember, this Coal Board show seems to be one of them.

"No, I don't know anything about coal, or labour relations. I leave all that sort of thing to the boys in the back room. Given good will, and a friendly chat round a good type of table, there's no industrial problem we can't settle. Always remember this—the main thing is to give Jerry a good kick in the pants wherever you may find him—"

A look of confusion, even of panic, seemed to come over the General's face for a moment. He recovered himself, however, as I left.

"Goodbye and good hunting. And jolly good luck to you whoever you may be."

Welfare doll

After the success of "Baby Doll" it was obviously only a question of time before the British Film Industry tackled the same agonising theme. "Welfare Doll" (Melodeon, Leicester Square) is the result.

In England, of course, the Deep South is not in the south at all, but in one of those Midland counties which are sodden and unkind. On the edge of the new housing estate a few decaying caravans and old bus bodies, gradually settling in the mud and litter, look forlornly out across the concrete posts and wire to the squatters' huts on the derelict airfield.

Here, in the most decayed of all the caravans, live a repulsive elderly couple, Stanley and Doris Gloater. They have not been on speaking terms since the failure of their budgerigar-breeding business 20 years before.

Their caravan is divided into two parts by a thin matchwood partition. Doris Gloater occupies the part with the television set. Stanley Gloater, unknown to his wife, has bored a hole in the partition, and through this he is able to watch a small section of the television screen.

Such items as "Spotlight on Smoke Abatement" and "Britain's Canning Industry" throw him into a state of almost uncontrollable excitement, and his shouts of anger and frustration disturb the whole neighbourhood.

So the Gloaters live apart, in a state of total deadlock, occasionally sleeping or eating meals of potato crisps, tomato sauce and individual fruit pies. It seems that only death can break up the pattern of their lives. . . .

One day a newcomer takes over a neighbouring derelict tram—Idris Boocock, 55-year-old Welshman from Canvey Island, successful budgie-breeder and man of the world.

He comes into Doris Gloater's life like a breath from the birdcages she has loved. What follows has a tragic inevitability. Stanley Gloater, mad with jealousy at the sight of Doris and Idris watching television together, deliberately uncages Boocock's budgies, symbols of the happiness he envies, and tries to push his tram into the River Trent.

There is a breathless chase round the housing estate before Stanley is led off to the Old Folk's Sunset Home at Retford, leaving Doris and Idris to watch the television in peace.

"Welfare Doll" is a film which has all the tender insight, the unearthly sympathy with the vanquished, which distinguished "Baby Doll". More: it is rooted in the very soil of modern England which we love so much.

Nidgett again

Versatile General Sir Frederick ("Tiger") Nidgett, of the Royal Army Tailoring Corps, is somewhat surprised, but by no means dismayed, by the news that he has not been made Labour Relations Officer to the National Coal Board after all.

Lady Nidgett was still packing from force of habit when I called at their Surrey home yesterday. I found the General in his study drinking light ale.

"Good morning to you. Sit you down," he said genially. "Matter of fact, I'm filling in time working on my autobiography till the next job comes along."

The General told me his publishers, Viper and Bugloss, had already paid him an advance of £25,000 on his book, which is to be called "Up Sticks and Away".

He seemed disinclined to say much about the actual contents of the book, however. Looking round, I noticed a meagre, dull-eyed and frightened little man in spectacles busily writing away in a corner.

"I think the publishers must have boobed badly somewhere," said the General. "They said they'd got me a first-class history don from Oxford to do the actual writing. He turned up just once, drank up most of my vino, and then sent this deputy ghost-chap in his place.

"He says his name's Julian Birdbath, and that he's written more than 70 books, but my lady wife, who goes in for literary wallahs, says she's never heard of him. Still, I suppose it'll all come out in the wash."

"Excuse me, sir," said Birdbath timidly. "This part about the Duke of Cumberland's visit to the Tailoring Corps Depot in 1943—"

"Now look here," said the General, and it was impressive to see the commander and man of decision emerge suddenly from the boyish, easy-going figure in the armchair. "Look here, Birdbath, remember what I told you about the chain of command, and stop dithering about like a wet hen.

"The man at the top has simply got to be able to leave the details to the staff chaps lower down." He turned to me impulsively. "Remember, the great thing is to hit the Hun for six wherever you may find him, and keep on hitting him good and hard. Good-bye, and cracking good luck to you all."

Memories of yore

Sir—I wonder whether the Dadshaw Gang, a bandit tribe now reported to be terrorising parts of South-Eastern Persia, are the same as the Dadshaws I used to know in the West Riding over 30 years ago?

Jonas Dadshaw and his wife Muriel were often to be met with at whist-drives and spelling-bees in the Bradford area in those far-off days, and I believe they won the Ormondroyd Cup for the best piece of raffia work three years running.

Mr. Dadshaw was full of ideas, and in many ways in advance of his time. One of his plans, I remember, was a new reversible time-table. "Dadshaw's Railway Guide."

But he never got over his disappointment when Alderman Foodbotham, then Chairman of the Bradford City Tramways Committee, turned down his plan to put potted plants on the upper decks of the trams.

I lost touch with the Dadshaws soon after that. But perhaps in the bitterness of their hearts they decided to emigrate to Persia, then regarded as something of an El Dorado by the go-ahead Yorkshire folk.

Can any of your readers enlighten me?

Yours, &c.,
EDITH GRAMPUS.
Ilkley.

The pursuit of space

There are little phrases which give one no rest. Symbolising precisely the inner futility of the age in which we live, they go on clanging and re-echoing maddeningly in the mind like so many cracked, tinny bells.

"*Social engineering,*" for instance: this embodies the pathetic fallacy, productive of so much human misery, that society is a sort of machine, working to known rules, to be controlled and regulated, repaired and improved by "experts," "planners" and other vain or malignant fidgets.

"*The pursuit of happiness*": a phrase none the less absurd for its long history, ignoring as it does the fact that happiness is never caught by those who pursue it, but comes only to those who stumble on it in the faithful performance of duties and obligations.

As grotesque as any, "*the conquest of space*": here we find enshrined the idea that man is doomed perpetually to be at total war with his environment, conquering or being conquered. No one asks what we are to do with space once we have conquered it. We are to conquer it for conquest's sake, spurred on by a reckless, unreflecting and all-consuming restlessness.

Social engineering, the pursuit of happiness, the conquest of space—this is the sort of rubbish which drums in the ears of Gadarene man and makes him deaf to warning.

Battles long ago

Sir—As the grandson of the Alderman Foodbotham referred to in your column, I cannot, in fairness to his memory, allow Miss Grampus's letter to go unanswered.

There are two sides to every question—a right side and a wrong side. My grandfather has often told me how, all through that blazing summer of 1925, Mr. and Mrs. Dadshaw persistently lobbied the Bradford City Tramways Committee.

Their proposals for the trams went far beyond the mere provision of potted palms for the upper decks. They envisaged hanging gardens of exotic design, a chamber orchestra, military whist-drives, and on Saturdays, after football matches, an Oriental slave-market with firework displays and processions of dwarfs and houris.

To my grandfather, his trams were a sacred trust. Rightly or wrongly, he believed that although this sort of thing might suit the public transport system of Shiraz or Ispahan, there was no place for it in Bradford.

If the Dadshaws, on their arrival in Persia, found it necessary to turn bandit, as Miss Grampus suggests, then it looks as if the Persian tramway authorities did not take to their ideas either.

However, let bygones be bygones.

Your truly,
MOSTYN FOODBOTHAM
Cleckheaton.

Nidgett in harness

The news of Gen. Sir Frederick Nidgett's appointment as Supreme Commander of the Expeditionary Forces which are to operate against the Imam of Todi sent me post haste to the "Tiger's" secret H.Q. I found him, as expected, calm and confident at the hub of a positive atomic mushroom of activity.

"Yes," he said, "it will be good to get back into harness again for a spell of real soldiering. Mind you, Operation 'Backache' is going to be no picnic. I shall not move until I have adequate forces at my disposal.

"So far the War House has agreed to mobilise the entire Home Forces, and they have ordered reservists to stand ready for recall to the colours. Troop-carriers have been shuttling men from Cyprus, Singapore, British Guiana and what have you to this country and back again for re-documentation and redeployment.

"All this makes a start. But we're not going to walk before we can run. Once bitten twice shy."

News from Todi itself continues to be meagre. It will be recalled that trouble broke out in this obscure and totally arid sheikhdom (population about 260, with large elements of goats and donkeys) when the 85-year-old, cantankerous, pleasure-loving Imam announced that a jehad (or holy war) would be declared unless oil was discovered in his domains forthwith.

The Imam's effective armed forces consist of the 35-strong Syrian-trained Todi Scouts, who are equipped with muzzle-loading arquebuses. It is thought, however, that arms are being smuggled from the Bojd over the rugged Jebel Snakhbar. Clearly Britain could not in these circumstances stand idly by.

As Gen. Nidgett told me: "Our chaps are all in great heart, fighting fit, rarin' to go, and mad keen to have a crack at the enemy. The object of the exercise, as I see it, is to hit"—here he consulted his notes—"to hit the Imam of Todi for six wherever we may find him—and whoever he may be."

Nidgett of Arabia

I have just seen a copy of a leaflet prepared by Capt. J. Birdbath, of the Psychological Warfare Branch of Gen. Nidgett's headquarters. Seven million copies have already been dropped on the territory of the Imam of Todi.

Capt. Birdbath, a noted lecturer and Arabist in civil life, believes he has found the answer to criticisms that our propaganda is out of date and that we have lost touch with the Arabs of to-day. A rough translation of the leaflet reads:

"Sons of the Desert! Hearken to the voice of Gen. Sir Frederick Nidgett, G.C.V.O., T.D., Terror of the Universe, before whom the waves of the sea retire and the stars of heaven bow down! Though he come with an irresistible host, attended by powerful djinns, Nidgett is your friend!

"The accursed Imam of Todi, grown old in evil, has betrayed you, and is even now preparing to hand over his dominions to the demons of Iblis, in return for a further supply of houris and false oil-share certificates.

"Drive out the infidel Imam and welcome Nidgett with wine and corn, with ivory and ebony and cedarwood, with gold and porphyry and with feasting and dancing and joyful shouts. And remember to hand in your flintlocks to the nearest Field Security Section.

"Fear not the magic birds which bring these messages. Like the giant roc of Socotra, which carried Sindbad of old, they are now in the service of the wise enchanter Nidgett. If you heed his words, they will do you no manner of harm. Tremble and obey."

"Yes," Gen. Nidgett told me yesterday, "Birdbath has done a magnificent job for this physiological warfare show. I'm recommending him for an M.B.E. We expect the leaflet will pull in Todi deserters right, left and centre. I've indented for 300,000 miles of barbed wire for prisoner-of-war cages and interrogation centres."

Nidgett victorious

As the minutes ticked away at "Nidgforce" H.Q. and N-Hour grew imminent, startling news arrived. A massive survey by reconnaissance planes, escorted by jet fighters and atomic bombers, had revealed that the 370 square miles of the Imam of Todi's territory were even more uninhabited than usual.

In fact there was nobody there at all. Goats could be seen browsing peacefully on the millions of leaflets dropped during the last few days as part of Gen. Nidgett's "softening-up" drive. The Imam and the whole population had evidently crossed the rugged Jebel Snakhbar during the night and taken refuge in the remote fastnesses of the Bojd.

In other words, "Operation backache" was off.

"Cracking good show," was Gen. Nidgett's command. "The object of the exercise, as I see it, was to get the Imam on the run. We've done just that. It's been a model police action, and it's proved that we still need the footslogger in this pushbutton age."

Norman the good

"The Monarchy," says the *New Statesman,* "is a part of the Civil Service." Yes, and the sooner it becomes so in fact as well as in theory, the better.

Happy those loyal subjects of the future who live in the reign of King Norman II, fourth of the House of Slough, and of kindly TV-loving Queen Doreen.

King Norman will be a model monarch. Beginning his working life as a postal sorter, he will have worked his way up through the local food and fuel offices, acquiring on his way an unrivalled collection of fountain-pens and propelling pencils, until he finally incorporates in his own person the mystique of Socialist monarchy.

His face, with the faces of Queen Doreen, Prince Barry and Princess Shirley, is familiar to all from a thousand official advertisements.

He is the first to switch off his electric fire at "peak periods". He never wastes water. He shops early for Christmas. He avoids public transport during rush hours. He promptly renews his TV and dog licences. Dutifully he invests his money in national savings certificates and dutifully he loses the lot.

How great the roar of cheering as he appears at the window of his council palace, file and date-stamp in hand, after the annual renewal of the regal permit, blue-suited, conscientious, smiling with egalitarian dentures.

Wake up, Britain!

Shouts Jack Moron

To-day the People of Britain are hopping mad. Men cannot look their wives and sweethearts in the face. Children eye their parents with mute reproach. Dogs and cats refuse their food.

Filled with shame and anger, we ask why a British space satellite, launched from British soil by British rockets, is not revolving round the earth to-day, transmitting British messages to Britain's people?

This wrong must be righted, and soon—or we, the British people, will want to know the reason why. Let us drop all other tasks, let us resolve neither to eat, drink nor sleep until Britain's flag flies in Outer Space. Here's what we can do to help.

Turf out the dreary pedagogues and dodos who still have the cheek to teach non-scientific subjects in our schools and universities. Let them make room for more space-engineers.

All churches, chapels, art galleries, museums, concert halls, private houses and other unessential buildings should be taken over as additional laboratories. Land now used for wasteful out-of-date farming should be taken over for launching sites. Animals, children and old people should be pressed into service. Women should be conscripted.

Maybe we can't afford a full-sized space satellite. But surely we can get some representative British object, some symbol of our way of life into an orbit round the earth immediately?

Wake up, Britain!

Atomic arcadia

After an accident yesterday at the atomic research station at Glumworth Abbey, a noted Barsetshire beauty spot, 300 square miles of country were heavily contaminated with radioactivity.

"There is absolutely no alarm in the district," said an Atomic Energy Authority spokesman: "All the farmers are absolutely delighted. They soon got used to the idea of pouring all their milk down the drains immediately after milking, and in cases where their livestock has had to be destroyed or their farmhouses pulled down, they have given cheerful co-operation."

"All my hair fell out yesterday," a typical Barsetshire farmer told me with a chuckle. "And, dang me, you should see old Grandad's wart—big as a house! 'Course we'm all tickled to death 'bout they three-headed calves and nekkid sheep."

"Aye, 'tes Progress, depend on it," said another farmer. "Just like what we read in the papers. Thanks to science, Man now has in his hands immeasurable powers for good or ill. It rests with Man how he uses these powers, whether he chooses to—"

At that moment a five-headed goat with eight legs ran at him from behind and butted him into a radioactive pond. Shortly afterwards a busload of scientists arrived and announced that the village was to be demolished and the inhabitants removed for experimental decontamination under laboratory conditions.

And everyone suddenly burst out singing.

1958

Cultprop

Mr. Malik, the Soviet Ambassador, thinks the present "cultural exchanges" between our two countries "totally inadequate" and wants them to be put on "a firm, permanent basis."

"Cultural exchanges" is one of those repulsive phrases which are

continually on the lips of Communists and of those who have been
infected by their jargon. It belongs to a world where people cannot
enjoy each other's art, or exchange ideas, or even play each other at
football, except under the supervision of officials.

There are people still living who can remember a Europe—and it
included Russia—where art meant joy and freedom, not political
propaganda, and where, since there was still a living culture,
heedless of frontiers, to be exchanged, "cultural exchanges" were
yet unknown.

Young England

Pupils at Bog Lane Secondary Modern School, Stretchford, are up
in arms against the headmaster, Mr. J. B. Dimwood. So are their
parents.

The trouble began when 15-year-old Ron Frabb was sent home
by the headmaster for wearing a plastic Bronx jacket embroidered
with musical notes, tartan jeans and an orange nylon day-glow wig
of "Tony Curtis" cut. He is leader of the school skiffle-group and
also of the "X Cert Gang," which is pledged to relentless warfare
against the school staff.

Ron's fellow-pupils, who have been demanding that guitar
lessons shall be included in the curriculum, boycotted the school
yesterday and paraded outside the headmaster's house, threatening his family with sharpened bicycle-chains.

Ron's father, Mr. Ted Frabb, boilerman and TV enthusiast, said
at his home yesterday: "It's a scandal. Ron is not going back to
school until old Dimwood apologises in the presence of a *Sunday
Defective* reporter. Teenagers demand freedom in this day and age,
and it's up to parents to see that they get it, and no mucking about.

"How can Ron ever hope to be a teenage idol and get in the big
money if he isn't allowed to dress as he wants? What is education
for? I've written to our M.P. about it, but if I don't get satisfaction
I'll do old Dimwood good and proper."

Mrs. Frabb smiled happily, and young Ron, who was sitting on
the floor in all his finery making casual passes at the cat with his
flick-knife, looked up and nodded agreement.

Ron Frabb's schooldays

On his return to Bog Lane Secondary Modern School from hospital, the headmaster, Mr. J. B. Dimwood, found his study occupied by Mr. Cliff Rampton, the variety agent, and by Jean Neck, a precocious fifth-former whom Mr. Rampton had taken on as a temporary secretary.

"I can offer you seven nicker a week and expenses," said Mr. Rampton as the headmaster appeared. "as a feed and spare gagman in 'Hotcha Paris Nights' opening South Shields Monday week. Take it or leave it."

As Mr. Dimwood hesitated, adjusting his spectacles, Mr. Rampton added "All right, sonny boy, leave it. And now run away and play at Greek literature or conic sections or something. I'm busy."

"In other words," explained Miss Neck, "Buzz."

As the bewildered headmaster turned to go, he bumped into Ron Frabb's father, who had called to discuss his share of the profits on Ron's £1,000 a week skiffle tour of the provinces. Unfortunately for Mr. Dimwood, Mr. Frabb's reflex-action at the sight of him was instantaneous and extremely effective.

Is this your surname?

If your name is Fruitperson, you probably had an ancestor who held his land under feudal tenure, being obliged to deliver a certain quantity of fruit to the Lord of the Manor annually. The seneschal on announcing the arrival of the fruit would probably say: "Here is the fruit person." Hence the name.

The name Musicseller, common in parts of Worcestershire, has no connection with music. It is probably of Gaelic origin, and means "one who removes the eyes of partially gnawed potatoes."

If your name is Sadcake, you may be descended from a member of the famous Red Indian tribe who emigrated to Manchester in the 1860's and took up birdcage manufacture in Salford. J. R. Sadcake, who played full-back for Accrington Stanley in the 1892 Cup Final, is probably the best-known scion of this dauntless race.

(Next week: McSeedy, Gongworthy and Lemonsodawallah).

Emancipation

Princess Laila Aisha, eldest daughter of the King of Morocco, is, I read, "one of the most dynamic personalities in the Moslem world to-day. She is 28, attractive and thoroughly dedicated to the idea of freeing her countrywomen from the veil, polygamy and subservience to their husbands." To this end, she wears a bikini and drives a fast sports car. She is also leader of a Girls' Organisation in Morocco which wears "an eye-catching uniform of white shirts and slacks and scarlet berets."

No doubt the women of Morocco will in due course emerge from the harem and have their emancipation. But they might as well realise now what they are in for. They might as well walk into the trap prepared for them not merely unveiled, monogamous and unsubservient to their husbands, but with wide open eyes as well.

The emancipation of women begins with bikinis, motor-scooters, tinned food, scarlet berets, free love and plenty of pocket money. And it ends with soap and water and uniform dungarees, as with shouted slogans the female forced-labour battalion marches past the ruined harem walls.

Ron Frabb's schooldays

The last day of the last term had come, and Ron Frabb, teenage idol of Bog Lane Secondary Modern School, stood before the headmaster, Mr. J. B. Dimwood, to take his leave and listen to a few words of fatherly advice before he went out into the great world.

Ron's frank boyish features were flushed, for he had taken the precaution of having a heavy drag on a reefer from the school tuck-shop before the solemn moment came. His newly-sharpened flick-knife gleamed in his hand.

In his phosphorescent Bronx jacket, skintight tartan jeans and built-up fetishist's boots, his abundant locks dressed in the fashionable Tony Curtis style and anointed with "Kasbah No. 3" unguent, he made a striking picture of contemporary youth.

For his part, Mr. Dimwood had prepared for the occasion as best he might. His poker, fire-extinguisher and heavy bust of Matthew Arnold lay to hand, and a touch on his bell would bring Plugden, the new caretaker and ex-heavyweight pugilist, post-haste to the study.

He did not realise, of course, that the bell-wires had already been severed by the enterprising Ron, and that Plugden at that moment lay bound in his cubbyhole, gagged with his own inkwells.

Mr. Dimwood's voice quavered with natural emotion as he began. "Well, my boy, your schooldays are now behind you, and you are going out into the world, as we all must. I know you will work hard in your chosen profession. Let me see now, what was it? Ah, yes, the Rock and Roll.

"Ah, Youth! Those dreaming spires! Those midnight conversa-. tions in panelled rooms, as Great Tom solemnly booms forth the witching hour! The line of festal light in Christ Church hall! Enchanted days on Cam and Cherwell! Yes, yes——"

"Cut it out, Dad," rasped Ron suddenly, "and try this for size." And before the headmaster could react, Ron had knocked him cold with a lead-weighted ginger-beer bottle.

With a final kick in the direction of the prostrate pedagogue, he rushed from the room, leaped into Mr. Cliff Rampton's waiting cyclamen and magenta Cadillac, and roared off to fame and fortune.

Honour school

The Nottingham students who are publishing an American style magazine which will "blow the lid off life at the university" are rather slow off the mark. At Stretchford University the School of Journalism, Advertising and Public Relations has more students than any other school, except of course those of Jazz, Ballet and Commercial Astrophysics.

As part of their degree course in J.A.P.R., students are expected to produce a scandal-magazine and to be fully proficient in the latest techniques of the smear campaign and applied pornography.

"A university must move with the times," says the Vice-

Chancellor, popular Sir William Goth-Jones. To set an example, he was himself involved in a particularly unsavoury scandal this year when he was found insensible, dressed in women's clothes, in a broom cupboard in one of the students' hostels.

Legacies

In the course of his inaugural address to the All-African People's Conference at Accra, Dr. Nkrumah referred to "the disastrous legacies of imperialism." Disastrous or no, these legacies are larger than he seems to realise.

The means of communication by which the conference was summoned; the network of transport by which the delegates were assembled; the language and the hall in which the proceedings were conducted; the very microphone into which Dr. Nkrumah spoke; these, for a start, are all among the legacies of imperialism.

Others were specifically mentioned in Dr. Nkrumah's speech. They include "the *bona fide* political and trade union organisations" which are struggling, and "the legitimate rights and aspirations" for which they struggle. They include not merely the possibility but the very idea of "an Africa free, unfettered and united."

"Disastrous legacies"? We shall see; but one would hardly expect Dr. Nkrumah to think them so.

1959

A group of calendars

Reviewed by Julian Birdbath

It was Goethe, I think, who said that one of the most moving experiences of the New Year was the arrival of the tradesmen's

hope it will be a better one than the planetarium a friend of mine
came across in a small town in New Zealand.

It had originally been a cinema. Now in extreme decay, an affair
of mouldering laths and plaster, with ancient posters of Pearl
White and Louise Fazenda flapping from the walls, it displayed the
secrets of the Cosmos.

A vast dome of tarpaulin represented the infinite reaches of
space; celestial bodies of fluctuating wattage moved uncertainly,
even jerkily across it; many of the constellations had lost a star or
two; Sirius, once the pride of Canis Major, had been blotted out by
a huge beer stain, the work of a careless maintenance man.

Many people must have imagined themselves in the place of the
Creator. This was just the sort of universe most of us would in fact
have made—rusty, shabby, creaking, its working parts protruding
and tied on with string.

The rows of plush tip-up seats were generally well-filled. "Le
silence eternal de ces espaces infinis m'effraie," the audience would
remark, as above their heads, with soft plopping sounds, the rats
leaped from star to star

Quoth the raven

"We live in an age," says Mr. Macmillan, "in which the voices of the
croaker, the moaner, the faint-hearted and the cynical are often
heard and are now, of course, amplified by all modern means of
communication."

I wonder which of these caps is meant to fit me? Croaker?
Moaner? I am not dismayed! I am in the best of company.

In the ranks of the croakers and moaners will be found some at
least not more faint-hearted or cynical than Mr. Macmillan, who
love England not less than he, who yet wonder whether she is best
served by those who ceaselessly flatter and soothe her, painting her
present in the most glowing colours, and beguiling her with visions
of a future yet more rosy than the past, to be won without specific
readjustment, sorrow, pain or effort.

Well may we croak as we survey the worsening state of the
world, the feebleness of our defences against it, our own dear
Europe half disunited, half united in slavery, the Common-

wealth—a great question mark, for all Mr. Macmillan's grand and windy words.

But we had better croak loudly, for the voices of the complacent are also "amplified by all modern means of communication."

Star-crossed

"We love each other. Nobody can come between us. But why, oh why can't they stop leaving us alone?"

This was the heart-rending plea of Len Nerp, 19-year-old turntable machinist and Gloria Waspthwaite, 48-year-old dry-cleaning manageress, in their Gretna Green hide-out yesterday.

Last week the lovers eloped from their homes in Brassgrove Park, S.E., and hitch-hiked to Scotland. There they intend to stay until they have made enough money from interviews and photographs to return to England.

But so far not a soul has interviewed them or taken their photograph. Not a single parent or guardian has pursued or threatened them. Not a single court order has been made against them.

What of the homes they left behind? "Good riddance to bad rubbish," said Gloria's mother, thrice widowed Mrs. M. Waspthwaite. "I have let Gloria's room to a very nice gentleman, a schoolteacher who is out all night and sleeps during the day.

"Now don't let that camera-thing off. The bang might wake him up."

"Len was always a trier," said his father, who lives a few doors away. "Two years ago he eloped to Gretna with a 65-year-old retired police-woman. And last year he was off again with two old age pensioners.

"I followed the errant trio to Gretna, but public interest was slack. From the financial point of view, the whole thing was a wash-out.

"I don't blame Len. He's doing his best to earn a decent living. But as for me, once bitten, twice shy."

It looks as if Len and Gloria may be in Scotland for quite a long time.

Book list

Sleeping Panzer: the Memoirs of Field-Marshal Erich Buber von Nittwitz. Viper and Bugloss, 25s.

Field-Marshal von Nittwitz comes late to the army of memoir-writing German generals. But then, though belonging to an old Junker family, he seems to have little Prussian forcefulness in his character.

Timid, hesitant, lazy, handicapped by a severe stammer and conspicuous at General Staff conferences by his scruffy, even dirty appearance, his rapid ascent to the command of the 17th Army Group is hard to understand.

His relations with Hitler were often strained. On one occasion he began to snore while the Fuehrer was explaining his plan to transfer the entire population of Northern Ireland to Moldavia. Hitler, dropping the Bokhara rug he was gnawing, seized Nittwitz's hat and bit off a large section of the peak.

Nittwitz's strategy in the German offensive towards the Caspian in 1942, which he tries to vindicate, hardly seems convincing. When the armies of Lessing, Wesker and Wolf von Mankowitz formed three sides of a quadrilateral round Rostov, Nittwitz, by falling asleep once again, left the trap unsprung, with disastrous consequences.

For the rest of the war, his role was to watch the Swiss frontier against the danger of invasion by the Helvetic hordes. His account of this period is confused by puzzling references to Marshal Macmahon, the Agadir Crisis and the defence of the Caprivi Finger.

What was Nittwitz's secret? Was he, as Dr. Trevor-Roper suggests, working for the British or perhaps the Irish Secret Service? His relations with Admiral Canaris are obscure, but so for that matter are his relations with Goering, Goebbels, Himmler, Hess, Ley, Frink, Pfaff and Ritter von Grundstedt.

Altogether, his memoirs can be said to cast no more than a pallid, fitful light on the rise and fall of the Third Reich.

Afoot in London

By "Wayfarer"

How many people know that behind an ordinary-looking sports

outfitter's shop in Boggis Hill High Street is the only coalmine in London entirely operated by the British Council?

Boggis Hill Main Colliery has a curious history. In Stuart times it formed part of the extensive South London coalfield which supplied "superior family nuttes" to the Royal household.

Cromwell closed it down as a "nest of Popery," but at the Restoration it was reopened and became a favourite resort of Court gallants on outings of pleasure, when light ladies would gaily operate the primitive pithead gear of those days, often with disastrous results for the miners down below.

With the coming of the industrial revolution and the opening up of the northern coalfields, Boggis Hill fell into disuse. By 1925, when the British Council took over, only a single demented miner was employed there.

Lumps of Boggis Hill coal packed in silver paper, with tasteful slips bearing quotations from the English poets, are now sent to all parts of the Middle East as part of a drive to publicise the British Way of Life.

The mine, with its remarkable baroque pithead baths, can be seen any Saturday morning on application to the Curator.

How to Get There. Trains every 20 minutes from Cannon Street to Hagstone Lane, through subway, turn right at the "Bella Vista" School of Ballroom Dancing, when you will see the miniature slagheaps rising over the burnished dome of the South-Eastern Gas Board Offices.

Brontes galore

Doreen Bronte: the Formative Years.
By Julian Birdbath, Viper & Bugloss, 25s.

Astronomers were able to deduce, from irregularities in the orbits of the inner planets, the existence of the planet Pluto before ever they observed it through their telescopes. Mr. Birdbath has performed a smiliar feat by his discovery of a fourth, hitherto unsuspected Bronte sister, Doreen.

Why have scholars and historians conspired to suppress Doreen Bronte's existence? Mr. Birdbath does his best to answer the question in this amazing literary detective story, whose first faint clues he came upon last year while examining old jam jars in the basement of Keighley Town Hall.

Doreen Bronte, it is evident, had little in common with her sisters. She was a brisk, bouncing woman whose insistence on keeping all the windows of Haworth Parsonage permanently open may have contributed, Mr. Birdbath suggests, to their early deaths.

She had little patience with their literary activities. Her own interests were mainly in dog-breeding, ballistics and light engineering. Mr. Birdbath reproduces a design for a primitive kind of machine-gun which anticipates Maxim. The Haworth girls' Small Bore Rifle Club, which she founded, was an interesting precursor both of the A.T.S. and of the Russian women's partisan groups of the last war.

Doreen Bronte seems to have been fond of disguising herself as her brother Branwell and drinking at the Black Bull in Haworth, where her anecdotes of Marshal Ney, delivered in a monotonous booming voice, frequently cleared the bar. It was after one of these visits that she vanished from the stage of history.

In his final chapter, Mr. Birdbath hints at the existence of yet a fifth Bronte sister, Dawn. But enough is enough.

THE SIXTIES

1960

Act now!

Yells Jack Moron

Once again the dread shadow of German aggression looms over the sleeping nations. Once again the tramp of jack-boots echoes through the cowering streets, and the rubber truncheon beats a ghastly tattoo on doors lit up by the flaring torches of Nazi Youth . . .

I have just been talking to one of the leaders of this reawakening horror. He is Bodo Neckhorst, 68-year-old ex-front-line post-officer in the Austro-Hungarian Imperial Army, now unemployed. He is self-styled Obergruppenhauptgehirnsturmfuehrer of the militant Klopstockjugend, a fanatical youth organisation.

A slight figure in rimless glasses, with a ramrod back and the typical unsmiling arrogance of his kind, Dr. Neckhorst wears shorts, he told me, made of human skin. On his head he wears a Viking-type pith helmet with horns made of warthog's tusks.

At a recent neo-pagan werewolves' rally in the Teutoberg Wald he was badly burned while trying to leap through a sacred tribal bale-fire.

Dr. Neckhorst is evidently not yet quite ready to defy world opinion altogether. At any rate he refused to allow me to meet any of his followers.

But I learned that the Klopstockjugend is linked to the Hegel-jugend, the Heideggerjugend and the Scholtz-Klink-Unity-Mitford

League of German Maidens in a sinister, growing network of evil which bodes stark menace to world peace and democratic values.

We must act now, to stamp out the Neckhorsts and their kind while there is yet time!

Mothers

What the Russian novelist Ilya Ehrenburg thinks to-day, the Kremlin can be taken to have thought yesterday. His reflections are thus of more than normal interest.

"So long as two military giants with enormous stocks of atomic weapons stand facing each other, it will hardly be possible to find in the world a mother who will be able to think calmly about the future of her children."

Mothers, I suspect, are not quite such fools as Mr. Ehrenburg hopes. Mothers are naturally suspicious of military giants. But they are shrewd enough to see that, if military giants there must be, two are better than one.

When one military giant with enormous stocks of atomic weapons stands facing another which, deluded by false promises, has thrown all its atomic weapons away—this is the time when sensible mothers will shake in their sensible shoes.

It may also be the time which Mr. Ehrenburg and his masters are waiting for.

Saturday bargains

"I must give my feet a treat," said Dad. He straightened his indestructible tie (permanent knot, washable, three for 5s.), removed his genuine 100 per cent British reconditioned Army boots (tipped heels and toes), picked up the nail-pliers ("ideal for tough, hard and ingrowing toe-nails") from the TV or coffee table and set to.

"Oh, do give over," cried Mum, who was trying to cut her own hair in the 3-way-chair 'designed by a doctor.' "How can I cut as I comb and save £££s with all this stuff flying about?"

"Adorable, irresistible me," carolled Carlene as she pirouetted round the room in her full-circle skirt of Princess Margaret Rose tartan, adorned with "beautiful jewellery" she had made herself.

"How do you like my new, full, high bosom look with deep, enchanting cleavage (19s. 6d., post 6d.)?"

Dad kissed his daughter. "You look like many famous film-stars, my dear."

"Well, Dad, you're not so bad yourself. Those high-ranking officers' long pants really suit you and you're so erect—every inch the real Guards officer!"

"Thanks to my 'anti-stoop' shoulder-braces," thought Dad.

The china rattled in the multi-purpose wall-cabinet as, with a volley of oaths, young Ron hit his head on the lintel, slid the length of the room on the hand-made Himalayan Numdah rug and finished up in the pet's bed (19s. 6d.).

"It's those —— elevator shoes," he cried. "Girls may love tall men, but I keep forgetting I'm two inches taller."

From the lounge floated sounds of auntie learning the piano by post. "Just think," said Mum, "she's only been at it a matter of weeks and already she plays correctly and enjoyably."

"She's a marvel," echoed Garlene. "When her time comes we'll give her a lovely memorial in best white Italian marble (£25 with 5 doz. letters)."

"I don't think we've ever had it so good," mused Dad. And from the top of the three-in-one writing bureau, book-case and record cabinet, Little Leo, the Fairy Shoemaker, "a beautifully-fashioned Irish leprechaun in SOLID METAL with GOLD-like finish," beamed down upon the happy scene.

Movement

"Christ! It's wonderful. This is something. Everyone seems so young, even the old. Everything is so alive and beautiful. At last I have some sense of belonging . . . It's great just to be here, with everyone else . . . Perhaps this C.N.D. weekend will combine and absorb the festival of Easter, the way the Christians absorbed pagan festivals.

"On the march! . . . These people are caught up in a common purpose, there is a movement afoot . . . They have worked through their personal *angst* and have joined in this fabulous charade that was set in by their children. Philosophies and families are galvanised . . . If He [Christ] were watching us, He'd approve. Why, He'd join in . . . It has spread, and everyone is caught up in it.

People with all shades of conflicting opinions, from all walks of life are united in a common purpose, at last. There is something to latch on to. The swirling mass of jubilant tired kids have made it—the days of apathy are over. They have a direction. No longer are they living for kicks, they are kicking for life."

The letters "C.N.D." are a clue. You have not in fact been reading the wild dithyrambs of some half-crazed, half-literate young storm-trooper, intoxicated by his first Nuremberg rally. No, it is only the playwright Bernard Kops describing in Tribune the effect produced upon him by the Aldermaston march.

God knows you might be forgiven the mistake. Here too, we find the same horror of being alone, the same worship of youth, the same desire to "belong," the same semi-blasphemous vanity, the same indiscriminate thirst for conformity, for a common purpose (the denial of liberty), the same blind longing to be absorbed in some "direction" (any direction?)

Our young people to-day are clearly just as disorientated as was the youth of Germany 30 years ago, just as free from inherited values and prejudices, just as sick, rootless and lost, just as lacking in sober judgment and self-reliance and in the capacity for thinking things out for themselves, just as ready to "go anywhere, do anything," just as ripe to be plucked by the first passing demagogue.

Thank God they have so far found to fill their empty souls no message more sinister than that preached by Messrs. Foot, Soper and Co.!

Space and butter

"Alexei," a sort of Soviet Man in the Street, was recently allowed to have a letter printed in a Moscow newspaper in which he asked whether rockets and sputniks were really necessary and said he would rather spend the money on houses and nurseries.

"A Moscow Engineer" then weighed in and ticked off Alexei in a seven-column official answer. "Alexei," he pontificated, "is uncultured if he prefers a full stomach to the search for knowledge."

I hope poor Alexei was cultured enough to spot the verbal swindle here. For although the search for knowledge is the engineer's, the empty stomach is Alexei's.

N.Q.O.C.D.

"Ughtred St. John Mainwaring," the electronic computer which handles the background research material for this column (no plebeian "Fred" or "Len" for us) is a unique piece of machinery.

Its carved mahogany case, its low, well-bred hum and subdued lighting as of the finest wax candles, amaze ordinary computer-operators accustomed to the naked valves, garishly flashing lights and vulgar clatter of their own machines.

Mr. Grylls, who is in charge of our computer, is an elderly clergyman and an authority on ecclesiastical law. While operating the machine he wears a special uniform of his own design and foreswears animal food.

The computer has a built-in code of manners. Recently, when a party of scientists from Stretchford University came to inspect it, one of them, with the facetiousness of his kind, fed in some jocular data, incorporating the question: "Who was that lady I saw you with last night?"

A million circuits were activated and with a speed far beyond the capacity of the human brain came the answer (with an instantaneous lowering of the temperature to zero): "Mr. Briggs, the door is open. Would you be good enough to close it when you leave the room?"

Home Guard stories

Readers of this column not only know what to expect but also know what is expected of them. This year being the twentieth anniversary of the Home Guard, they have been bombarding me with

Home Guard stories by the sackful. Here are a few of the most notable:

He blew his top

Sgt. Holdsworth, who commanded the H.G. detachment at Breathbury Old Sidings, Staffs, invented a combined respirator and mapcase so large that he used it as an individual air-raid shelter. One night, on an exercise, we filled it with rhubarb sandwiches and one of the lads did his imitation of a Heinkel 87. Sarge blew his top all right!

—B. JARRETT, SUCTION ROAD, WEDNESBURY

Absent-minded

During a day on the ranges, our 2 i/c, Cpl. the Rt. Hon. the Viscount Haversnake, then 88, accidentally shot dead every man in the detachment except myself. Talk about laugh!

—E. PARR, NOSING, ESSEX

It's a free country

When an elderly woman wearing jackboots and a swastika armband made a parachute descent near Gogweston Abbas in Dorset, most of us thought the invasion had started and our H.G. sergeant, Jack Illweather, had the church bells rung.

The woman explained that she had been doing this for years, for exercise, long before the Nazis were thought of, and saw no reason to stop now. Were our faces red!

—P. H. SYPHON, BLANDFORD

He had his chips

During a street-fighting exercise we ran short of practice grenades and our officer issued us with hot baked potatoes instead. Hearing a choral version of "Down Mexico Way" coming from an open window, I lobbed in a potato and to my amazement the whole lot went up. It was a grenade factory.

—F. BROOTES, NUMB ROAD, S.E.

Forging ahead

Trevor Dimwiddie, 35-year-old blond-bearded British underwater motor-cycling champion, had to turn back with engine trouble on his attempt to cross the Channel underwater yesterday. Crowds lined the harbour at Eastbourne as the 28-year-old, black-haired, Leeds-born ace emerged from the sea.

A wall of water surged inland and demolished several tobacco kiosks. Previously the 40-year-old, clean-shaven Waltham Abbey man's attempt had raised freak waves and clouds of steam in the Channel. There were protests from officials on a pleasure cruise off Dungeness and storm cones were hoisted at the Burling Gap orographical research station.

"Who's going to pay for all this?" asked a spokesman. But 23-year-old, crew-cut Glaswegian Dimwiddie was unrepentant. "I had bad luck," he told a Press conference.

"Sea-bed conditions were absolutely first class when about six miles out I tangled with an underwater rubbish dump not on the Admiralty charts and my 600 c.c. all-British Black Panther developed 'jabber'.

"The controls became red hot. I couldn't breathe. Something, some inner voice, told me to call it a day. I probably owe my life to that.

"I'm all set to try again to-morrow. I must and will beat this hoo-doo and put this Britain of ours fairly and squarely on the map of underwater cross-Channel motor-cycling."

Any offers?

I met an interesting man yesterday. He is Dr. Abdul Ngong Castrumba, a dark-complexioned, luxuriantly-bearded man of indeterminate non-European race, wearing a peaked forage-cap, thick pebble glasses, a double-breasted jacket, a dhoti and riding-boots of military style.

He is a freelance, all-purposes revolutionary leader, "ready," he says, "to go anywhere at a moment's notice to seize power and drive the imperialists and colonialists out of anywhere."

When I called on him, he was practising a 36-hour speech, with appropriate gestures, before a looking-glass. He showed no sign of hoarseness or muscular exhaustion.

"The imperialists and colonialists," he was shouting, "have never given me any instruction in the vital functions of government, such as how to take over their property without compensation, massacre them, rape their women and chase them out of any country they have got into.

"I've had to learn all these things for myself. That is the supreme crime of imperialism and colonialism.

"I only want peace," he went on, his voice rising to a scream, "but I shall make war. If anyone refuses to have the freedom I offer, I shall throw him into gaol. I want co-operation with Europeans. If they try to co-operate, I shall kill the lot of them."

Does any non-European country, now writhing under the sway of the colonialists and imperialists, require the services of Dr. Castrumba? If so, I understand his rates are moderate. The first instalment is, anyhow.

Land's End

The Last Church. The Last Inn. The Last Grocer's Shop. The Last Telephone Kiosk. Though plastered with these announcements of imminent finality and roaring with ultimate motor-cars, the road to Land's End has the right feeling of being on the edge of the world, high and bleak among small Celtic fields, radio masts and primeval moors.

Then comes the End: the Last Hotel (whoever stays in this strange building, it would be an unforgettable experience) the Last Snacketeria and the Last Car Park. There are the Last Signposts, pointing to New York in one direction and in the other to any town of your choice. And then the Last Rocks plunge to the sea.

Worn shabby by the friction of millions of shoes and trousers and skirts, they are not like other rocks to look at. Orange peel and cigarette packets litter their crevices. There is a continual click of cameras and buzz of transistor radios among the ancient granite.

"Mum!" shouts a voice, "can I take a photo of you and dad sucking your lollies?"

Yes, it is all a disgrace and a desecration. But I am not at all sure I agree with people who would like to sweep away this all too human rubbish, put up tasteful green notice-boards and admit only those who could guarantee appreciation of the once more majestic scene.

This is England's End. And it may be right and fitting that modern England should end in a torrent of litter, shouting, iced lollies and mechanical uproar spilling down over the rocks and into the inviolable sea.

Huff and puff

Mr. Khrushchev has to "huff and puff", according to "seasoned observers", because he cannot afford to lose face in Russia. He has to be sensitive, so they say, to "the thoughts and reactions of the Russian populace".

I have seen this before, and more than once, too. In Sunday's *Observer* it was stated that Mr. Khrushchev was in "a touchy, unpredictable mood and under real pressure from Soviet public opinion".

Such, I take it, is the view emanating from the British delegation now in New York: thus, in particular, the view emanating indirectly from Mr. Macmillan.

It is a comforting, cosy sort of view, bodying forth as it does the wishdream that Mr. Khrushchev really means all the nice things he says in private, whereas the nasty things he says in public are no more than concessions to "Soviet public opinion".

The only snag is that Soviet public opinion does not exist. To say that Mr. Khrushchev is "under real pressure" from it is thus to say no more than that he is under pressure from his own dark and sinister impulses.

There are those in Russia who are entirely subservient to Mr. Khrushchev's every whim. They do not count.

There are doubtless those in Russia—though we hear little of them—who shiver in their shoes whenever he blows his top, just as Germans shivered under Hitler. We know from experience that they don't count either.

And there are those—the vast majority—who know nothing about anything. Is it from these that the pressure comes?

Belshazzar's feast

Kenneth Tyman, the dramatic critic, complains of the lack of true, "nonconformist" satire in the London theatre and cabaret. By contrast he praises its practitioners in New York, from the "liberal nihilist" Mort Sahl downwards.

To call night-club liberal nihilists "nonconformist" is nothing but a perversion of language. In fact, nobody could possibly be more conformist than they are.

They conform exactly to the fashionable desperation of their audience, its smart hatred of civilisation, its intoxication in the West Side dance of death, its Gadarene rush to destruction. That is why, far from being mocked and driven into the wilderness, they have grown rich and popular and fat with long-playing records.

The role of Mort Sahl at Belshazzar's Feast, in that most expensive of Babylonian night-clubs, would have been to make liberal nihilist jokes about the writing on the wall, to the huge delight of his sophisticated audience.

What is wrong here?

"Aid for the Underdeveloped Countries" is one of the great rallying cries of to-day. This idea is a soothing, often anaesthetic balm for the agonised guilt of liberal consciences. It is also a heady intoxicant for technologists eager to get on with the work of transforming the world.

Ancient civilisation and primitive tribes alike, they infer, must be industrialised as quickly as possible, for "industrialisation," it is said, "is the sole hope of the poor."

The same liberal people will maintain that colonialism is a curse and must be abolished. Yet if what they say about the urgent need for industrialisation is true (and it is as much as one's life is worth to question it), then the underdeveloped countries may be doing themselves a great disservice by getting rid of their Western rulers.

The inventors and developers of scientific techniques, forming coherent and at least potentially efficient governments, are hastily expelled by nationalist agitation, only to return in reply to anguished appeals next day in a confused, wasteful and often impotent form as officials of the United Nations, rival fighters in the Cold War or both at once.

If, as we are continually told, the industrialisation of the under-developed countries is absolutely all that matters, then this seems a remarkably circuitous way of going about it. The under-developed colonial countries might have done better to stay colonial.

Toy psychiatrist

At last we in Britain are catching up with this Day and Age (writes Doreen Gaggs). I spent a fascinating hour yesterday in Hambridge's new toy department. It's the first in Britain to have a resident psychiatrist.

Dr. Kiosk's job is to see that parents don't just buy any old toys their children may fancy. Grave harm may be done to a child's future development unless its early history, traumas, complexes and so on are taken into account. So no toy may be sold until Dr. Kiosk has carried out a psychiatric examination.

He's very quick at this, he tells me; a fifty guinea deep analysis takes only a few minutes. Normally he uses hypnosis; the new wonder drugs, electric shock treatment, or, in a few cases, lobotomy, take longer and are correspondingly more expensive.

While I was there, one four-year-old (he looked quite normal, I must say) wanted a teddy bear. Dr. K. soon put a stop to that. The child, he established by a quick examination, was hyperpyknic and a suppressed ursophobe; the only suitable toy was a miniature electronic psychiatrist.

As the child was led away clutching his new possession, I realised how crucial this experience was going to be for his future development.

Another thing: whereas the teddy bear cost £5, the toy psychiatrist, plus Dr. Kiosk's fees and commission, cost £80. So almost everybody was happy.

Crisis city

To-day, Stretchford is a city of sullen anger (write a team of "Way of the World" Sports Correspondents). Everywhere, in room-at-the-top mansion and council house, at trolley-bus terminus, in undertaker's parlour and select snug, there is only one topic of conversation.

Shall Albert Rasp, star goalkeeper of Stretchford United (871 goals scored against him this season) be sold to the Italian Ugolino Wanderers Club for an undisclosed sum, believed to be in the region of half a million pounds?

Rasp's own lips are, except for a small aperture, entirely sealed. "It's all the same to me," he told us yesterday. "I like Indians, though I don't much go for the language. I met a Japanese at Blackpool last summer. He seemed all right."

Now a persistent rumour is sweeping Stretchford: that far from receiving a penny from the Italian club, Sir Roland Grampus Smith, United's able chairman, after unsuccessful attempts to have Rasp stabbed, shot, poisoned or sold into slavery, is paying a vast sum just to have him taken off Stretchford's hands.

A deputation of United supporters called on Sir Roland last

week for an explanation. They had the doors shut in their faces, while warning shots from a 25-pounder were fired over their heads.

One thing is certain. In a city torn by bewilderment, indignation, wrath, anguish, passion, fury, self-pity, endemic alcoholism and a helpless sense of injustice, anything can happen.

Barbarism

"After last week (writes a science journalist) there will be two kinds of people in the world: The Gagarins, whose health, age, training, nationality and good fortune will have combined to secure their place among the elite . . . and the rest of us . . . Now is the time to consider what it all means to us underdogs."

So on the one hand we have glorious Major Gagarin whirling round in his gadget-infested container, and on the other hand we have you and me and Gen. de Gaulle and Stravinsky and Eichmann and Henry Moore and Donald Hume and Dr. Schweitzer and Greta Garbo and the rest of the dull, indistinguishable mass of underdog humanity.

This method of classifying people might be carried further. It means, logically, that any acrobat who has ever been fired out of a cannon is the superior of Shakespeare, Beethoven and Cardinal Newman.

We ought to resist this barbarian view of the world for all we are worth. Those who hold it are growing in power and impudence every day.

Now write on

"Soup! Teeth! Free hair-restorer!" The low growl of the crowd of hunger-maddened operatives rose to a whining scream as, brandishing staves, ratchets, iron bars, paving-stones and bicycle-pumps, they pressed ever nearer to the great gates of Grindrod's Mill.

With a clang that echoed the iron determination in his heart, Ephraim Grindrod threw over the lever that operated the massive inner gate. Feeling a little safer now, he retreated to the card-winding room, peering out through the smoke-grimed window where, on that far-off summer evening in the year of the Chartist Petition, he had plighted his troth.

The scene before him now was ironically different. Every moment the crowd grew denser; the dark, hessian-clad figures, with here and there a wild-eyed harpy wearing nothing but a string-bag, seemed to close up into a thick, impacted mass that had an identity, a warped collective soul of its own.

In the middle of the crowd, like a lump of gristle in a Lancashire hot-pot, Winnie Cadwallader, the mad Welsh fiddler from Laister-dyke, sat inaudibly playing a full-sized concert harp. So Winnie was heart and soul with the rioters too? Ephraim bit his lip. With a sudden convulsive jerk, he threw over another lever.

Clouds of steam poured from the reciprocating donkey-engine. What a grand machine it was! Old Ephraim Grindrod in Waterloo days, first of his line, friend of Trevithick the engineer and patron of Tom Paine the brandy-guzzling philosopher, had built even better than he knew.

Slowly the whole mill-yard, with the now bewildered mob in it, began to revolve on its hidden turn-table. Ephraim smiled grimly. Faster! Faster! He noticed that the shouts that came to his ears were now tinged with alarm. Had he a chance of holding out till the Militia arrived? Or would the boiler burst?

[*With the compliments of the "Way of the World" fiction-writing Service (West Riding Saga Division)*].

Megalomaniac days

As I was being driven slowly along Fleet Street the other day in my bullet-proof, purple Rolls-Royce, half enjoying the sullen murmur of the crowds as the motor-bicycle out-riders skilfully forced them out of the way, I found myself speculating, not for the first time, on the mysterious workings of Privilege.

How had it come about that I was riding here at ease, admired and envied by all, needing only to seize the speaking-tube and convey my wishes, even the most capricious, to Bennett the principal chauffeur, to have them instantly gratified? I knew, for example, that if I suddenly ordered him to drive me to Harrogate or

Trucial Oman, he would obey either command without a flicker of hesitation.

I looked through the windows at the hosts of the unprivileged, wondering idly what it must be like to share those lives of anonymous toil. What would it be like, for instance, to be that somewhat worried-looking man in a mackintosh who had just alighted from what is, I believe, known as a "bus" and seemed to be making his way, with many a hesitant and bewildered gesture, towards his place of humble though doubtless meritorious employment?

Was it possible, I wondered, for me to forget for a moment my Olympian status, this life of mine so utterly removed from all the cares and responsibilities of the vulgar, and, by one immense, concentrated effort of empathy, to *be* that man?

It was.

Puzzle

That the Communists and fellow-travellers of England should further Soviet plans by all means in their power is natural and even right. It is natural, though not right, that they should find numerous brainless dupes to help them in their work.

What is neither natural nor right is that they should find intelligent, liberal-minded Englishmen unwittingly helping them.

After all, it is all there in black and white. There is no secret about it. There are thousands of voices, both living and dead, particularly dead—many of them intelligent liberals—to bear witness to Communist aims and methods. And, whatever you may suppose, the "Chinese Wall" of Berlin was not invented by Senator MacCarthy.

What is the explanation of this extraordinary, blind obstinacy? It cannot even be explained, at the lowest level, as an instinct of self-preservation.

The well-known practice of the Communist military bureaucracy, when it takes over a country, is to liquidate the liberals first, as having on the whole, the greatest nuisance potential. E.g., I would expect Canon Collins to be shot at least ten minutes before I was.

Believe me, this would be no consolation.

News from the courts

James Bonnington Jagworth, 42, described as a motorist, of Staines, was accused at Nerdley (Staffs) Magistrates' Court yesterday of driving without due care and attention.

Sgt. E. Harmer, of Stretchford City Police, said he saw Mr. Jagworth pass three other cars on a blind corner leading to a narrow railway bridge in a built-up area of Soup Hales at over 70 mph. After an 80 mile chase he caught up with him near the Welsh Border.

Accused of exceeding the speed limit, Mr. Jagworth said: "You say I was doing 70 mph. Rubbish, I was doing 95. What's more, in my new Boggs Yobbo convertible I can do over 130."

When arrested, Mr. Jagworth took a truculent attitude, and said repeatedly, "Do you know who I am? You'll hear more of this."

Mr. Jagworth, who conducted his own defence, stated in court: "I am appearing here as the representative of the whole persecuted body of British motorists. What sort of car do *you* drive, anyhow?" he asked the chairman, Dr. Ellis Goth-Jones.

When Dr. Goth-Jones admitted shamefacedly that he owned a 6-year-old Snail Popular Saloon, but seldom drove it as he found the roads too dangerous, there were titters, and some booing, from the gallery. After receiving an apology from the Bench for the waste of his time, Mr. Jagworth left the court to resume his interrupted journey.

Awake!

There is an old prophecy in Bradford that at a time of supreme peril for the city the 22-stone, iron-watch-chained, indigo-waistcoated Alderman Foodbotham will awake from his age-long sleep in his granite mausoleum on Cleckheaton Moor and ride forth in a spectral tram to save his people.

When, not long ago, the beautiful smoke-blackened heart of Bradford was torn out to make way for cheap cardboard skyscrapers, many thought the Alderman's moment had surely come. A local newsagent, who dared to penetrate into the mausoleum and look on that awful majesty, blew several notes on the Alderman's magic horn, but without result.

But now Alderman Foodbotham has a personal rather than a

civic reason to wake at last. The Conservative party conference at Brighton has actually passed a monstrous motion urging the Government either to abolish aldermen altogether or to ensure "fair representation for substantial minorities."

Substantial minorities, indeed! When Alderman Foodbotham, in 1921, was reproached by some puny Socialist councillor for himself taking up all the seats on the aldermanic bench and being both majority and minority, one roar, in a voice like Lister's Mill working at full pressure, was enough to disintegrate the wretched fellow and reduce him literally to material for the City Cleansing Department.

I doubt if the Alderman, when he awakes, will care to descend on such a centre of southern daftness as Brighton. That will not be necessary. No seismograph will be needed to register the earth-tremors of his northern rage.

Hear all sides

The GPI Television Network weekly discussion programme, "Hear All Sides," got off to a good start yesterday evening with a lively free-for-all on Berlin, nuclear tests and the Cold War.

Taking part in a well-balanced programme were Eric Lard, the avant garde playwright; Mrs. Dutt-Pauker, the Hampstead progressive thinker; Sir Osric Fenton, the Left-wing actor-manager; Dr. Abdul Castrumba, the freelance revolutionary leader, and Mr. J. L. Smith, an elderly retired newsagent from Stretchford.

I thought Mr. Smith, who suggested that we ought to stand by our Allies and not accede to all Communist demands, got very much the worst of the argument, partly owing to a speech impediment, partial illiteracy, and a recent course of electrical shock treatment.

The Chairman, Sir William Goth-Jones, had to intervene when Sir Osric called Mr. Smith "a common little horror," while Lard spat on him, shouting "Rat! Slimy pillar of the Establishment!" and Dr. Castrumba pulled out his sub-machine-gun.

There was general agreement when Mrs. Dutt-Pauker said that as a typical English housewife she would welcome the Red Army to our shores after the liquidation of the reactionary forces.

Immediately after the programme, a GPI spokesman reported, their switchboard was jammed with angry calls from Left-wing sympathisers who had evidently misunderstood their orders and were protesting against the wrong programme.

1962

Rentacrowd

I have just received an advance copy of the Spring Catalogue of Rentacrowd Ltd., the enterprising firm which supplies crowds for all occasions and has done so much to keep progressive causes in the public eye.

The new catalogue contains all the popular standard lines for the home market—the easy-terms "Aldermaston," the "Trafalgar Square" in various sizes (with or without small Fascist counter-demonstration in separate container), the "St. Pancras" anti-rent protest set (with assorted kiddies in push-chairs), and the well-tried overseas models, the "Kassem" Howling Mob No. 2, the "Merdeka" and "Lumumba" Super-Raving Anti-Colonialist Mob No. 4, etc., etc.

Progressive people who for one reason or another prefer not to stir from their own homes can now order small, hand-picked luxury mobs with more literate and sophisticated slogans and with banners designed by well-known experts in decor.

The Rentacrowd people emphasise that you should place your order in good time this year, to avoid disappointment. The demand for mobs is constantly growing and there is already a danger that it may exceed the supply.

Rentacrowd even anticipate a situation in which the whole human race will have become one huge, protesting, demonstrating mob; then Rentacrowd, its work well done, will simply wither away.

Art for the people

Several readers have taken me to task for objecting to Arnold Wesker's schemes for "bringing art to the people" by means of trade union festivals. What possible harm can there be in that, they ask. Let me explain.

Art, being a living thing, cannot be organised and imposed by "cultural reform," as if it were some kind of suffrage. It is something that individuals have to discover, and if they are fortunate, produce, for themselves. And this possibility is just as open to a member of the working-class as it is to a member of any other.

What is art? The transfiguration of the world by the power of imagination? But what Wesker means by art, and what, presumably, he wants to bring to the people, seems to be a matter of trite, easily understood, contemporary social "messages."

The argument can be summed up neatly, as it happens, in Wesker's own play "Roots," with a conclusion opposite to that which he intended.

Here the heroine, born on a Norfolk farm, returns home from London to bring metropolitan enlightenment and cultural awareness to the backward rustics. But what she brings them, in fact, is nothing but a thin, indigestible compound of "progressive" ideas and self-conscious, third-rate cultural small-talk.

The rustics, quite rightly, prefer to remain sunk in hoggish lethargy, interrupted only by enormous meals, doltish personal remarks and, of course, work. They do not know it, but their instinct is right.

There is far more health, more nourishment for life, more hope for art even, in their ignorant stupidity than in all the wretched amalgam of Hampstead coffee-party clap-trap they are offered in its place.

Now write on

"Oh, I do wish I could understand the Feudal System." Jehane the Fair gazed out wearily from the casement over the broad lands of her husband, the Lord of Dancreville, where peasants, pygmy figures gnarled and bent with back-breaking toil, were working under the hot sun in the long strips of field that stretched away to the dark rim of the forest.

She saw Humphrey, Lord Dancreville's steward, a parchment in his hand, walking with his finicking gait through the jumble of peasants' huts below the castle-walls, avoiding the piles of garbage, dead dogs, illuminated manuscripts and broken abaci flung down by frustrated peasants whose efforts to understand the Feudal System had come to as little as the Lady Jehane's.

"By Our Lady, Master Humphrey," a thick-set, gnarled-headed villein caught the edge of his fine woollen jerkin, "it passes the wit of man. Thou sayest I be bound to gave a quarter of all my beans and sunflower-seeds to the Lord Dancreville and five-sixteenths of my monthly curds and whey production to my Lord Abbot of Bromsgrove in return for part scutelage on the comman land—."

"No, no, no," the Steward interrupted testily, "thou hast got it all wrong again, chucklehead. Rights of scutelage and murrage are held by the Lord on behalf of all villeins *in toto.* Every leveret caught between Lammastide and All Saints goes to my Lord Abbot, and one tenth of the dried nettles of all men in possession of a longbow — 's Blood, now thou'st got *me* all moithered too—."

Slowly, shouldering bill-hooks, mattocks and wooden ploughshares, the peasants crowded round, each shouting his accustomed arguments and contributing to the general immemorial confusion.

Then all at once, above the hubbub that rolled across the fields, mingling with the din of church bells and plain-song and the clashing of Lord Dancreville's armour as he practised sword-strokes against himself in the closet next door (he had long since given up trying to understand the system himself), a single heartfelt shout came to the Lady Jehane's ears.

"Roll on the Renascence. . . ."

[Compliments of the "Way of the World" Fiction-Writing Service (Historical Novel Division)].

Glory

A friend of mine, a military historian, was talking the other day about the role of the cavalry arm in nuclear warfare. I was surprised and gratified to hear that it had any role; but he pointed out that a determined charge of cuirassiers might well overrun a battery of nuclear artillery before it had time to work out the complicated calculations required before it could press the button.

A glorious thought—a symbolic triumph of the rich, human past over the tinpot, scientific present! I see the overalled, bespectacled, scrub-haired technicians, part-time social psychiatrists to a man, peering myopically at the knobs and dials on their devil's box of tricks. Suddenly a strange, multi-coloured blur, like the tiger moth's deep-damasked wings, appears on their radar screen. The sound of silver trumpets bursts their plastic headphones.

Alarmed, they scurry here and there with slide-rules and oscilloscopes. Too late! Next moment the thunder of hooves and the wild neighing of chargers is on them, a whirl of nodding plumes and gleaming breastplates, and the terrible flash of the sabres that cut them down is the last thing they know.

Rebuke

"The Bible does indeed contain a great deal of wisdom, but to proclaim as a perfect model a man who chose to be crucified for the sake of others does not set a healthy example for society" (from a reader's letter in the *Observer*).

1963

Survey

Should a suitor ask the girl's father for her hand in marriage? In a typical survey which took me through 2,000 miles of sun-drenched English countryside (writes DOREEN GAGGS, the Woman Who

Understands) I put this question to a typical cross-section of men and women. I believe some of their replies, frank, unsparing, will give the fuddy-duddies food for thought.

"Don't make me laugh!" turntable minder Gloria Norp, 18, of Bevindon New Town, told me. "Don't you realise we are living in an age of sexual revolution, when traditional beliefs and customs are increasingly coming to be questioned and if necessary rejected by the younger generations? Suitors, fathers, marriage, hands, what does it all *mean*?"

"How stuffed-shirt can you get?" asked Marylou Boggis, 22, who models outsize sports-clothes for a Liverpool store. "If any boy friend of mine asked my father for my hand in marriage, I'd paste the living daylights out of them both."

But Les Das Gupta, 46-year-old bookmaker's machinist, of Toadsway, Nerdley, took a more conventional view. "I courted a local girl-machinist for 17 years," he told me, "before I plucked up courage to ask her father, a typical British trade unionist of the old school, with strongly progressive views, for her hand in marriage. Unfortunately I decided to wear an old Calcutta chief tramways inspector's uniform, handed down in my family for generations, for the interview. Dad thought I was a Spanish general and didn't he just fly off the handle! Once bitten, twice shy," Les added ruefully.

But Lorna Hornblow, 26-year-old teenager, who lives at Numb Lane Caravan Site, Canvey Island, had the last word. With a newswoman's flair, I happened to call at the very moment when her father, ex-wrestling champion James Hornblow, 56, was asking her suitor, Ron Ghaistrill, 17-year-old part-time youth-organiser, to accept her hand in marriage. "Why don't you drop dead?" Lorna asked me amid an excited buzz of conversation.

What do *you* think?

Compelled romantics

The white Southern Rhodesians can hardly be called a romantic people. Yet their cause must surely appeal irresistibly to those like myself who instinctively support the weaker side. One of their politicians, Mr. Gaunt, has described their situation as analogous to Dunkirk. This is not altogether absurd.

Here is a group of British people like ourselves—only more so, since they represent a simple, rather suburban attitude to life which is vanishing in our own country—with almost the whole world against them.

They face the fanatical power of black nationalism; tongue-tied themselves, they face the supremely vocal, embattled Left-wing moralisers of the world, the daily propaganda which seeks to persuade us that their mild, innocent, paternal rule is one of the most vicious tyrannies the world has ever seen.

These simple farmers, shopkeepers, tennis-players and devotees of afternoon tea are trapped in a situation—perhaps a heroic role—which does not suit them and which they are only just beginning dimly to understand. The most unromantic of people, they may soon acquire the romantic dignity of all those who, though their cause seems lost to start with, resolve to stand and fight.

Letter from a pygmy

Sir—You express surprise in your column at the news that pygmy forces in the Congo are using modern weapons. This is typical of the obscurantism and reactionary thinking which make you a laughing-stock throughout the forests of Central Africa.

The days when pygmies went about eating missionaries and using poison blowpipes are past. Science and technology are rapidly carrying the pygmies, like everyone else, forward into the Space Age.

New pygmy housing estates, power-stations, motorways and even a pygmy plastic handbag factory are planned for the Congo. I myself am the first pygmy sociologist to work in England, where I am doing research into the social implications of gigantism. My younger brother is head of the first pygmy psychiatric clinic in Kivu province.

We pygmies may be—in fact are—of less than average stature. But we are determined to play our full part in building a new world where the most advanced weapons as well as the other gifts of technology will be the birthright of all.

Yours faithfully,

"PROGRESSIVE PYGMY."
Chalk Farm.

Jellifer's diary

Thursday. 6.45 a.m. call. Worked at home all morning sorting out invitations (783) for the day. 1.15 p.m. lunched at the Hengrove Club with Mrs. Anthony Badgerton, the Piedmontese Ambassador and the Marchesa Balbergo, Lady Mudhoe, Father Grampus and Lord Gorbalstoun. 1.20 Lunched with Lady Jean Halibut-Smith, organiser of National Press Intrusion Day. 1.30 lunched with Sir William and Lady Goth-Jones, Dr. Bruce Westside and Mr. Terry Hungermeier, Mr. Julian Glasse-Derkeley and Lady Serena Burstleigh-Jones. 1.45 owing to oversight lunched with Mrs. Anthony Badgerton, &c., again.

On to the Barchester Hotel for a meeting called by Lady Crypt-Harris to discuss details of a film premiere (*Wittgenstein and the Vampires*) to be given next month at the Odeon theatre in aid of World Deaf-Aid Week. Then back home for a hurried bath, breakfast, lunch, change, &c., and on to Bilton Crescent where Mrs. Jill McInnes-Gammersjoeld was giving her first cocktail party of the season, a gracious, glamorous affair with a large number of beautiful older women and pretty girls—I noticed only one really hideous guest.

Twenty-seven more cocktail parties, then on to the delightful 21st birthday dance Mr. and Mrs. Olaf Dankshaw gave for their eldest daughter Tryphosa. Dinner with Lady Susan Hemp, another dinner with Mr. and Mrs. Bertram Murderhouse, back home for tea, bath, dinner, supper, change, &c., then to the first night of Brecht's play at the Misfortune theatre, where I noticed Lady Jock MacWeirdie and a gay crowd of guests still having lunch in the stalls, while forty-five cocktail parties, eleven debutante dances and a meeting in aid of Gossip Columnists' Mental Health Year were going on around them. . . .

(Acknowledgments to *Queen* magazine.)

Clairvoyant

Our grandchildren, said Lord McCorquodale in the Lords debate on birth control, will have to face a world population of 12 thousand million, still growing at an ever-increasing rate. How does he know this?

The figure is, of course, arrived at by extrapolation from the present world population and its ever-increasing rate of growth. It rests, in fact, on a belief that it is possible to foretell the future.

Lord McCorquodale would probably be the first to be sceptical about this belief, if it were based on the use not of statistics but of gazing-crystals or Tarot cards. But a veneer of science does not make the belief less dangerous and absurd.

Our ancestors had their own superstitions. But unless they were millenarians, they would have been amazed at the idea, now generally accepted without question, that it is permissible and even desirable to turn the world upside down and alter the manners and customs of whole nations for the sake of a future which, whatever statistics may show, remains unknown.

1964

Sunshine and shadow

The response from readers to my request to send in their Best Holiday Stories (First Prize: a free fortnight's holiday on the glamorous, sun-drenched Persian Gulf Riviera) moved me beyond words, reports MUNGO CLANGE, whose "Tidings of Joy" feature brings daily solace to millions of people and to many dogs, cats and budgerigars.

In spite of the postal strike, sacks of letters, redolent of human joy and heartache, of sunshine and shadow, have been pouring into this office daily. Here are a few of the best entries received so far:

Two years ago, when my wife Thora (she won the Glamorous Granny contest at West Hartlepool in 1959 in the face of stiff opposition), myself and Baby Ron, aged 26, were at Torremolinos, we asked a Spaniard we found hanging about aimlessly on the beach the way to the nearest Bingo hall. To our surprise he took to his heels and ran screaming into the sea, where, I believe, he was later drowned. Foreigners are a queer lot and I shall never understand them. (J. S. BREATH, Phantomsby Park Caravan Site, Wolverhampton.)

I am a State-registered claustromaniac and xylophage but am employed, on medical advice, as a greenkeeper at the local golf-course. The best holiday I ever spent was in July, 1928 when my son Fred accidentally locked me in a broom-cupboard at home and went off on a fortnight's holiday to Whitley Bay. When released I was fighting fit and had gained two stone. (NORMAN SOCK, Gidea Park.)

Every summer my wife and I take a boating holiday on the Manchester Ship Canal, savouring the quiet charm of this unspoiled corner of Old England. Last year, as we went slowly past the Trafford Park Industrial Estate, we saw a boat coming from the opposite direction, rowed by several youngish women wearing crowns and dresses of old-fashioned cut made of what I recognised (I am in the clothing trade) as white samite.

They went past at a fair lick and my wife (who is highly strung) maintained that there was a body in the boat. We wondered later whether to inform the police, but live and let live is my motto. (MAX NOBESPEARE, Belper.)

Pleasure dome

Stretchford City Council has set up a committee, headed by dynamic, go-ahead Cllr. Gordon Nadir, chairman of Nadirco Enterprises, to plan a Pleasure Area, taking in the Stretchford

Green Belt and eventually surrounding the city with what a public relations handout describes as a People's Girdle of Ecstasy.

"The most urgent problem of the age," Cllr. Nadir told me yesterday, "after the problem of profit, is the problem of leisure and, consequent on that, pleasure. I believe our plan for the Stretchford Pleasure Area will go far towards solving these problems simultaneously.

"That it will be a really imaginative plan, geared to the People's needs, is shown by the names of those who are advising us—such distinguished people as Sir William Goth-Jones, Vice-Chancellor of Stretchford University, Dr. Bernard Goth-Jones, Director of the Goth-Jones Drama Foundation, Dr. Lloyd Goth-Jones, the eminent architect, and Dr. Freudina Goth-Jones, the erotician and social problematologist—all of them directors of Nadirco Enterprises.

"We shall take as our over-all model and inspiration the well-known Pleasure Dome and adjacent grounds of Xanadu, once the property of the late Emperor Kubla Khan, described in a handout written by an English public relations executive, the late S. T. Coleridge.

"This will, of course, be adapted to modern conditions and modern needs. Sinuous rills, incense-bearing trees, romantic chasms and cedarn covers will be provided in full measure, as specified, but they will be interspersed with capacious car-parks, fun-fairs, teenage battle areas where live ammunition can be used, fooderamas, electronic bingo halls, underwater motorcycling courses, old time dancing centres, garagomats, vendomats and everything that the people of Stretchford can desire or Nadirco Enterprises can contract for.

"Our guiding principle will be: Pleasure on the prow, and Profit at the helm."

Shares of Nadirco Enterprises boomed spectacularly on the Stock Exchange yesterday and are still rising rapidly to-day.

Mystery intruder

Bruce Carbon, 24, described as a New Thinker, of Pembroke Road, Lampton-on-Hoke, was charged at Nerdley Magistrates Court yesterday with loitering on enclosed premises.

Det. Sgt. J. Mackenzie, 40, of the Nerdley police, said that in the early hours of Sept. 2 he found Carbon trying to climb up a nuclear accelerator at the Nerdley Institute of Advanced Technology. When cautioned, Carbon, who appeared to be in an excited state and whose breath smelled strongly of newsprint, said we were living in a time of rapid and exhilarating change.

"It is up to every one of us," he added, "to be pacesetters, to show that as New Thinkers we have sloughed off the dead hand of the past and are reaching forward towards the horizons of the technological future. Why don't you join me in this exciting crusade?"

When Carbon pointed to the accelerator and offered him a hand up, he arrested him. When formally charged at the station, accused climbed on to the Superintendent's desk, waving his arms and emitting a loud humming noise. Taken to a cell, he exploded.

In court the accused, who asked for 153 similar offences to be taken into consideration, stated: "Eton and Harrow ... automation ... breaking free of outmoded ideas ... a new dynamic Britain ... grouse-moors . . . social progress . . . above all, New Thinking demands New Thought."

Binding Carbon over, the chairman, Dr. Ellis Goth-Jones, 58, said we were living in a time of rapid and exhilarating change. A new, dynamic Britain was on the horizon. He himself was, on the whole, just as thrilled about this as anyone. But people should not take the law into their own hands.

On the ohm farm

The bounteous, golden, chemical-rich harvest was gathered in. Harvest Home, with its quaint, immemorial ceremonies of Costing the Net Yield and Plastic-garlanding the Last Spray Gun was over. The last visiting agrotechnological statistician had departed, and Seth Roentgen, Britain's greatest scientific farmer, settled down in his office for a brief moment of leisure.

Outside in the mellow September sunlight the stubblefields, saturated with benzoamyl-toluene, shimmered with drowsy hues of purple, yellow and green. An electronic scarecrow boomed at intervals from a treble-yield garden-croft and gathering helicopters, out on a practice run for the winter spraying, roared in the intimidated skies.

Idly the agrotechnician took up a leaflet just delivered, redolent of the immemorial garnered wisdom of Earth. In rare moments of comparative idleness like these, such was his favourite reading.

"Vaccines," he read, "Sevlam, Dyslam, Quadlam, Pulklam, Blacklam, Breglam, Leglam." The words came like a litany, like the low, rapt whisper of mellow, fruitful Autumn itself. "Furasol, the newest nitrofuran . . . Loxon . . . Mintic . . . Thibenzole . . . Phenothiazine . . . Halophen, the first non-toxic bactericidal sterilising agent . . ."

Lulled by the timeless words, he let his head fall on his breast for a moment, and passed into a misty, autumnal dream of overheads and expenses, of vast chemically fertilised fields, yielding 4,000 per cent. net profit, that stretched to the blue horizons of the world.

A voice boomed over the loudspeaker: "General alert! General alert! Scarlet pimpernel believed detected in Field 49, Section 17E!" In a flash Farmer Roentgen was on his feet, dreams forgotten. Reaching for his personal atomic spray-projector, he strode purposefully out to scotch the threat of this potential loss of 0.0000019 per cent. of planned productivity.

A barefaced lie

Frank Harris, as everyone knows, was a bounder and social climber of the first order. In his so-called autobiography, "My Life and Loves," he boasts of his invariable success. I am glad to say that there was at least one occasion when he was not successful.

One day in 1907 I was in the library at Simpleham when Venables, the butler, announced: "A Mr. Francis Harris to see you, sir." I looked at the man's card with distaste. It was of large size, engraved with florid vulgarity, gold-edged, and bore the inscription: "Frank Harris, Genius and Lover of Women."

A loud booming, whiffling noise was coming from the ante-room and there was a smell of pomade and expensive cigar-smoke. "I do not know Mr. Harris," I said with freezing hauteur, "Nor, on the evidence I now have about his character and antecedents, do I wish to know him. Kindly convey that message to him, Venables, and ask him to leave Simpleham at once. If he refuses you may eject him, using the maximum of force. If necessary, get Bennett, Dodds and Hargreaves to help you."

In the event, Venables exceeded his instructions, stuffing Harris up a chimney in the unused East Wing, from which he had to be removed by block and tackle.

Needless to say there is not a word about this incident in Harris's autobiography. Instead there is a long, boastful account of a week-end at Simpleham in 1909, when King Edward is said to have been a guest—a typical absurdity, since I always made a point of cutting that monarch whenever I saw him.

A great debate

Moving the second reading of the Discrimination (All Purposes) Bill, Mr. A. Grudge (Lab., Stretchford North) said that if Britain were to maintain her standing in the eyes of the non-aligned world and move rapidly forward into the Space Age, it was essential to stamp out all vestiges of discrimination whether on grounds of race, sex, religion, age, moral character, intelligence or anything else.

It was intolerable, to give a few examples, that one-armed Pakistani women were excluded from the Oxford Boat Race crew; that magistrates, in open court, publicly discriminated between honest people and so-called criminals; that Calvinistic Methodist children of low intelligence were excluded from the higher grades of the Civil Service.

We must build a Britain in which everyone pulled together. If we could not make everyone alike (and personally he hoped that Science would soon make this possible), at least we should treat them alike.

Sir Rufus Grunt (C., Natterhurst) said that he hoped the Bill would deal with the possibility of flogging everyone, not merely violent criminals, periodically. A good sound tanning never did anyone any harm; if he might say so, he was himself a living proof of this. If he could not get anyone else to flog him, he flogged himself every day.

Miss Edith Sandpiper (Lab., Shuffham) complained of sex discrimination in such places as men's Turkish baths, which deliberately excluded women. She herself, as a test case, had recently entered a men's Turkish bath in London. At sight of her all the customers fled and one of the attendants fainted (laughter).

Sir Rufus Grunt: They thought she was a Turk (laughter).

Mr. A. Grudge: That is a perfect example of the sort of racial discrimination we are trying to deal with. How would the Hon. Member, if he were a Turk, like to have such offensive remarks made about him? (Labour cries of "Cyprus!" "Suez!" "Smethwick!" etc., etc.)

Wing-Cdr. H. J. Wolfram-Jones (C., Nerdley) said that the problem of discrimination was closely bound up with juvenile delinquency, road accidents, old age pensions, the 11-plus examination, steel nationalisation, alcoholism, indecent films and the present flood of printed filth. He believed that unless this country devoted itself to the ideal of service it would perish, as the Roman Empire perished. But he did not think more motorways and shorter licensing hours were necessarily the answer.

The debate continues.

1965

Greetings

Welcome to 1965! As the New Year bells, tape-recorded by British technological know-how, ring out from tower and steeple over Britain's smiling, chemical-envenomed fields, messages come vibrantly from famous men and women who are sure, whatever happens, to play a leading part in the stirring news paragraphs and television interviews that lie ahead.

"Coats off!" clarion-calls Gen. Sir Frederick Nidgett, leader of men and expert on industrial relations. "1965 will be a year of unexampled prosperity for Britain if we resolve to pull together right, left and centre, in every direction, and on all sides of industry. Let's get our backs stuck well into the cutting edge of an export drive with a sense of purpose and vision, and hit the Luddites and the Dismal Desmonds a shrewd wallop where it hurts most."

"The old year has been a happy one for all who love revolution, massacre, rape, destruction, hate and the progress of mankind," says Dr. Abdul castrumba, freelance, all-purposes, revolutionary leader, who is on holiday in go-ahead Zanzibar. "But there are still so many countries crying out in agony to be liberated from peace and quiet that I am confident the New Year will be happier still."

"Let's make 1965 a really trendy year," is the message of top model, TV star, fun-person and pace-setter Giselle de Frabazon. "Let's concentrate on the things that *really* matter to Britain—the new fur table-legs, Zambian cookery, de Sade on ice, pop sculpture, stuffed insects, a National Fun Centre and—long overdue—a Ministry of Trends."

"My message for 1965," says Sir William Goth-Jones, Vice-Chancellor of Stretchford University, "is simple. We must resolve, individually and as a nation, to show more respect to engineers. Try giving up your seats to them in trains and buses: in restaurants, offer to pay their bills for them; if you're married, offer them your wives and daughters. Only thus can Britain survive in this technological age we love so much."

Norman the good

The Duke and Duchess of Kent, who have been presiding over Gambia's independence ceremonies, are reported to have delighted the Gambians by their informality. Perhaps we should take another look into the future, into Good King Norman's Golden Time, when a Socialist Royal family will display an informality of which we can hardly dream.

February 18, 2005
Duke Len of Erdington, brother of Queen Doreen, accompanied by the Queen Gran, arrived this morning in the steam dredger *J. J.*

Mendelson at Warbey Island, an isolated atoll in the Pacific, the last fragment of Britain's former colonial empire to gain independence.

As he waded ashore to be received by Dr. Ghost, Warbeyan Prime Minister and President-elect, the Duke delighted onlookers by taking informal swigs from a bottle of National Austerity Gin. As he inspected the guard of honour, he slumped informally to the ground and was dragged informally to his feet by the Queen Gran.

That evening, at a State banquet, the Duke drank the health of the new nation and, ignoring his notes, made an informal speech which included anecdotes about the social life of sales representatives in the Midlands. The Queen Gran's shouted interruptions, though informal, made parts of his speech inaudible, but an expurgated transcript was later made available to the Press.

At midnight, after a march past by a detachment of the Royal Socialist Antinuclear Air Force, which had been carrying out leaflet distribution duties on the island, the Duke, in a moving ceremony, lowered the Trades Union Jack, while the purple and yellow 18-starred flag of Warbeya was simultaneously raised aloft.

The Duke's informal gesture in getting his braces caught in the ascending flag and being hoisted, struggling and shouting incoherently, to the top of the flagpole delighted the crowd so much that the Queen Gran's informal comment to Dr. Ghost, "I don't like black men, and never did," passed almost unnoticed.

Doreen Gaggs talking

To judge by the raised eyebrows and crooked little fingers among the fuddy-duddies whenever some 13-year-old schoolgirl announces her engagement (writes DOREEN GAGGS), you'd think we were still living in the days of King Stephen.

I've even read about so-called teachers who ordered girls not to wear their engagement-rings in class, because it might cause jealousy among the other non-engaged girls. My goodness, how anti-Life can you get?

Luckily, not all schools are as stuffy and snob-ridden as that. I've just taken time off from a long week-end at my friend the Marquis of Stretchford's big country-house in Staffordshire, to visit a really splendid, forward-looking school not far away. It's called Bog Lane Secondary Modern.

Here's a school that's really living in 1965. Nearly all the girls are engaged, of course, mostly to boys who are fellow-pupils. The result is that instead of spending their schooldays in snobbish, stuffy fact-grubbing, they're learning to live in this day and age—and learning fast.

I looked in on one class which was a positive blaze of jewellery. Many of the girls were engaged to more than one boy, and some were wearing as many as six engagement rings at once. The room was a babble of excited conversation about stones, settings and above all, how much cash boy-friends who hadn't been switched on enough to knock off the rings from jewellers or pawnbrokers or by "doing" private houses had paid for them.

Suddenly, in one corner of the room, I noticed a wispy teacher and one ringless, lank-haired, bespectacled girl, both without make-up, dimly trying to read out of some dust-laden textbook or other.

The snobs and the anti-Life brigade were still at it! My heart sank. I only began to cheer up again when I went round and inspected the really up-to-date school premarital family planning clinic, the marriage guidance bureau, the psychiatric screening centre, the infants' home and the mental hospital.

Struggle for power

A new television serial deals with the struggle for power on a London newspaper. I have a draft for an even more absorbing serial about the struggle for power in this column. It reveals labyrinths of the human heart so murky that even the GPI Network may hesitate to broadcast it.

Set among the rambling corridors and mahogany-infested offices of Simple House, it presents a set of characters all the more incompatible, all the more bent on doing each other down and snatching supreme power because of the subtle family links between them.

There is managing director Ezekiel Bradshaw Simple, square-jawed, frock-coated man of adamant, a Yorkshire ironmaster and lay preacher who refuses to co-operate with the Government's economic policy until factory hours are increased to 14 hours a day, with compulsory Bible readings night and morning. There is personnel manager John Ruskin Simple, nature-lover, organic food and pure water propagandist and Luddite, who organises nature-rambles for the workers on which they are encouraged to dynamite pylons and dig up airfields and motorways.

There is sinister, black-clad, race-conscious Houston Stewart Simple, head of research and archives, who collects photographs of German generals and is drilling his elderly, bespectacled assistants as stormtroopers for an eventual putsch.

Another executive is clerical reactionary J. M. de Maistre Simple ("Posed as Cardinal: Six years for 'Impudent Fraud'"). There is Chief Welfare Officer Ieuan ap Iorwerth Simple, Welsh nationalist and pan-Celtic agitator, with his glamorous girl personal assistant, long-haired harpist Rhiannon Morag O'Raghallaigh. And ever moving behind the scenes is the chairman of the board, Lord Algernon Simple, an aristocrat of immemorial lineage who conceals under his monocled, languid, effete exterior a talent for ruthless intrigue second only to that of Lloyd George.

The tortuous manoeuvres of these characters in their single-minded pursuit of power reduce the novels of C. P. Snow to the level of Noddy in Toyland.

Bookshelf

Nembutalov and the Development of Anarcho-Syndicalist Economic Theory, 1848-1900.
By Wolfgang Braunzwerg. (Norm and Graph, 84s.)

Dr. Braunzwerg, who is Lecturer in Political Theory at Bevindon University, has worked for 10 years to produce a book which is not only of definitive importance for the specialist in the history of anarcho-syndicalism, but will also fascinate the general reader.

Taking a deep breath, Dr. Braunzwerg plunges into the strange, murky world of 19th-century revolutionary life in Russia, which, as he says, "manured the ground for the events of 1917." Here we glimpse, flitting through a lurid gloom haunted by Tsarist agents, professional conspirators, mad beggars, and fanatics from every part of the revolutionary spectrum, such figures as Sekonalov, Benzedrinov, Phanerganov the dialectical spiritualist, Prince Andrei Dexedrinov, ineffectually plotting to overthrow the Tsar on his estate of Oblovonka, and of course, Nembutalov himself.

It is a stuffy, oppressive world of violent controversy and furious political passions (when Nembutalov sent Marx a copy of his 250,000-word pamphlet *The Roots of Political Inertia*, Marx publicly described him as "an old surgical boot" and "a decaying cabbage-stalk of the bourgeoisie").

There is welcome human interest in the equivocal relations of Nembutalov and Benzedrinov with the enigmatic Ukrainian terrorist Anna Drinamylenko, who when not cooking enormous pots of sunflower-stew for the conspirators, spent her time, often to their alarm, manufacturing infernal machines. The fiasco of her attempt to assassinate Pobedonostsev, the dreaded Procurator of the Holy Synod, in 1890, when his bodyguard was merely showered with stew, led to an open breach and to Lenin's sardonic comment: "Plain cookery is the enemy of the world revolution."

The proof-reading for such an expensive work might have been more thorough. On p. 386, "Lenin" appears as "Lemon" and on p. 419 as "Lonegan," while "Kropotkin" appears as "Corcoran" throughout.

Nature notes—

by "Redshank"

At a time when so many of our old country customs are sinking into the limbo of forgotten things, it is heartening to find that some show unexpected powers of resistance. My own corner of the countryside is particularly rich in these age-old survivals.

Strolling through the hamlet of Kingston Blatt at noon yesterday, peering occasionally at thatched eave or telephone kiosk for signs of early nest-builders, I knew from the loud humming proceeding from Fred Mangle's cottage that the old man, always a staunch upholder of country ways, was "telling the bees" again.

Readers of the novels of Mary Webb, a favourite authoress of that great country-lover the late Stanley Baldwin, will remember this Shropshire custom by which the head of a household solemnly told his bees the tidings of such important family events as marriages, births or deaths.

This custom, like many others in our neighbourhood, has been subtly modified to-day. As the bees buzzed drowsily about his head, occasionally settling on the old pianola (in rosewood case) or the daguerreotype of Lord Raglan on the wall, old Mangle was telling them about current divorces in the neighbourhood or about which of the village lads had formed new pop groups. This he varied by readings from the latest county statistics of vandalism, illegitimacy and alcoholism as set out in a Government report.

A happy blend of old and new, I thought, as I walked away towards Blumber's Meadow in search of the first shy pipits, accompanied by a few old-fashioned, prim-looking bees which evidently found the recital too much for their queasy apian stomachs.

Think on

That a writer of television scripts about comic policemen should be made a Life Peer is absurd enough. That he should lay down the law on television drama to the Royal Society of Arts is worse.

Lord Willis criticises what he calls the "wet set," that is, people who believe television may have evil effects. "What I find strange and disturbing," he says, "is that so many people seem to imagine the audience can be made savage, or promiscuous, or criminal by one programme, but not made to think by another."

Who imagines anything of the sort? Who doubts that television audiences can be "made to think"? The really important question is: Made to think *what*?

For most of the people responsible for the "serious," "iconoclastic," "thought-provoking" television programmes we are told so much about, to think is to think Left-wing. There is no other kind of thinking.

It is to think that the civilised traditions still remaining in England are mostly mere antique snobberies, to be uprooted and swept away; that religion is an outmoded sham; that every man is entitled to make his own code of morals, or even do without one altogether; that there is not much to choose between the Russian and American systems of government; that the white South Africans, *per se*, are the wickedest people on earth; that the hope of England and the world is the United Nations; that . . . you can easily go on with the list for yourself.

The process of stuffing television audiences with these opinions, while hardly ever even suggesting that any other opinions exist, can be called "making them think" if you like. But there are other, less indulgent, ways of describing it. One of them is "brain-washing."

Provincial news

"Way of the World" Reporter

Last Saturday's pretty wedding at Nerdley All Saints (Staffs) of blonde, attractive model Shirley Globes, 23, daughter of 51-year-old Mr. Norman Globes, a local turntable overseer, to tall, brown-eyed, 27-year-old spongecake executive Kevin Breath held some unusual features.

The bride could not bear to be parted from her pet warthog, five-year-old, African-born Mazeppa, during the ceremony. So, with the smiling permission of the go-ahead Rector, 53-year-old, Harrogate-born nuclear disarmer the Rev. Austen Fredds, Mazeppa joined the wedding party dressed as a bridesmaid, in shot pink and electric blue lamé, with matching handbag.

The Rector stipulated that the warthog should not enter the churchyard. But owing to a last-minute confusion of identity with one of the other bridesmaids, 26-year-old red-haired paperclip factory underlooker Mavis Tuber, Mazeppa not only took her place at the ceremony but attempted to sign the register and kissed both the bridegroom and the best man, 29-year-old, heavily-moustached cold chisel tester Howard Trembath.

As the bride and bridegroom drove away, amid a veritable raging inferno of good wishes, for their honeymoon at Barrow-in-Furness, Mazeppa tried to follow. A further confusion of identity occurred when the Rector, trying to restrain the animal, seized grey-haired, wartime Church of Scotland canteen manageress Mrs. Beryl Globes, 48, and a fracas broke out in which dark-haired, Yarmouth-born supply teacher Davina Bloatch, 35, damaged her hearing-aid.

Arts

There were angry scenes at a Stretchford City Council meeting yesterday when the question of the annual grant to the Stretchford Municipal Symphony Orchestra was discussed.

Alderman J. S. Goat (Lab.) said that he was second to none in his conviction that to foster the arts was an essential plank in the wind of change which was creating a democratic Britain of equal opportunity for all.

He thought, however, that the proposal to provide and maintain a personal coat-peg, at a cost of 15s a year, in the dressing-room of Sir Jim Gastropodi, the orchestra's permanent conductor, was an insult to the ratepayers. When two-thirds of the world's population were on the borderline of starvation, as a result of 13 years of Tory misrule, it was an inversion of priorities and a case of midsummer madness.

Cllr. D. Croake (Con.) said that although he was second to none in his love of music, he thought that Sir Jim Gastropodi's choice of programmes left much to be desired. The incessant performance of music by German and other Continental composers suggested a bias against the Commonwealth. It was, he thought, part of the current betrayal of this anchor-stone of world peace and prosperity.

Alderman R. Gogden (Lab.) said that although he was second to none in his determination to put Stretchford fair and square on the cultural map of Britain, he believed that the orchestra's annual grant should be withheld while it continued to operate a colour bar.

The string section of the orchestra did not include a single coloured immigrant, and although a Pakistani triangle player had been engaged it was only too noticeable that in many of the works played he was deliberately excluded from active participation for long periods at a stretch. Here was a matter which should goad the conscience, not only of musicians but of all who wanted Britain to retain the moral leadership of the world.

Jude obscurer

In the semi-darkness, on this occasion only moderately inspissated, of the small front parlour of a council-house in Melchester New Town, in Wessex, a young man of the artisan class, well-made and alert, yet with a certain shade of melancholy habitually wreathing his strongly-marked features, sat watching a television-set.

Jude Fawley was a devotee of the new "University of the Air." Indeed, since it had been introduced on the new BBC channel by a Socialist Government bent on improving the minds of the humbler classes, he had largely given up his books.

The flickering, bluish light of the set, ever-changing as the images of scientists, complex mathematical formulae or vast technological installations ebbed and flowed on the screen, was enough to feed his dreams. As often, he now found himself unconsciously giving vent to these aloud.

"Just wait, just wait, that's all," the young man now muttered. "I shall be a great nuclear physicist yet. I know it. I shall have my own department, my own staff of white-coated assistants . . . I shall build my own nuclear power station . . . over at Winfrith maybe, out on the heath yonder. . . .

"How does the Second Law of Thermodynamics go? . . . ah, yes . . . mass . . . energy . . . velocity of light . . . bombarding the nucleus. . . ."

A sudden screech from the next room, uttered in the unmistakable accents of a female native of the Vale of Blackmoor, brought him painfully back to reality.

"Jude! Jude! Come and see if 'ee can mend thik spin-drier! 'Tes to-brasted again! And all along of 'ee staring in a swoundy dream at thik telly all day long!"

Jude rose warily to his feet as Arabella, with her arms akimbo, entered the room like a whirlwind. Instinctively, with a protective gesture, he made as if to shield the television screen, on which a bald biochemist was now displaying a diagram of enzymonucleic acid, from his wife's wrath.

But he was too late. With a smart click of the small, fluted knob, Arabella had switched channels. A slow, almost sensuous smile,

80

derived partly from satisfaction with the new programme itself, partly from pleasure at once again frustrating her husband's dreams of self-improvement, spread over her face as, in tremendous, deafening volume, the strains of "Juke Box Jury" flooded the room. . . .

(Acknowledgments to Thomas Hardy)

Fun with the void

It is pointless to complain that many contemporary works of art, in the theatre or other media, are meaningless. Their meaninglessness is their meaning.

Sometimes with talent and skill, sometimes with modish, mechanical facility, sometimes with neither—and sometimes even by accident—these works portray a universe from which meaning has drained away from material objects and from men themselves. If they are effective works of this kind, they can move us by the terror of an emptiness from which everything but terror has disappeared. If not, they appear merely silly.

There is nothing new in this view of the universe; it is a common, perhaps universal experience for men; it has appeared, at any rate incidentally, in many great works of art throughout history. What is new is that the mass media of communication have vulgarised it and made it fashionable.

It has become material for technical exercises by pseudo-artists without feeling or talent, substitutes for experience as superficial and stereotyped as any drawing-room comedy. The Void is now "with it".

Boon

This week the Ministry of Aviation carried out tests in connection with its project for a new airliner which will be able to cross the Atlantic in under 10 minutes. It uses a new "miracle fuel" which gives out a smell described by Government aromatologists as "mildly unpleasant" to "nauseating" (with stench-indices ranging from 14.2 to 107.6 on the Horrorwicz Scale).

The tests are regarded as "highly successful". A few hundred thousand telephone calls in protest were received from people, described as "mainly cranks and neurotics", living over an area of

200 square miles. Emergency hospitals were set up to deal with two or three million cases of nausea and vomiting.

A Ministry of Aviation expert who was present stated that when the new airliners were in full operation the smell would pervade the whole of the country. They were working on a scheme to issue special masks to the whole population, including new-born babies. Alternatively, they might introduce some substance such as phenylacetobenzine into water supplies. This would destroy everyone's sense of smell altogether, at some risk—well within the limits of tolerance, of course—of side-effects such as brain damage and sexual impotence.

The smell, he said, would probably persist for about 200,000 years. But, as everyone would realise, this was a mere flash compared with the unlimited aeons of technological progress before us.

"We have clearly got to get used to living in a superaromatic age," he explained. "I think everyone will agree that what we have smelt to-day is not intolerable. Personally, I rather like it," he added smilingly, as, green in the face and retching, he staggered towards the nearest Government experimental vomitorium.

Lucky winners

As we expected, our competition for the best answers to the question "Why do I like 'Way of the World'?" (with prizes of a week's holiday either in Salford or on the Persian Gulf Riviera) produced an avalanche of entries. Here is a selection of winners' views:

"What I like about 'Way of the World' is that it gives the views of all sides without fear or favour and is completely free from prejudice or bias." (Mrs. J. Bootle, Tamworth.)

"Apart from the excellent sports coverage, gardening hints and really informative articles on ballroom dancing, I enjoy your column for its cheery, sunny attitude to life, such a welcome contrast to the moaners and groaners who are far too vocal to-day." (Fred Hashimoto, St. Austell.)

"To me 'Way of the World' comes like an old, understanding friend, breathing the nasturtium-scented heartache of old-world cottage gardens, bringing daily balm and solace with tender smile or booming laugh to young and old." (Miss Vera Slabb, Goole.)

"Such writers as that brilliant husband and wife team Jack Moron and Doreen Gaggs express everything I am thinking far better than I could express or even think it myself. Their fearless, hard-hitting exposures of the bestial menace of the Eternal Hun should be compulsory reading for everybody. More power to all their elbows!" (R. H. Crevice, "Bashteuton", Numb Lane Caravan Site, Canvey Island.)

"Thank goodness one columnist has the guts to stand up for the eternal verities of life—the rounding up, flogging and hanging of all niggers, wogs, dagoes, Welshmen, Irishmen, and other 'lesser breeds', wherever they may be found. If you would advocate sending the whole lot back to Palestine, where they belong, I would like your column even more." (L. Scream, Bevindon Airport.)

"I am 94 and my eyes are not what they were. Every morning I get my 11 great-grandchildren to read your column to me in unison, as loudly as possible, till I feel the top of my head coming off, after which I make a hearty breakfast." (J. H. Vector, Barrow-in-Furness.)

How it was

I was sitting in the tastelessly furnished lounge of the Adlon Hotel, Berlin, having tea, as usual, with Adolf Hitler and other Nazi leaders, on that day in February, 1933, when the news of the Oxford "King and Country" motion came through.

The Führer was just starting, with evident relish, on his sixth enormous cream bun when Dr. Goebbels came clumping in, obviously in a state of high excitement.

"My Führer!" he shouted almost hysterically. "England is finished! Kaput! The students of Oxford University have just declared they will not fight! Nothing now stands in the way of German mastery of Europe, of the British Empire, of the world . . ."

"Hold on a bit," Goering put in, with, of course, a fat laugh. That there was little love lost between him and the diminutive club-footed doctor had long been obvious to me. "My Luftwaffe . . ."

Goebbels shot him a venomous glance. Rosenberg was already droning on about the proportion of pure Germanic blood among the Oxford undergraduates. Even if they would not fight for King and Country, he thought, they would gladly fight for Führer and Reich against the Judaeo-Plutocratic-Bolshevist world conspiracy, if the issues could be properly explained to them.

Seyss-Inquart and Heydrich suggested that Oxford should be bombed immediately. Himmler favoured more subtle methods, such as the planting of Nazi members as college servants and landladies and as potmen in the mediaeval taverns of the age-old Nordic city.

Suddenly Hitler himself, who had apparently fallen into one of his shamanistic trances, quelled the uproar by rapping the table with a huge chocolate éclair.

"Simple," he commanded, "you are an Englishman. Give us your opinion."

And that is how I was able, by feeding these naive, thick-skulled, ill-educated Teutons with information even more totally misleading than they already had, to ensure that when they started their inevitable war it would be at such a colossal disadvantage.

A new star

Over the cultural horizon of Britain, now the cynosure of the world, rises a new star (writes art-critic Neville Dreadberg). He is bearded, stocky, 27-year-old Neville Dreadberg, who has exploded into success—personal, social and financial—as current rave of the pop art "scene" with his show of "structural" stale confectionery sculpture at the Kevin Blatsch Gallery.

The first artist to explore the inwardness—and the essential anguish, loneliness and non-communication—of cream buns, éclairs, custard tarts, liquorice all-sorts, chocolate caramels and

similar artefacts, Dreadberg is a man of the *avant garde* with fingers deep in many different pies.

He is directing a film he has written about the sex-life of alienated Lesbian boiled-sweet factory workers in the Midlands. His GPI Network TV series on the Theatre of Stale Confectionery starts next month. An opera, "Marshmallow 46", with Dreadberg's libretto and musique concrete ("porno-realistic with sadistic overtones" is his own description) is also "boiling up" in his restless mind. His pornographic novel "Naked Humbug" comes out in July both in London and New York. Rave reviews, mostly by Dreadberg himself, have already been organised.

Unconcerned with political or social questions, Dreadberg believes that present Western policy is unmitigatedly evil and that Britain, "guilt-ridden and sodden with puritanism, censorship and hide-bound conventional morality", is an impossible country for an artist to live and work in.

Outrage

A keen student of my own dreams, I have generally been able to count on one dream of ideal landscapes (down, Dr. S. Freud and other known troublemakers!) about every fortnight.

In such dreams I generally travel in an idealised Derbyshire or Massif Central of France, in Tuscany, Spanish sierras or Himalayan valleys—or perhaps in a subtle mingling of some or all of these—in an idealized 18th century conveyance over idealized 18th century roads and accompanied by idealized 18th century servants.

The other night, for the first time, a new and disturbing element entered the dream. I was passing, late on a fine summer evening, through a wild, solitary upland region with only a few shepherds' huts to be seen, and with fine jagged peaks, admirably arranged, in the distance.

Suddenly, descending into a shallow valley, I came upon a small housing estate, unmistakably English from the television aerials on each smug, planner-spaced house and the bluish flicker to be seen through each uncurtained window as the democratic occupants took their ease with foil-wrapped TV snacks beside them.

A signpost by the roadside pointed to the "Industrial Estate" and, inanely, the "Frank Cousins Radio Rentals Factory".

Struggling up from my rugs in anger and alarm, I ordered the coachman to whip up the horses. But before I woke from what had become a nightmare, I could see in the distance, in a noble mountain valley, the unmistakable outlines of a people's fun installation.

The explanation may be that I read, in the course of duty, too many newspapers. But that democracy, not satisfied with ravaging our waking lives, should begin to invade our dreams as well is an outrage.

Unfortunately, as someone said of the weather, one hardly knows to whom to complain.

Pop notes

by Jim Droolberg

The Filthy Swine, with their folk hit "My Girl's Head Comes to a Point" again head the Top Twenty this week. The Bedbugs' "Chewing Old Socks With You" goes down to third place and Cliff Alopecia moves up with "Individual Fruit Pie of Love".

Wanda Drainstorm's "My Old Plastic Granny" stays steady at

number four and the Cockroaches have rocketed up from eleventh to fifth place with "Love Crawled Under the Door".

The Drips, whose "Softening of the Brain" kept fifth place for three weeks running, suddenly collapsed and fell out of the charts altogether. Their manager has had them destroyed.

Tempter

"It's high time you had a new image. Don't you want to be one of the Get-up-and-Go People? Wouldn't you like to be written about in *Queen* and *Town* as brilliant, dynamic, exciting, controversial, trend-setting, pop, op, camp, kooky, kinky, *avant garde?* Wouldn't you like to be enormously, but enormously rich and go to first-nights and parties all the time with hairdressers, writers, fashion designers, actors and fabulous models?

"Wouldn't you like to take a holiday in Turkey, drive a white Q-type Jaguar and be photographed by Lord Snowdon? Wouldn't you—"

Breaking off a paragraph about Brass-Rubbing in Shropshire between the Wars, I looked about my office, unable to discover where the relentless voice, bright yet with a strange, droning quality, was coming from.

Everything seemed to be in order. The grandfather-clock showed the correct time and the correct phase of the moon. My reference books—Burke's Landed Gentry, Jane's Fighting Ships, Spurrell's Welsh Dictionary, the Almanach de Gotha, Blunt's Dictionary of Religious Sects, the Army List for 1907—were all in their proper places. So were the engraved portraits of Hölderlin, Bruckner, George Gissing and other culture-heroes. Nothing had changed. Yet the voice still droned on. Now it seemed to come from everywhere at once.

"Why don't you drop all this reactionary whimsy about standards of civilisation, England, rural landscapes, comparative philology, the Luddite Front and the coming feudal society? It's not going to get you anywhere, you know.

"Just put yourself in my hands. In two days I can give you an entirely new image. Integration, experimental theatre, motorways, fun-people, the lot. I can—"

The voice died away into an electronic hum, merging with the accustomed noises. I searched the room, peering into drawers, under typewriters and, particularly closely, into waste-paper baskets. There was no sign of the speaker.

When the Devil tempted Faust, he appeared in the form of an energetic and witty man of the world. To Ivan Karamazov he appeared as a slightly seedy minor official. To others he has appeared as an empty cupboard, or as a dirty sheet of newspaper blowing along the road.

It might be possible to cope with these. But what can be done with a Devil so confident of being unanswerably with-it that he does not even trouble to manifest himself at all, but simply pervades the air we breathe?

New style

Nadir Hostelries Ltd., an enterprising subsidiary of the Nadirco Empire, is rapidly extending its operations over the Midlands and beyond. It is taking over higher-grade hotels by the score and assimilating them to what its publicity handouts call "the dynamic, new-style pattern of 20th-century British hotel management".

During a visit to the Stretchford area, I called for dinner at one of these hotels, the Old Post Horn, a famous coaching inn at Lampton-on-Hoke, notable for its associations with Dr. Johnson, Dickens, Thackeray, Mrs. Gaskell, Arnold Bennett, W. J. Locke, Hubert Crackenthorpe, Scriabin and others. When I was last there, it had been a comfortable, rather old-fashioned place with good food and drink and pleasant service.

A dynamic blast of 20th-century cooking met me as I went in. The horse-brasses and prints of hunting mishaps on the walls were now interspersed with arrowed signs: "Dr. Johnson Steak and Chicken Bar", "Mrs. Gaskell Chicken and Steak Bar", "Arnold Bennett Scampi Bar", "Thackeray Steak and Scampi Bar", "W. J. Locke Scampi, Steak and Chicken Bar", and so on, quoting fixed prices for the appropriate food (plus glass of red or white wine, "country-fresh roll and butter, traditional old English cheese-board and schooner-size cup of Gaelic coffee").

At random I entered the Dr. Johnson Steak and Chicken Bar and was at once caught up in a dynamic meal-producing machine. "Our object," said a notice on the wall, "is to streamline high-class catering-operation in accordance with the new demand for speed and convenience. We estimate that you can enter this room, sit down at a streamlined, easy-to-sit table, give your order, eat a dynamic, easy-to-eat dinner, settle your easy-to-pay bill and be out again in 25 minutes. Eventually it is hoped, for your convenience, to cut this time to 12½ minutes flat."

My own time in the room (I did not even sit down) was 25.07 seconds by my stop-watch. As I left, fending off a streamlined demand to pay a bill, I noticed that one guest had got so confused by the speed of the service that he had eaten his bill and was trying to pay the waiter in scampi, perhaps causing a bottleneck in the dynamic, 20th-century accounting machine.

But most of the diners looked contented enough, if stunned. They had better be. Soon, if Nadir Hostelries' plans of expansion go through, there will be nowhere else for the middle classes to eat, apart from lorry-drivers' cafes and five-star restaurants. But who are they to think they have a right to choose?

Romance

Rumours that Mrs. Dutt-Pauker, the 53-year-old Hampstead thinker, is thinking of marrying for the third time have caused surprise and some bitterness in Left-wing circles. Surprise, because she has the reputation of being faithful to her second husband's memory; bitterness, because of her impressive financial resources, which, meant for all mankind, may now go to benefit one man.

By inheritance, by 35 years of progressive thinking, by a Left-wing flair for the stockmarket and by sheer forward-looking greed, she has built up a considerable fortune. As well as her large house in Hampstead, she has a country house in Dorset, Beria Garth, another in Wales, Glyn Stalin, and another in the West of Ireland, Leninmore.

Her first husband, whom she met and married during the Spanish Civil War, had to be accidentally liquidated in Barcelona in 1937; at the same time her name became linked with that of Walter Ulbricht, then working in Catalonia, with whom she shared a romantic passion for the techniques of terrorism. Though love faded, as love will, they have always remained good friends. He still sends her a coloured picture postcard of the Berlin Wall every May Day.

But the love of her life was her second husband, bespectacled, four foot ten Ernst Dutt-Pauker, a typical swashbuckling Highlander, stalwart of the Siege of Madrid, hero of a thousand purges, friend of Bela Kun, Yagoda, Beria and Gerö, and at one time motoring correspondent of the *Daily Worker*.

His study in Mrs. Dutt-Pauker's Hampstead house is still kept just as he left it at his death: on his desk a half-completed plan for a people's re-educational labour camp on Exmoor lies next to the stuffed head of Marshal Tukhachevski and a silver-mounted upper set of Marx's false teeth.

Can any individual man, however bold and resolute, many people are asking, take over, as well as Mrs. Dutt-Pauker herself, this glorious but overpowering heritage of progressivism? Isn't there rather a case here for a people's collective, an object lesson in the building of Socialism?

Pioneer

A newly discovered manuscript of Leonardo da Vinci shows sketches of an indisputable bicycle-chain. But according to the Rev. W. S. Smailes's too little-known book "Awheel in the High Renaissance" Leonardo not only invented the bicycle-chain but actually constructed a bicycle.

In all essentials the same as the modern machine, Leonardo's bicycle was made of iron, with engraved bronze handlebars, richly gilded leather saddle and toolbag, ratchet-operated back-pedal brake and wooden spokes and tyres.

The bell was of heavy bronze, with a deep-toned, melodious note. The pump, a complicated apparatus worked by water-power, added considerably to the weight of the machine and, as Leonardo mentions in his journal, was one of the technical snags which cost him most trouble to iron out.

Ludovico Sforza, Leonardo's patron, was delighted with the machine. Visions of cyclists' touring clubs, cyclists' battalions (perhaps armed with Leonardo's projected water-powered machine-gun) and bicycle-chain-swinging Milanese juvenile delinquents whirled through the tyrant's keen brain, continually exercised with the problems both of peace and war.

But after trying out the bicycle himself in the foothills of the Alps, Ludovico suggested that some sort of three-speed gear would be an improvement. And why, he asked acutely, was it necessary to carry a bicycle-pump at all?

But Leonardo had alredy lost interest, his restless genius turning to thoughts of charcoal-fired refrigerators and armoured trams.

Ugliness is fun

Sign of the times: the proliferation of hideous, distorted toys for children and of correspondingly hideous, distorted cult-objects for adolescents and grown-ups.

There are now animated toys, pop-singers and other entertainers, whose whole raison d'être seems to be a deliberately cultivated self-conscious repulsiveness of appearance, manners and habits.

Whenever anyone objects to this strange cult which reverses all accepted human values, even those of commonsense, he is instantly showered with catch-phrases—"square", "anti-life", "jealousy of the new freedom and straightforward sincerity of the young" and similar modish bits of clap-trap.

This simply will not do. There is something deeper here than a stale old newspaper controversy about the war of the generations. It is the discovery that the perverted love of ugliness which is in everyone can be exploited, like any other impulse, for entertainment and profit.

There is no need to believe in a deliberate conspiracy to corrupt the young by presenting ugliness as fun, making them believe that to enjoy it is a sign of sophistication and freedom from outworn conventions. Those who engage in this branch of commerce may well be unaware of its meaning. It is time they began to think about it.

Ugliness *is* fun. It is an infernal joke which we can all share only too well. If it were not it would have no power to corrupt us.

Cannock Chase

When I write about some interesting or attractive and little known part of England I usually avoid mentioning it by name, knowing that thousands of motorists and nature-lovers will otherwise converge on it within seconds and ruin it for good.

In the case of one place, Cannock Chase in Staffordshire, there is no need for secrecy. It cannot be ruined. It is too horrible already. Yet it has a curious beauty.

This is not the beauty of "unspoilt countryside", of State amenity areas held up for official admiration and celebrated, often in embarrassing prose, in thousands of illustrated books about the Heritage of Britain.

Cannock Chase has the mysterious beauty of paradox. In a small space it contains many of the troubling juxtapositions and incongruities of modern England; and its gloomy groves and haunted lay-bys are littered not only with picnickers' waste-paper but with half-grasped symbols that still the mind with wonder.

It rises out of the prosaic North Staffordshire plain, east of the new M6, a long, low plateau, dark and strange, one of the aboriginal waste places of England, a mediaeval hunting-ground, haunt of hermits and charcoal-burners, never ploughed and probably uncultivable. Part of it is still wild, untidy forest, part tidy Forestry Commission plantations. There are coal-mining towns and villages with slag-heaps, Victorian miners' cottages, red-brick chapels, dank, peeling pubs, decaying newsagents, acrid fish-and-chip shops, roads "liable to subsidence". There are also smart council houses and walls scrawled with "Release Mandela" and the C.N.D. sign.

There are fine old parks, Shugborough and Beaudesert, part rotting, part furbished for the pleasure of Midland trippers. Round a corner of a forest road, lined by squalid-looking patches of seeding fireweed, where a notice says "Drive Carefully: Deer," is a lonely settlement of prefabs, with suspicious-eyed women hanging out washing. One of the huge new Post Office Radio totem poles, worshipped by the forest people, perhaps, as a fertility symbol, rises above the trees like an installation from another planet.

Cannock Chase is, in fact, an unholy mess. But it is also profoundly poetical. It has a powerful spirit of place, it is immeasurably ancient and English, yet both the old industrial desolation and the new technological contraptions merely serve to make it seem more haunted still.

It is a troubling, even frightening place too. It could give a susceptible person quite a nasty turn. After a visit, it is advisable to take a cup of tea in a nice hotel in the nice cathedral city of Lichfield nearby and regain a feeling of safety, as if awaking from a mysteriously important dream, by listening to the smooth gossip of clergymen over home-made rock-buns.

Bogeyman

"Could it happen here?" is the cliché-question invariably asked by Left-wing publicists whenever the name of the celebrated bogeyman Senator McCarthy comes up in book, article or television programme. A more pertinent question would be: "Should it happen here?"

The penetration of the life of this country, in every particular and at every level, by disloyal agencies has probably gone much further than McCarthy would have imagined possible.

An English McCarthy would have to be a man of genius. Being English, he would of course be more intelligent, more civilised and more honest than the original American bogeyman. But he would also have to be able to face from the outset, with superhuman patience and unerring astuteness, the biggest organised campaign of misrepresentation in the history of the world.

Among all the free countries of Europe, the mind of England is most nearly in the grasp of those who have no loyalty to any country, but only to some world order of the future, whether Communist or other. Is it likely that they would easily give up such a prize?

Could it happen here? Should it happen here? Or is it already too late?

1966

Afoot in London

by "Wayfarer"

How many people who pride themselves on their knowledge of our vanishing London know that behind an ordinary-looking billiard-hall in Gormsworth Broadway there still lingers on the only Indian fishing village left in the South of England?

First founded in the 15th century by one of those enterprising groups of Indian fishermen, mainly from the Coromandel Coast, who slipped into England almost unnoticed during the confusion of

the Wars of the Roses, the colony at first "flourished exceedingly".

Queen Elizabeth, who had been given an enormous ruby and "xij baskettes of skate" by the village headman when she paid a surprise visit to the settlement in 1591, later granted it a charter of incorporation.

By this the fishermen were given the sole right in perpetuity to take rock salmon, hake, cod, narwhal, swordfish and whale from the Thames within 25 yards either side of the old Gormsworth Soapball Factory.

After its apogee in the early 17th century, the settlement gradually declined. Cromwell frowned on it for its "lewd Hindoo idolatry". William and Mary tried to annul its charter. George III made no secret of his indifference.

By Victorian times the colony had dwindled to no more than six families, all called Viswaswami. Tennyson visited it in 1869, but failing to strike fire for a reflective poem on the subject, retired gloomily.

Carlyle denounced its "amphibogulous nautch-girls with their poppadum millennium". Swinburne, over-excitable as always, fainted on the spot when he came here with Watts-Dunton in 1894, and had to be revived by inhalations of spiritualised fishglue.

Today only a single fisherman, 85-year-old Mr. M. K. ("Jack") Viswaswami, remains to dream of the old days as he sits in the rain, chewing betel-nut, rolling chapattis with his feet, reading the Football Special and occasionally casting a mouldering fishing-net in the direction of the Odeon Cinema, on the crumbling wharf which once blazed with all the colourful life of the Indian Sub-Continent.

How to Get There: No. 112a bus from Cannon Street to Gormsworth High Road, turn left at the "Unity" Budgerigar Accessories Shop, then through the Victoria Temperance Billiard Hall (guide advisable, 5s.), when you will see an intricately-carved sandstone *stupa* rising over the prefabs immediately ahead.

Sweet tooth

The average weekly consumption of sweets per head in Great Britain, it is announced, far exceeds that of any other country in the world. What is more, I have the impression that we are continually drawing even further ahead in this Gadarene rush towards moral and dental decay.

A sign of the times: perhaps the most shameless and indecent of all television advertisements are those which show grown-up men and women, often quite intelligent-looking and respectably dressed, sucking and munching sweets with expressions of delighted greed.

It is now becoming quite a common sight in our streets to see a middle-aged man and wife with their faces pressed to a sweet-shop window. "Look, Mummy!" the man cries, his childish treble, oozing through a mouthful of caramel, to his wife, who if anything is dribbling down the glass even more disgustingly than he is.

"Look! scrunchy, munchy, extra-sweet marshmallow-flavoured butterscotch, with a delicious, luxury centre of squelchy, melchy milk-chocolate! Yum, yum!"

Hand in sticky hand, jaws working, eyes bulging, the nauseous pair grope towards the shop doorway, as the very skies of England begin to rain syrup in delicious, large-size, extra-value drops.

Secret of happiness

For "many deprived, frustrated women, who find no happiness in their marriage, no fulfilment in their home life . . . shopping is sex compensation," says Lady Dartmouth.

Dr. Heinz Kiosk, Chief Psychiatric Adviser to the South-Eastern Gas Board, comments: "With remarkable creative insight, Lady Dartmouth has massively pinpointed one of the key problems in sexual relationships today.

"There is, however, a reverse side to the problem. For many women who feel deprived and frustrated by the lack of shopping activities, sex, marriage and home life are themselves merely inadequate forms of compensation.

"On my advice some of my women patients have found happiness and fulfilment by making their husbands dress up as shop-assistants when they return from work.

"The husband's sales-talk, forceful yet subtly flattering, as he tries to sell his wife the dining-room curtains or a complete set of Nevil Shute's novels, the pleasant rattle of the cash-register, the glow of satisfaction that comes from an evening of hard bargaining, with real money changing hands—all this makes an ideal formula for happy and fulfilled marriage in the 20th century."

Old mitre

The Episcopal Bishop of California, Dr. James Pike, is publishing a book, already creakingly heralded as "startling, disturbing, con-

troversial, sensational, a theological bombshell", etc. etc. In this he explains that "Jesus was in every sense a human being just like we are".

"Under Pike's pen," says a newspaper article, "Jesus becomes very much a man struggling with a man's ideas against the times, leading civil disobedience movements . . ."

I'm afraid Dr. Pike's bombshell is very old mitre indeed. In English theological circles it will scarcely blow up even a single choir-stall. The book seems to be mainly a watered-down version of "God the Humanist" by Dr. Spaceley-Trellis, Bishop of Bevindon, a book which, thanks to the hard work of a first-class Press agent, really did cause a sensation when it came out several years ago.

In this Dr. Trellis explained that Jesus was a brilliant technologist of Left-wing, humanist views who was disgusted by the neglect of technology and social advance in the Roman Empire owing to its out-of-date class-structure.

He and the "first-class sociological research-team" He gathered round Him, called the "12 Disciples" by backward-looking, myth-bound people at that time, conducted a vigorous civil disobedience movement for better scientific education, as well as for "one man, one vote" and nationalisation of the commanding heights of the Judaean economy.

Only historical factors prevented them from campaigning for racial integration, "free elections" in Vietnam, majority rule in Rhodesia, blockade of South Africa and the abolition of public schools.

Such, according to Dr. Trellis, is the essential heart of the Gospel. The rest, as we now have it, is mainly superstitious, pre-scientific speculation about human behaviour, mythical "super-natural" beings and so on. All this was inserted by reactionary clerics and other instruments of the Establishment anxious to slow down Man's onward march to the Humanist Millennium.

Personal

Progressive Woman, 36, experienced demonstrator (six Aldermas-ton marches, over 300 hours picketing South African Embassy in two years, etc., etc.) would like to meet Anti-fascist Man, about 40, view friendship and marriage. Interest in Communist Chinese nightsoil collection methods desirable. Box 482.

Retired Bengali terrorist, 57, ex-Indian National Army, B.SC. (Chittagong), sly disposition, experienced amateur explosives expert, permanent curry-stains, wishes contact British Woman second-hand clothing dealer preferably Mancunian, of similar interests and background, view matrimony. Box 483.

One-legged Widower, 65, five foot one inch, 18 stone, chronic indigestion, Left-wing views, reduced circumstances, with large collection of old copies of *New Statesman,* would like to meet beautiful, politically conscious Girl, 18-25, perfect health, amiable disposition, large private income, country house, university degree, driving and pilot's licence, nursing experience, etc., etc., view marriage. Box 484.

Lonely? Repulsive? No friends? Why not join the Brassgrove Park Progressive Circle, Ulbricht Road, London, S.W.46., and meet others like yourself? Combined teach-in, short story reading and humanist tea-dance every Sunday. This week: Rhodesian Sanc-tions Excuse-me Dance. Box 485 for particulars.

Tidings of joy

by Mungo Clange

"Bless you, dear, and good luck!" The voice of a little old white-haired lady, neatly dressed in widow's black, rang out amid the cheers of the crowd of businessmen, teenagers, nuclear physicists, ballet dancers and ordinary, decent British escaped lunatics who gathered at London Airport yesterday morning to see Mr. Harold Wilson off on his fateful visit to Moscow.

Amid the thousands of handkerchiefs, Commonwealth flags, dusters and wet face-flannels that waved for our Prime Minister, her little scrap of lace stood out for its spotless whiteness and for the subtle, nostalgic hint of old-world lavender it wafted on the spring-like air.

Suddenly she turned to me. There was a hint—more than a hint—of tears in her keen blue eyes. But her voice was firm, and the jab of her frayed but well-kept handbag in my ribs was surprisingly painful.

"You believe in him, don't you, as I do?" she asked me. "You believe he'll speak for Britain, and come back with peace in our time?"

She laid a hand on my sleeve, and her worn gold wedding-ring, symbol of a faith more powerful than death, bit into my wrist remindingly. I nodded wordlessly as hot tears—I'm not ashamed to say it—came into my own eyes.

"Cheer up, sir," said a deep manly voice. I looked up to find a typical big, broad-shouldered London bobby standing by, waving a big, typical handkerchief at the departing plane.

"I know how you feel, sir. But it won't be long before he's back." I could swear there was a sob in his own voice.

Far away in the now hushed crowd a dog barked movingly and a single cow mooed, bearing mute witness that, for all the cynics and scoffers may say, the heart of Britain still stands firmly grounded in the living rock.

Lost cause

"The grouse moors and the deer forests . . . must be put to more productive use. No tears need be shed for any knickerbockered gentleman displaced in the process. Redundant miners are compelled to make much sterner adjustments to the needs of the twentieth century."

This is a passage from an article on economic planning in Scotland, which explains, with proper relish, why it is desirable to cover the beautiful wildernesses of the North with gloomy forests of newsprint and plywood-trees, with pulpmills and ski-runs and horrible, juke-box-crammed tourist hotels; and why the inhabitants must either accept the disappearance of their present way of living or do the other thing.

But when any people, whether knickerbockered gentlemen or redundant miners, are ordered to "adjust" themselves to "needs" and sacrifice themselves for some cause, they are at least entitled to ask what those needs really are and whether the cause is really a good one.

The needs in this case are (of course) those of economic planners, bent on the total, efficient exploitation of natural and human resources in the Highlands. The cause is that of ever-increasing production, of an ever-rising "standard of living" without regard to the consequences for human beings—the cause, to put it in shamelessly old-fashioned terms, of Mammon, Mammon newly armed with scientific curiosity and scientific greed.

Luddites of the World, Unite! Redundant miners and knickerbockered gentlemen alike, with all the familiar little worlds they know, may indeed go down before this monster, as the old Luddites went down before. For the foreseeable future, their cause seems hopeless. But what decent man ever refused to fight for a good cause because he knew it was a lost one?

Norman the good

March 15, 2006.

There were angry scenes in Parliament yesterday when Mr. Frank Ghoules, Member for the Stratford Division of the Oxbrum Conurbation, asked Sir Fred Briggs, Minister of Exports, for details of King Norman's sales mission to the United States.

Why was it necessary, he asked, to equip King Norman at the public expense with a new plastic suitcase for carrying his samples? What orders for garden gnomes, bird-baths, children's toy windmills and other key British manufactures had he in fact received?

What truth was there in the report that when King Norman entered a store on Main Street, Mountainville, Arkansas, and opened his sample-case he had been forcibly ejected and subjected to unmentionable humiliations?

Why had the Government decided that the Queen Gran and Duke Len of Erdington should accompany the King as assistant sales representatives, although neither of them had attended a training course at the University of Salesmanship at Blenheim? (Shouts of "Answer! answer!").

Replying, Sir Fred said that he believed trade followed the flag. When the time came to review the results of the Royal sales mission it would be found that a magnificent job of work had been done by all concerned.

The incident at Grand Rapids, Michigan, when the Queen Gran was accused of stealing a novelty tartan handbag from a supermarket, had been greatly exaggerated and had in fact increased the respect in which the ordinary American held our Socialist Monarchy.

Duke Len of Erdington had also shown himself a first-rate ambassador for British trade, with a convivial manner defiant of stuffy protocol and a repertoire of dubious anecdotes second to none.

The whole mission would, he believed, prove the greatest boost to British prestige since the decision to hand over the Isle of Wight to the United Nations as a base for the Organisation for African Unity.

Among the fine words

Senator Robert Kennedy's address on progress and internationalism at the University of Capetown is already being equated in some quarters with the Sermon on the Mount. To criticise any part of it, however mildly, therefore, is to risk equating oneself with the Powers of Darkness.

Nevertheless, the risk had better be taken. Here is one short passage from the Senator's collection of fine, resounding words:

"Only earthbound man (in the age of global technology and communications) still clings to the dark and poisonous superstition that his world is bounded by the nearest hill, his universe ended at the river shore, his common humanity enclosed in the tight circle of those who share his town and views and the colour of his skin.

"It is . . . the task of the young people of this world to strip the last remnants of that ancient, cruel belief from the civilisation of man."

It does not seem to occur to the Senator that if the Afrikaners, young or old, the Irish, the Welsh, the Nagas, even the English and Americans cling to their various tribal, national, parochial attitudes, it is not necessarily out of poisonous superstition and ancient cruelty, or out of hatred and fear of other people. It may be because they feel, dimly but instinctively, that their individuality and identity, their familiar environment, all the things they—and those dear to them—personally know and understand, are threatened with absorption, forcible or otherwise, in a strange, remote, inhuman international order.

That order, being world-wide, will be unchallangeable, without appeal, with powers of life, death and coercion unimaginably greater than any yet known to mankind.

It is all very well for Senator Robert Kennedy to look forward to that global, scientific order and wonder how any sane man of goodwill can have doubts about it, let alone dislike or oppose its coming. He and his friends, or people like them (if things turn out no worse), may be its masters. We shall not.

New Left

Mrs. Dutt-Pauker, the Hampstead thinker, became a grandmother yesterday when her daughter Deirdre, who is married to red-bearded, Leftish, G.P.I. Network television producer John Armature, gave birth to a son at St. Ulbricht's Anti-colonialist Nursing Home, Highgate.

The lusty, red-haired 13lb. 8oz. boy will be called Bert Brecht Mao Odinga, and has already been entered for a primary school in Holland Park, Eton and Stretchford University.

The entire birth was televised on close circuit and was watched by Deirdre's mother and husband and by a large invited audience which included playwright Eric Lard; Flemish teratologist Dr. Max Laryncx; writer and TV personality Doreen Gaggs, who is to write a series of articles in *Handbag* magazine; psychiatrist and erotician Dr. Heinz Kiosk; and avant-garde self-publicist Neville Dreadberg.

A highlight of the show was the age-old but ever thrilling

moment of the baby's first cry as he entered into the world: "Blockade South Africa—Now!"

Gillian ("Sneer with Mother") Paste, a well-known fellow-producer at G.P.I., is to edit the show as a film, to be called "The Birth Game". Several Labour back-bench M.P.s have offered to sponsor a Bill to make it compulsory viewing for every man, woman and child in the country with penalties of fines or imprisonment for non-attendance.

Document

From the *New Anglo-Saxon Statesman,* May 12, 1066: Anglo-Saxon Socialists, who were far from happy about the policies of the late King Edward, with his embarrassing confessional habits, his absurd over-emphasis on church-building and his backward-looking attitude to the problem of religious education in the schools, are keeping an equally wary eye on the policies of King Harold and the true blue, class-obsessed Anglo-Saxon Establishment figures who surround him.

At the moment, foreign policy is the main worry. Making great play with a few threatening noises emanating from Duke William—obviously intended for internal Norman consumption in the present shaky state of the Norman economy, with its falling production figures—King Harold, after a perfunctory debate in the Witenagemot, has moved substantial forces to the South Coast "to keep an eye on the Channel".

To withdraw men from essential productive work on the pretext of meeting an imaginary military threat, at a time when it is essential, because of the balance of payments crisis, to make ruthless cuts in the arms programme, is bad enough. The suspicion that the whole operation may really be designed to boost the morale of the mead-quaffin', huntin' and shootin' landowners of Kent and Sussex makes matters worse.

In any case, Anglo-Saxon Socialists are more and more coming to wonder whether, as regards the things that really matter—raising living standards, improving agricultural techniques, providing crèches and discussion groups for working peasant-mothers in the villages, the fight against class-privilege—there is much to choose between the rule of Harold Godwinsson, William of Normandy or, for that matter, Harold Hardrada of Norway. Time will show.

Ceremonial

"It's time they put a stop to all this old-fashioned dressing-up. As I see it, it's just tasteless ostentation and waste of money in the present crisis of the world predicament and the population explosion. Why don't they save the money and send it to relieve the starving millions of India?"

These words, or words like these, may be heard from many a sour-faced lover of humanity as he scowls at a newspaper photograph of the annual procession of the Knights of the Garter at Windsor, or of some other ancient ceremony. Some people who ought to know better may well agree with him.

It is doubtful whether any money which might be saved by abolishing the Order of the Garter would in fact be sent to relieve the starving people of India, or whether the starving people of India would get it if it were. But let that pass.

What the grumbling lover of humanity really dislikes about all this ceremonial is not that it costs money, but firstly, that it is ancient, and secondly, that it is beautiful. He is ready to applaud the outpouring of a hundred thousand times as much money on what is new, ugly and even more useless every day of his life.

No country can exist entirely without ceremonial. What many a lover of humanity really wants, whether he knows it or not, is to sweep away the traditional English ceremonial with all its subtle symbolism, and substitute a kind of ceremonial he can really understand and respect: an up-to-date, universal symbolism of naked power—marching files of drab-uniformed Socialist militia, tanks with grim-faced, steel-helmeted crews and monstrous rockets moving past the base where the Masters of the People, wearing their ritual grey suits or dungarees and eyeing each other shiftily, take the salute.

What the scorner of ancient ceremonies wants in his heart, he may well get. Unfortunately we who do not want it will get it just the same.

He lisped in slogans

Bert Brecht Mao Odinga, the progressive baby who was born to Deirdre Armature (formerly Dutt-Pauker) at St. Ulbricht's Anti-colonialist Nursing Home last Wednesday, is already showing signs of unusual powers.

Weighing 13lb. 8oz. at birth, Bert has put on 5lb. in less than a week. Yesterday he began screaming furiously when a Spanish nurse, who had got a job at the nursing-home by falsely pretending to be an underground anti-Franco worker, approached him. He was only pacified when the girl, unmasked, was sent packing.

Later, when Mrs. Dutt-Pauker, taking time off from picketing the Portuguese Embassy, called in to admire him and hand him some toy leaflets about West German militarism, Bert snatched her ball-point pen and began drafting letter after letter to *Tribune* on different progressive topics at a speed which had the grown-ups dizzy and gasping with admiration.

"At this rate," breathed Deirdre, her face glowing with a mother's happiness, "he'll be able to go on next year's Great Easter Peace March to Aldermaston all by himself."

Beyond time

The recession of the railways, except for a few showy new trains for businessmen, into dimness and hopelessness has one pleasing aspect. In their very shabbiness and pathos they are becoming homely, lovable and haunted all at once.

There is one suburban station I use occasionally where the staff now seems to consist of only four people: a mild-looking, white-haired old British railwayman, soon due to retire; a middle-aged Irishman who looks like a Victorian caricature in *Punch,* evidently a monoglot Gaelic-speaker; a volatile but bewildered-looking Indian and an elderly woman in gym-shoes and a blue overall.

These four take turn-and-turn about with the station duties, ranging perpetually about the gloomy, dank, peeling halls, stair-cases and passageways of their mouldering House of Usher.

Thus you will sometimes find, late at night, the elderly woman collecting tickets, while the Irishman makes tea by the oil-lamp in the porters' room, the Indian leans on a broom on the platform, staring at the rails with a wild surmise, and in the distance the old railwayman can be heard singing hymns in his sleep.

Another time the Indian will collect the tickets, slowly reading each one to himself in a vibrant monotone, while the Irishman leans on the broom, the elderly woman makes the tea and the old railwayman paces up and down the narrow wooden platform like a sea-crazed ship's captain in a storm.

So they live, forgotten by the world and forgetting it, surprised and even, to judge from their expressions, faintly irritated every time a train actually stops at their decaying platforms. Like all people in such situations, isolated and obscurely menaced by change, they draw ever closer for comfort, resentful of outsiders.

But since the Indian is the youngest, most active and most intelligent member of the group, his influence, I have noticed, is growing. The subtle ambiguities of Indian philosophical thought, its serpentine speculations on the nature of reality, of time and of the world, are taking hold, and the station is sinking into ·a dreamlike state where East and West may perhaps be one at last.

The other day, when I asked the aged railwayman whether my train would stop at platform 1 or platform 2, he simply replied, nodding obliquely, "Yes". Then, as a sense of timeless mystery enveloped us both, he stalked slowly away past the rusting cough-lozenge machines to the door marked "Lamps".

Eros planned

Unmarried young people, says Sir Theodore Fox, Director of the Family Planning Association, should be left to decide for themselves whether they should have sexual intercourse. But he adds two conditions. They should understand "what they are doing to each other and to themselves" and they must always use effective contraceptives.

Poor young people, who thought they were going to be free to enjoy a pagan world of love and pleasure where moral restraints had vanished and all might do as they pleased! It is not going to be quite like that after all!

Pursued into the bedroom by experts brandishing pills and coils of ever new design, questioning them about their attitudes to each other, observing their love-making like any scientific process and measuring the degree to which they achieve a psychologist's idea of a "mature, meaningful relationship," they will find they have exchanged one system of restraint, moral, religious, instinctual, for another system, social, secular, rational.

They will find that new Family Planning Expert is but old Priest writ large—and not only writ large but armed by the State with powers of compulsion few priests have ever dreamed of.

A Great Year

A year has passed since Rhodesia declared her independence. In England, has there ever been such a great year for sheer, unremitting humbug? Has hypocrisy ever produced a crop so fat, glistening, bulging with nourishment for fools?

All year long our Socialist Government (often abetted by our Opposition) has slithered from one shifty expedient to another in its efforts to keep on doing and even saying several incompatible things at the same time. All year long the Left-wing militarists of Hampstead have howled for war, encouraging others no more militarily competent than themselves, but much more liable to get hurt, to howl for war too.

All year long progressive clergymen, progressive students, progressive journalists, progressive window-cleaners, progressive thinkers and non-thinkers of every kind, hardly any of them knowing anything whatever about the situation at first hand, have spouted about the unique wickedness of the present Rhodesian form of society.

A whole year has passed; and Rhodesians, white and black, are not merely still there but are almost exactly the same as they were before, peaceful, prosperous and quite reasonably content with their imperfect, unfashionable, paternalistic system.

Merely to exist straight-forwardly in a world of lies has a kind of dignity. When assailed by shifting and inexplicable phantoms, it may not be the highest, most romantic sort of heroism to keep on calmly and obstinately living as you choose; but it is something.

Problem Corner

by Clare Howitzer

"My boyfriend, Jim, is a manic-depressive, one-legged, homosexual dwarf. He wears kinky boots, carries a flick-knife, sucks ice-lollies

all the time I am talking to him and is very hairy. I am wondering whether my love for him is just a passing teenage infatuation or whether we can establish a normal, adult, satisfying, psychologically complete love-relationship, like you said in your article last week.

"Do you think it is the real thing for me this time?" (Sandra Cloggie, Barrow-in-Furness).

Clare Howitzer replies: I certainly do. You have got a real winner there, Sandra. My advice to you is to write a T.V. play about Jim right away before some other girl can do it first.

Talking Point

In advanced industrial societies even the petty bourgeois managers of licensed premises have a close reciprocal nexus with the banking and financial elite. By this the latter decline to serve alcoholic beverages in banks, while the former, in return, decline to provide facilities for money transactions through the medium of bills of exchange—Karl Marx.

Forward-looking

Stretchford Education Committee has published, with justifiable pride, its final scheme for comprehensive schools in the area.

It proposes to amalgamate the 400-year-old Nerdley Grammar School, St. Bogwena's Roman Catholic School and Bog Lane Secondary School, adding for good measure over 30 other educational institutions including Stretchford College of Art, the Victoria Road Nursery School for Autistic Children, now run on

Freudian principles by Mrs. Rosamund Goth-Jones, the Gloria Refayne Charm School for Models, the Sadcake Park Rabbinical Students' Training College, the Darby and Joan Sunset Home for Old Folks and the Approved Schools for juvenile delinquents at Hokewell Court and Soup Hales Priory.

With more than 126,000 pupils the new school—it will probably be called the Ron Frabb Comprehensive School in honour of Bog Lane's most distinguished pupil—will be by far the largest, and therefore the most advanced, in the whole country.

Acclaiming the scheme as "magnificently imaginative in its dedication to the principles of social justice, and a heartening pledge of the Socialist Britain that is to be", Sir William Goth-Jones, Vice-Chancellor of Stretchford University, yesterday condemned the "snobbery and stick-in-the-mud prejudice" of parents and others who have expressed doubts about the scheme.

The headship of the new school will be a key appointment. With such figures as Mr. J. B. Dimwood, present headmaster of Bog Lane, obviously out of the running by reason of their backward-looking attitude, possession of Oxford or Cambridge degrees or incompetence at Karate and Korean all-in wrestling, the job may well go to Dr. Kev Burst, at present head of Stretchford University's Department of Youth Studies and Comparative Vandalism.

Catching up

The G.P.I. Television Network is putting on a new programme, "Keep Left with Mother", for children under 5, who have been shamefully neglected in this field up to now.

Pretty, blonde, moustached 24-year-old Gillian Paste, the producer (all the studio people, who adore her, call her "Pasty"), was enthusiastic about the idea when I saw her yesterday.

"We want to get rid of all the silly fairies, elves, talking animals and the rest of the out-of-date make-believe which has cluttered up children's T.V. so long," she told me. "The only animals in the new programme will be experimental laboratory ones.

"Children nowadays are sick of fairy stories—even our previous series 'The United Nations Elf' was adversely criticised at a T.V. seminar for Hampstead children last month.

"Children want to be down-to-earth and practical and play their part in building Socialism. They are interested in things like comprehensive schools, nationalisation, family planning and World Government. We shall include, for example, a series about a typical 4-year-old, Jim, who wants to go out and fight the White Rhodesians.

"Political bias?" Gillian laughed infectiously. "How can the programme be biased when all shades of progressive opinion will be represented?"

Dr. Heinz Kiosk, the psychologist, who is advising Gillian on the programmes, looked up from a child he was putting through abreactive treatment for suspected Conservative tendencies to nod cheerfully in agreement.

1967

Last of the few

Sheppey Rural Council in Kent are said to be using a "spy plane", which circles the island at 500ft., to spot illegal building. They are still a long way behind the Stretchford Borough Council, which at one time kept a whole squadron of war surplus reconnaissance aircraft, plus a few bombers and fighters, for this purpose.

Gradually the squadron dwindled. Some of its planes seized up in their hangars and became unusable through rust, or their crews became too old, drunk or incompetent to fly them. Some made forced landings on the city outskirts and were immediately stripped bare by souvenir-hunters. Two were shot down in one day ("Black Monday") by the crack potato-gun marksmen of Bog Lane Secondary Modern School.

Now the only survivor is tough, swashbuckling, grizzled, 60-year-old, self-promoted Group Captain "Jumbo" Goth-Jones, Second World War veteran and black-sheep brother of Sir William Goth-Jones, Vice-Chancellor of Stretchford University.

"Jumbo", whose reminiscences of old flying days are much valued by connoisseurs of boredom and obsolete idioms, over the odd noggin of directors' bitter in the Town Hall canteen, still takes off on the odd solo mission. Then the strange, irregular droning of his ramshackle machine with its whirring camera, circling over the Stretchford Green Belt, often at "nought feet", strikes terror into the hearts of illicit pig-keepers, unlicensed caravan-site promoters, faithless housewives and their dustmen lovers alike.

For all his blue-eyed, alcoholic stare, shabby uniform and disreputable manner, "Jumbo" knows his job. When one of his panoramic photographs is developed and interpreted by the experts in the Planning Department, the illegal lean-to shed of some old-age-pensioner allotment-holder is sure to stand out clearly, while of the vast fun-palace and multi-storey vendomat run up in the Green Belt by Nadirco Enterprises on the site of some demolished ancient monument there is not a trace.

Unknown goals

In a last, desperate effort to restore Stretchford United's fortunes, Sir Roland Grampus-Smith chairman of the club, decided that Albert Rasp, its famous goal-conceding goalkeeper, should write a best-selling novel. As Rasp is illiterate, the well-known ghost-writer Julian Birdbath was engaged to write it for him.

The result was not quite the simple, fast-moving story of football, women, booze and bottle-throwing Sir Roland expected. Toiling away in the disused Derbyshire lead mine where he lives, Birdbath poured all his lonely anguish into the first "avant garde" football novel, "The Disconnected Goalposts", full of alienation, homosexuality, sadism, heroin-addiction and psychosomatic diseases.

Krebs (he has no first name) is goalkeeper of a mysterious unnamed team, and lives in a state of such total non-communication that he cannot distinguish between the goalpost, the ball, the bellowing crowd, or even the sinister policemen and press-photographers who squat intermittently on the touchline, sometimes vanishing into thin air.

Throughout the book, which ends in mid-sentence in the same broken words with which it began, Krebs blunders through an evil miasma, where he meets and tries to talk with various grotesque figures—S., the necrophagous team manager, scuttling spiderlike in his glass wheel-chair; N., the dwarf transvestite centre-forward; V., the opposing goalkeeper, a perverted hunchback who is trying to escape from the world of football altogether by digging a hole in his penalty area.

To add to his difficulties, Krebs, who has no roof to his mouth, changes sex several times.

When Sir Roland read the completed manuscript, he ordered Birdbath to be paid off, then disembowelled. But in fact the book may do quite well, bringing Rasp a modest fame and Stretchford United a new image ("Kafka ... Beckett ... Pinter ... Burroughs ... the pioneers of non-communication are joined by a new explorer of the anguished post-Christian world of professional football" — *Observer*).

Leadership

A Town Clerk, says a report on the staffing of local authorities, should not necessarily be a lawyer. The important thing is that he should have "distinctive gifts of personality and leadership".

To 25-stone, crag-featured, iron-watch-chained, grim-booted Alderman Foodbotham, at the height of his power as Chairman of the Bradford City Tramways and Fine Arts Committee in the great days, the only important thing about a town clerk was that he should do as he was told.

If that condition was fulfilled, he did not care whether the town clerk was a lawyer, a boilerman or an unemployed birdseed-tester. To make sure, he made the appointment himself, usually from members of his own household.

Normally the appointment was accepted without question. But there were some murmurs of dissent from Labour members of the council when in 1920 he made one of his superannuated carriage-horses town clerk. In a thunderous, overwhelming speech which is still quoted in local government circles as a model of how to silence opposition, the Alderman scornfully asked if they were so enamoured of progress that they would prefer him to appoint one of his vast indigo-coloured Rolls-Royces as town clerk instead?

As the abashed radicals, whining thinly, slunk from the chamber, the new town clerk added a fresh smart to their humiliation by a ringing neigh of triumph. And at that moment, with a proper sense of what was fitting, a single sunbeam struck nobly through the stained-glass windows, illumining horse and alderman together in the purple gloom.

For your bookshelf

The Nerdley Scene.
Edited by Jon Glasse-Derkeley. (Viper and Bugloss, 30s.)

After the Liverpool Scene, the Manchester Scene, the Stoke-on-Trent Scene, the Barrow-in-Furness Scene, the Darlington Scene, the Sowerby Bridge Scene and the rest, comes the Nerdley Scene.

The well-known cultural entrepreneur Jon Glasse-Derkeley must have shifted as many scenes as any man living since the scene industry first became a key economic growth-point; he is to be congratulated on his enterprise in cornering one of the few remaining English provincial scenes not already exploited or booked by rival practitioners. It must have been a very near thing.

What is there about Nerdley, a medium-sized, rather more than usually dim industrial town in Staffordshire, which has made it, for a few minutes, the cultural centre of England (Murray Fringeberg, the American poet, has called it "the paradisial navel of the human world"), humming with pop, marijuana, L.S.D., sawn-off guitars, Youth in revolt, photographers, television cameramen and all the other features of the English folk tradition? Is it just something which has happened? Or is it just something which has been made to happen?

Certainly, as Glasse-Derkeley makes clear in his introduction to this glossy, finely illustrated book, the pop poets of the Nerdley Scene—Julian Macnumb, Jim O'Vacancy, Rodrigo Otiose and the rest—are at least the equal of any possible rivals in the luxuriance of their hair and beards, the photogenic extravagance of their dress (for his poetry readings Macnumb habitually wears a purple-dyed plant-pot on his head; O'Vacancy's saffron bonze's robes are stuck all over with multicoloured boiled sweets), and—perhaps the most vital breakthrough of all—in the significantly trivial inanity of their poems.

"Yet it would be a mistake," says Glasse-Derkeley, "to think that the Nerdley pop poets owe their motive power solely to the Wilhelmina Stitch and Patience Strong revivals. There are other elements: cracker mottoes, quick repartee heard in local authority

homes for the deaf and dumb, puns and jokes based on memories of
TV commericals (O'Vacancy's poem "Fry's Turkish Disgust" is a
brilliant example)—the rich, warm, pavement-mirrored, sporadic
neo-existential consciousness of an urban ambience, rootless yet
rooted—all this is basic to their demotic assertion of new values."

Well said. The only question is: where do we—or rather where
does Mr. Glasse-Derkeley—go from here? It would be sad if in the
end, all other scenes exhausted, he were reduced in baffled rage to
making an embarrassing scene himself.

Twain

United Europe; a wider Holy Roman Empire; a New Order without
the Nazis; a federation of European nations with a place for
England, France, Spain, Wales, Slovakia, Brittany, Lithuania,
Flanders, the Grand Duchy of Muscovy and all the rest; a forest of
ancient flags on a green ground; an Empire of extreme diversity,
prosperous but aware that prosperity is not all; peaceable but
unchallengeably strong in its own defence; a Europe taking its
place once more as the natural centre and summit of the world . . .

The Common Market; greater efficiency in a larger economic
unit; bigger and better feats of technology; bigger and better pan-
European industrialists; a nation of shopkeepers joining a continent of shopkeepers.

Are these two ideas of Europe—they are, I suppose, roughly Mr.
Wilson's and mine—utterly incompatible? Is there no hope of
getting something of both? Even if Europe, by a miracle, were
United, could *they* be?

Aristotherapy

Among those who habitually use bogus titles in England, the new
edition of Debrett reveals, there is one psychologist. I am surprised
Debrett knows of only one.

A "Way of the World" Medical Correspondent comments: As the
number of psychiatric patients increases among all classes, more
and more are finding that they can only discuss their troubles
freely with a psychiatrist who, if he is not actually of noble birth,
at least pretends to be so.

So the old type of guttural, bearded, white-coated Central European psychiatrist is giving place to an urbane, ermine-robed, coroneted figure whose very brass plate at the door "His Grace Dr. the Duke of Cumberland, K.G., M.D., D.P.M.", inspires confidence and is almost a cure in itself.

Once the patient is on the couch, the psychiatrist's easy talk of shooting, fishing, genealogy and estate management soon calms his disorientated mind and leads him insensibly into that world of hierarchy and privilege, now revealed as normal and healthy, he has already glimpsed in his unnecessarily guilt-ridden dreams.

There is a new school of psychology which holds that most neuroses are directly traceable to the advance of democracy, the disappearance of landed estates and the decline of the class system. Hence the new caste of noblemen-psychiatrists, technically bogus for the moment but destined, perhaps, as their power and affluence grow, to form a genuine new hereditary landed aristocracy themselves.

St. Ebbe's

It is sad to hear that St. Ebbe's, the oldest quarter of Oxford, is to be demolished this autumn. I could sooner have spared some of the colleges.

Thirty years ago, when tired of my fellow-undergraduates, I sometimes used to visit a small, shabby, wholly undistinguished pub I had discovered somewhere in that maze of shabby, undistinguished streets of brick, the dankest, most permanently autumnal part of the dank, autumnal city.

Here, in a brown parlour with a cracked, out-of-tune piano and dusty photographs of jockeys on the walls, I played a simple variant of dominoes for half pints of beer with undersized, secretive men who sometimes changed the rules, such as they were, in mid-game.

Some of them, men with flat, dark, opaque eyes in sallow faces, descended perhaps from the marsh-dwellers of Otmoor, may have been related to college servants, judging from the bags of assorted food—mostly cold anchovy toast, or, in the summer, lobster mayonnaise and strawberries—they often had with them. Their conversation was often about missing bicycles, varieties of soap or the best ways of catching rats.

It was hard to say if these strange people accepted me. Sometimes, bemused by beer and dominoes, I passed into a mystic trance in which they seemed not so much people as a crowd of rain-worn sundials and clock-faces, whose sighing breath lifted the frayed linoleum at my feet in a soothing, rhythmic motion. They did not seem to mind.

I believed these people were the real inhabitants of Oxford, the aboriginal people, living a more intense life than dons or undergraduates, destined to survive unchanged, with St. Ebbe's itself, long after the upstart University had passed away. Evidently I was wrong.

Unique

"Whatever the rights and wrongs of its original foundation, Israel is now a sovereign State exactly like any other, with the same right to exist as any other." Such is the orthodox liberal assumption, found equally in the columns of the *New Statesman* and in the House of Commons.

It sounds reasonable enough. But like most orthodox liberal assumptions, it does not bear examination. For one thing, if Israel really were a State exactly like any other, its extinction as a State, however unjust and outrageous, would not be—as we are told it is—"unthinkable".

Other States have lost their separate identities in our lifetime. Do you remember the sovereign States of Estonia, Latvia, Lithuania? Their extinction was not only thinkable; it was thought, and promptly done.

Far from being a State like any other, Israel is a State quite unique in the world. What other State in the modern world has been established as a refuge, for the ingathering of a people dispersed for centuries, in a region foreordained, in order to fulfil an ancient prophecy?

To think of Israel as a State in the sense of Belgium or Nicaragua—no more and no less mysterious and significant—is to take an absurdly shallow view of human history. Can even the most bigoted secularist, the most obstinate rationalist, Jew, Arab or other, whatever side he may be on, really believe it?

Smile

In summertime on Bredon, and indeed at any other time, a strong, squat, technological tower of concrete, topped by radio aerials and a red, winking light, surmounts the ancient earthworks, the holy well, the woods, combes, sheep-runs and lovers' walks.

It does not matter. On a fine June day this part of England, indeterminately Worcestershire, Warwickshire and Gloucestershire, even now looks rich, beautiful and good enough to eat. Its meadows are still spread thick with clover and buttercups, its lanes are still a tangle of grasses and flowers, its villages still look almost laughably English, like a child's jigsaw puzzle, complete with ancient church, cottages, lumbering farmers, a sheepdog racing on the green.

Stinking cars rush by the meadows. Above the flowery lanes, on every hilltop, stands some steel-masted contraption. Television flickers through the cottage windows. Yet this rural world, already written off as an anachronism, may have more power of survival than we think.

The world of the professional Old English heritage writers is one thing. These real woods, fields and tangled flowers are another. In June, this is a "smiling countryside" if ever there was one. But it may be smiling not only from joy but from strength.

There is something very tough here, something indestructible, as if the earth itself were determined to survive, with its beauty, richness and fecundity, our masquerade of poison and electronics.

What do you think?

asks Virginia Ferret

Prominent journalists in every field—Middle Eastern affairs, Soviet affairs, military affairs, medicine, theology, sociology, famine relief and sport—hastily dropped whatever they were doing yesterday and hurried from all over the world to the Press conference announced by Cliff Rampton, Ron Frabb's manager, in the vast £500,000 Ionian white and gold audience hall of the pop star's £15 million London headquarters.

Dressed in a £45,000 suit of white samite encrusted with emeralds, Ron addressed them from his £10,000 marble and £3,000 lapis lazuli throne.

"Last Thursday," he read slowly from a prepared statement, with some prompting from one of his linguistics experts, "last Thursday at 10.45 p.m., I smoked a mixture of dried carrots, aspirin, old handbags, sardine oil and wallpaper.

"I did not do this for kicks or sensationalism," he went on. "I did it, seriously, deliberately and of set purpose, as part of my lifelong quest to find myself. I believe the experience has sort of helped me to find myself, or something. I have summoned you here today so that you too may try to sort of find yourselves. And I hope this finds you as it leaves me at present."

As his voice died away, echoing solemnly through the mighty hall, shocked speculation broke out. Questions were hurled at him from all sides. Was he speaking *ex cathedra*? asked a theologian. What sort of wallpaper did he use? asked an interior decorator.

Wasn't he setting a terrible example to teenagers? asked several women experts on drug-taking and teenage ethics. Would millions of teenagers who looked to Ron as the ultimate sanction of morals now take to smoking not only carrots and handbags but anything they could get their hands on? There had already been reports from Nottingham and elsewhere of teenagers smoking their grand-parents.

Representatives of greengrocery and handbag trade journals disagreed. But it was Jack Moron, world-famous science writer, who had the last word.

"To Ron Frabb, pop star, multi-millionaire and B.F., I say this, straight from the shoulder and with no holds barred. Belt up! Come off it! Pipe down! Stand up and shut up! Get knotted!

"And, Ron, get this straight," he added, then suddenly slumped to the ground unconscious amid the sound of breaking bottles and a renewed buzz of speculation.

What do YOU think? Or have you decided by this time that there is no money or future in thinking at all?

Dr. Henbane talking

Good morning. Quite a number of worried people have been writing to me for hints on how to cope with the hot weather. Mrs. F. S. of Aston Garfinkel (Notts.) is typical. "The other day," she says, "my feet got so overheated that they left charred patches on grass as I walked along, and partially melted asphalt. Now I face a bill for damage from our local council."

Her problem is not as uncommon as she may think. Trabb's Foot (or pedal hyperpyrexia, as we medicos call it) is a recognised condition. In the old days it was slow to yield to treatment. Patients usually wore a clumsy type of surgical boot with a compartment containing cold water, which had to be continually renewed as it turned to steam.

Today, a course of injections of a wonder-drug—borboromycin or one of the newly synthesised amphibogulene group—plus a few days' rest, should do the trick.

Another, related foot trouble is Pedal Effloritis (also called Herbaceous Foot or Olwen's Syndrome, after an early Welsh sufferer). The patient, usually a young and attractive woman, finds that beautiful white flowers spring up wherever she walks, causing social embarassment and loss of self-confidence.

This complaint, fortunately very rare nowadays, is one of our current medical puzzle-points. But there's no doubt that the backroom boys who are now working on the problem will come up with a cure sooner rather than later. Good morning.

Thank you so much

Race riots like those in America could start here, says a report by the Youth Service Development Council, if young coloured immigrants are not "integrated swiftly into society". This may be right or wrong. But since such integration (what precisely does it mean, anyhow?) is no more than a remote possibility, we had better prepare ourselves.

In a few years' time, as we sit smoking our legalised hashish and watching our colour television sets, vaguely hearing the howling of the mob and the crackling of flames approaching from the distance, we must not forget to say a heartfelt "thank you" to all those who will have made this possible.

To the politicians of all parties and the civil servants who quite unnecessarily allowed vast numbers of unassimilable immigrants to pour into this country and pretended that nothing untoward was happening: to the conspirators who did not mind what was happening so long as it helped to mess up England: to the progressive thinkers who assured everybody that all would be well if we would only be nice to each other (true)—and that if we were not nice to each other we could be made to be nice to each other by law.

To the professional integrationists who hold that anyone who believes there is any difference between one race and another is a Nazi and a diabolist: to the journalists who even now write solemn articles about psychopathic racial agitators as if they were responsible statesmen; and to others, deceivers or deceived, too numerous to mention.

We must say thank you, in fact, to all those who knowingly or unknowingly arranged this interesting little sociological experiment on the English people. We turned out not to be angels in heaven, as was evidently expected, but merely human beings on earth. But would any other nation have done better?

I remember

"Take a look at these papers. I pinched 'em from the Foreign Office. Complete figures of Canadian enriched zirconium production for 1948. Yours for £1 7s. 9d. You could flog 'em to the Commies for double that." Burgess's voice, with its "improved" Manchester accent, was as ingratiating as ever. Tittering drunkenly, he threw some crumpled papers in my lap, then slumped from his chair to join his unconscious friends on the floor, his head on Maclean's chest and his feet dealing Philby's left ear a painful buffet.

Looking back to the post-war years, I quite enjoyed those evenings at the Gargoyle in the company of Burgess, Maclean and Philby. But one thing about the trio rather irritated me. This was their own story (which began as quite an amusing joke, but when endlessly elaborated became a bore) that they were employed by the Foreign Office or the Intelligence Service but were really Soviet agents.

Everybody at the Gargoyle knew they were employed by the Band of Hope to drink ostentatiously and noisily in public and thus spread the gospel of temperance among people who might otherwise never have heard of it. I believe they drew a nominal salary and were allowed a small expense allowance. As their capacity for drink was moderate, it cannot have cost their employers much.

This particular evening, I remember, was much like any other. Burgess, after drinking a few miniature bottles of brandy, had challenged Maclean to a fight and for a few minutes the two of them had pushed each other into the band alternately, smashing mirrors and washbasins over each other's heads while "Kim" Philby climbed on to a table and, defying gravity in the engaging way he had, tried to fall through the ceiling.

As the trio slumped to the ground, Dylan Thomas, another member of our circle (who, I believe, really *did* have an important job in the Foreign Office) wandered over to our table and was instantly bitten in the leg by the semi-conscious Maclean.

The poet staggered back in alarm, dropping the battered cardboard suitcase he always carried. It burst open, showering the room with empty Guiness bottles, B.B.C. scripts and the complete South Korean order of battle. How would Dylan talk his way out of that, I wondered.

Fortunately, at that moment a new group of Gargoyle habitués appeared in the doorway. I recognised Philip Toynbee, Ernic Bevin, Bram Stoker, W.J. Locke, Herbert Morrison, Ernest Dowson, Matisse, Verlaine and Rimbaud . . .

Tomorrow: A Midnight Feast at the Admiralty.

Enlightened dread

I can still watch Harold Wilson on the television screen with diminishing enjoyment of a skilled but now almost worn-out act. I can still watch George Brown with a certain disgusted amusement. But Roy Jenkins gives me the creeps.

There is nothing personal in this, of course. Nor is Jenkins' face at all frightening in itself. Why then, as he emits, in that smooth, too-educated voice, that endless stream of liberal platitudes, does his face, so smooth and enlightened, fill me with dread?

It is because of what I think I see behind him, peering over his liberal shoulders—coldly calculating faces and wild, half savage faces, the faces of those who for their different reasons hate our society and our country beyond measure and are filled with an exultant lust to destroy them both.

I see Jenkins, or someone like him, as the last Prime Minister of England. Still he mouths smoothly on, civilised, earnest, well-intentioned, tolerant of everything but illiberal intolerance, still confident of his own enlightenment as bestial cries of hate overwhelm his voice, fire devours his image and England falls apart.

Mystery intruders

Are the eight mysterious Pakistanis who landed on a beach in Kent the other day part of a large-scale operation to divert attention from the whole-scale smuggling of white people from the Midlands into Pakistan? One man who thinks so is ex-Chief Superintendent "Big Bill" Henhouse ("Henhouse of the Yard").

As we talked yesterday (writes "Way of the World" Special Investigator VERNON BROOTES) in the modest, well-kept garden of his Norbiton home, littered with trophies of his 50 years' war against crime—gelignite-blasted safes, rusting handcuffs, the mummified corpse of a favourite "old lag"—revelations, many of them sensational, flowed like melting ice-cream.

Who were the 24 mysterious middle-aged Englishmen, said by local fishermen to speak with a "marked Black Country accent, with diphthongal peculiarities and labio-fricatives most probably indicating the Bushbury-Willenhall area", who were seen landing from a dinghy near Karachi, then hurriedly making their way into the Sind Desert?

What is the explanation for the growing popularity of Bingo in parts of the Indus Valley? Who put up, at dead of night, a prefabricated British Legion hut, with the sign of a well-known

Midland brewer hanging outside, on the outskirts of Peshawar?

Who are the "big boys" behind the racket? That is what Henhouse means to find out. He believes they operate from headquarters in Dudley Port, Trieste, Shiraz or all three centres, and that they use the Island of Socotra, in the Arabian Sea, as an entrepot for the despatch of the Midlanders to Pakistan, either on board ship or carried, like a well-known former illegal immigrant, Sinbad the Sailor, on the back of a giant roc.

Emergency

"Raise high the Great Green Banner of Peter Simple's Thought!" "Down with the social engineering freaks and monsters!" "Raise the stones and expose the creeping technologists to the Eye of Heaven!"

These are a few of the spontaneous cries (announces a Columnar Spokesman) now being chanted by crowds of peasants, fishermen, carpenters, organ-builders and market women in towns and villages throughout this column. Their peaceful, orderly though enthusiastic meetings are joined by smiling, gaily-uniformed secret policemen, keen-eyed beadles of the Prince-Archbishop and men of the Columnar Imperial Guard on furlough.

The people's indignation was first aroused by the discovery of an illegal institute of advanced technology in a remote part of the column. Then came reports that large numbers of foreign sociologists, behaviourists, statisticians and other mechanistic bandits had infiltrated its mountain borders. At the thought that the "bad old days" of science might return, there was a momentary surge of panic and despair.

This was succeeded by a stern, calm determination to root out the technological puppets and destroy their works wherever they might be found. Today the whole population stands ready, armed with the infrangible iron bars of Luddite-Obscurantist Theory, to meet the threat to Church and State and protect from the disruptive forces of the past the green meadows and grey-walled cathedral-cities of the feudal present.

Dance of death

"Vulgarity, ridicule and spectacle. These are the three absolutes of the New York underground drama today," says a newspaper article. "It is an increasingly successful formula."

The article describes some of these dramatic offerings. "At the moment you can see two plays dealing graphically with narcissism and rape . . . 'Conquest of the Universe' is . . . played in a style of exuberant lewdness . . . Unnameable acts are casually performed on stage and in the final scene nine new-born infants are carved up with a dinner knife. The whole thing is hysterically amusing."

The whole thing must certainly be hysterically amusing to the single-minded enemies of the United States in Moscow and elsewhere, who will conclude, rightly or wrongly, that a nation which permits such increasingly successful spectacles will neither survive nor deserve to do so.

As for us in the West, less single-minded and more sophisticated, what should be *our* critical reaction? We may search for appropriate phrases . . . "alienation" . . . "problem of non-communication" . . . "neo-expressionism with dadaist elements" . . . "Theatre of the Abominable" . . . "fearless confrontation in theatrical terms with the human predicament in the post-Christian era" . . .

But at the back of them all there seems to nag at the mind some other critical reaction, older, simpler, and more universally applicable than any of these both to art and life. What can it be? "Deliver us from evil"?

Absolved

In the dream, the huge, dark figure which confronted me had an expression stern and authoritative, yet pitying and kindly; its features, familiar but subtly changing, recalled now Dee Wells, now Dr. Edmund Leach, now Sgt. Dixon of Dock Green.

"Very well," I said at last. "I confess. You are right. All the progressive thinkers are right. Everything I think and everything I write is due, simply and solely, to my obsessive hatred and envy of the young.

"When I am not hating and envying the young, I am drooling over my memories of the War (the happiest time of my life, since I not only experienced order and discipline but could indulge to the full my wish to hurt and kill).

"Often, I am lucky enough to be able to combine my only two remaining emotions at one and the same time. As I shamble through the streets in my shabby mackintosh and wide flapping trousers with turn-ups, I see the young in one another's arms or, bright-eyed with compassion for all mankind, separately rattling Oxfam collecting boxes. 'Stand to attention and say "sir" when you speak to an officer,' I bark, unaware of my own breaking, papery, senile voice.

"The only answer is a pitying smile or a mocking 'Move over, Dad' from boy or girl. With lips pursed and disapproving at blond hair and miniskirts (though groaning inwardly with dismal lust) I pass on, brooding on declining moral standards, the ruin of England and the collapse of Western civilisation.

"I am, of course, an unconscious hypocrite. It is only my envy and hatred of the young which makes me pretend to think Beethoven a better composer than the Beatles. It is only my envy and hatred of the young which makes me pretend to believe Soviet Russia is a more dangerous threat than South Africa, Rhodesia, Portugal or Greece to the remaining liberties of this country.

"It is only my envy and hatred of the young which makes me pretend to fear the advance of technology, of universal urbanisation, of a scientific attitude to birth, love, death; in short, to fear the glorious and happy future the young will inherit. It is only my . . ."

But the compound figure, which now seemed to have put on the infectious smile of Sir Hugh Greene, was already raising an absolving and progressive hand. I woke as winter dawn flared at the windows and an early jet-liner passed with its rending scream across the sky.

1968

Numinous

Our own age has taken solitude and quietness from places like Stonehenge with technological contrivances—motor-roads, car-parks and "visitors' facilities". Now, by a further use of technology, it is trying to put solitude and quietness back, shove our present day out of sight by installing subways for visitors and moving their facilities underground.

But all it can put back is a simulacrum. The *feeling* of solitude is gone. A modern visitor can no longer feel the sacred awe his forebears felt when they first trod the turf of the great plain and first set eyes on the grey, fabulous stones. He knows the refreshment kiosks and Ministry of Works administrative offices are not far away. He knows he is in a museum.

It may be that a feeling of strangeness, if not quite of the old kind, could best be restored to Stonehenge if all attempts to institutionalise it with tasteful archaeological treatment were dropped, and our up-to-date sort of nature were allowed to take its course.

Surrounded by council houses, condemned as an incomprehensible nuisance or piece of rudeness by spin-drier-loving housewives, or standing strangely in some factory executives' car-park, its very origin and nature almost forgotten, Stonehenge might once again assert, if only to a few people, its irrational and numinous strength.

Yarn

"I believe it was right . . . the principles we have proclaimed . . . consistent with our honour . . . the bar of world opinion . . ."

As the Prime Minister's stirring words boomed through the quiet club smoking room, a reminiscent gleam came into the keen blue eye of old "Skipper" Stannard, a lean weatherbeaten man with that indefinable air about him of one who has ploughed the seven seas.

"The Bar of World Opinion," he mused, sipping his tall whisky-and-soda. "How it all comes back to me . . . What tales I could tell about that place . . ."

"Come on, Skipper," urged Pip Lethbridge. "Spin us a yarn." We all crowded eagerly round.

Stannard sucked his pipe ruminatively. "It was a rum joint," he began, "and no mistake—New York East Side, right down in the slums on the river. A gloomy Swede kept it when I knew it—Dag the Drag they called him; a queer chap for the job you might think, but then it was a pretty queer job. A Burma Wallah has it now, they say . . ."

"Tell us more", chimed in "Staggers" Horniblow, all agog, ordering another round of stingers.

"To be quite blunt," the Skipper went on, "the Bar of World Opinion had a bad reputation. Can't say why, but every sort of riff raff found its way there from all quarters of the compass—black, white, khaki and how's your uncle. Flashy sort of women—you know the kind"—we nodded man-to-man agreement—"and the worst kind of rotters—bar-flies, chaps on the run, remittance men, fancy blokes, lounge lizards and all that . . .

"Well, one night there was a regular Donnybrook Fair going on in the place. Dag had locked the bottles away, and about 30 darkies were going hammer and tongs for some poor Belger, and chairs and glasses were flying in all directions, when suddenly the swing doors flew open and a great roar split the row— *'Bejabers*! And is there any of youse gossoons would be afther a *rale* foight?'

"And there in the doorway, fists at the ready, stood the mad fighting Irishman! Conor the Cruiser we called him, a bit of a Bolshie if you ask me, always in some scrape or other, always ready for a glass or a girl, always ready with a tall story—he had Paddy's gift of the gab, you know, full of blarney, and the prince of good fellows to boot. Well, to cut a long story short . . ."

People and parties

Inspired by the current boom in D. H. Lawrence (drools REX HICKFIELD), I dropped in on Connie Mellors (Lady Chatterley that was) and ex-gamekeeper and nature-writer Oliver Mellors in their Kensington flat. I found her just as I remembered, still beautiful in her late sixties, elegant, yet with a hint of sadness in her blue-rinsed hair.

I asked if she'd been consulted about the Royal Court productions of Lawrence's plays or the filming of "Women in Love" at his Nottinghamshire birthplace. She shook her head.

"I'm afraid these 'avant garde' people don't want to know me now," she laughed. "I suppose they think I'm 'square', not 'with it', almost a part of the Establishment." She laughed again.

"One television producer did come to see me, to offer me a small part in some programme they were doing about David's—I mean D. H. Lawrence's—life. I'm afraid Oliver was really awfully rude to him. He's been terribly difficult about the BBC, you see, ever since they dropped 'Woodland Ways', his children's natural history series, you know."

She smiled ruefully as her husband, still tall, erect and handsome, wandered in from his study next door, a suspicious look clouding his mane of white hair.

"Look here, Connie," he began. "I must say it's a most ghastly bore—I mean, er, dunna thee worrit, little lass," he said, recovering himself at sight of me. His voice died away in an incoherent mutter, in which I could just distinguish the words "blood", "oneness" and "grey modernity".

"You see how it is," Connie said ruefully, as he wandered vaguely out of the room again. She sighed. "I sometimes think Sir Clifford has had the best of it. He's still living down in Nottinghamshire, you know, and tremendously active. I believe he runs a youth club at Eastwood and takes a great interest in jazz and protest and drugs and theatre and all that sort of thing.

"Did you read that series of articles he wrote in the *Sunday Defective*: 'How I Got Switched On at 85'?"

Heroic days

Bournemouth councillors are indignant at a film by Lord Snowdon, which they say gives a false impression of Bournemouth as a "bath-chair town". "The other day," says the chairman of the entertainments committee, "we tried to find a bath-chair. We couldn't. This is just about the most virile town in Britain."

Curiously enough, I remember Ernest Hemingway saying the same thing to me 20 years ago when I stayed with him at his ranch near Branksome Chine. "Bournemouth makes a man live good, eat good, drink good, write good, love good, shoot good," he told me as we sat on the veranda gulping down slug after slug of his own special "Sandbanks" cocktail ("equal parts rye, bourbon, slivovitz and brandy on the rocks"), and firing off our elephant guns at anything that moved.

There were plenty of bath-chairs about in those days, but anyone who imagined their occupants lacked virility was in for a big surprise. Ernest himself, arriving at Bournemouth railway station hot from his liberation of Paris, had made the mistake of hiring a bath-chair and having himself pushed by a beautiful, blonde nurse through the centre of the town, with his typewriter and guncases following in another bath-chair behind.

He had not gone far, he told me, before he was challenged by three octogenarians in bath-chairs for possession of his own bath-chair, nurse and all his possessions.

"They fought good," he said ruminatively, scratching his chest. "But I fought gooder. They died good. I guess the whole goddam town was at the funeral. 'Ernesto', some big noise—Alderman Pickles or some such name—said to me at the graveside, 'Ernesto, *hombre,* you know something?' 'I know nothing,' I said. 'Nothing, Nada. I know it good'."

He sent his great booming, virile laugh echoing over Bournemouth; and that great, booming, virile town of sand, pines, bath-chairs, beards and he-men returned it with interest.

Spectral thoughts

"A spectre is haunting Europe—the spectre of student power," says Paul Johnson in the *New Statesman,* absurdly parodying the opening words of the Communist Manifesto.

Among the students of Paris, he rhapsodises, there is a "pentecostal" mood. "In the overflowing lecture halls and corridors every conceivable topic is examined: forms of revolutionary action, birth control, free love, the role of parents, the uses of exams, Vietnam, marriage and divorce, the nature of the university."

Over this festival of reason broods the lovable figure of Cohn-Bendit, "this jovial young Robespierre with his flaming red hair and piercing blue eyes", who like all such legendary heroes "makes the impossible become possible simply by doing it".

Inspired by this romantic personage, "the students fought all night on the barricades on May 10; the next day the Government capitulated".

While Johnson exults over the birth of a new world and the humiliation of that bourgeoisie of which he is himself a flower, less excitable bourgeois may raise doubts. Nor is it necessary to condemn the French students out of hand—some of their reputed ideas, such as their hostility to industrial mass-society, should appeal to all rational people—to see that the Editor of the *New Statesman* has avidly swallowed at least two new and excitingly fashionable myths.

One of these myths is that it is to the students of Paris that the French Government has capitulated. The other and more danger-ous myth is that the French Communists are just as scared of these students as the French bourgeoisie is supposed to be.

What have the Communists got to be scared about? What are student insurrections but one further stage, perhaps the penulti-mate, in the progressive ruin of the West? Whatever the students themselves may hope to achieve—and not all their hopes are bad ones—what can they achieve in fact but destruction and disorder?

There are those who, whether they have planned that disorder or not, will know how to take advantage of it. They are experts unsurpassed at that game. And behind them, in the last resort, is a power rather more formidable than the stormtroopers of Cohn-Bendit.

The spectre which is haunting Europe is the same spectre which has been haunting it for 50 years. It is the spectre of the Red Army.

Picketing on

A plague of demonstrators is now infesting every part of life. At York they have been picketing churches which are said to be redundant. At the back door of the Minster, some carried a placard reading "Why? A rich church, a poor world".

So long have such propagandists been arguing, and without contradiction, that the existence of beautiful old churches, with their treasures and rituals, is an affront to the world's poor, that almost everybody has now come to believe it.

I have read of some film which is being made from a novel about the Papacy. The climax is a scene in which the Pope, warned that the starving millions of the world will rise in warlike fury unless the Vatican is instantly abolished, sells all the Church's treasures and gives the money to the poor, thereby, it seems, ensuring eternal peace and plenty for all.

This preposterous scene is meant to be taken quite seriously. But the idea that the dispersal of all the churches of the world, with all their treasures, would do anything much to "solve the related problems of poverty and war" is at best a grotesque simplification; at worst, an enormous lie. It is not the poor who make war; but the rich.

When York Minster was built, few people, if any, thought it a waste of money or an affront to the poor. It was a visible symbol of the splendour of God, and this, if it is anything, it still remains. Far from being an affront to the poor, it is an affront to the rich, to the powerful, to the secular rulers of this world who, believing that no other world exists, must measure everything in terms of this world's use, whether in peace or war.

No wonder they, with their well-meaning dupes and unconscious abettors, want to destroy such monumental symbols, and to build instead their own even more gigantic monuments of utility and power—factories, barracks, traffic complexes and power-stations—for a wholly secular world.

In that world there will still be poor to be affronted. But if the reformers have their way, no symbols of supernatural splendour and beauty will remain to turn their hearts to what may lie beyond it.

Go into a Post Office and buy a stamp

... Or buy a colourful postal order, or ask for a free, exciting Road Fund Licence or Premium Bond form. Go on. Spoil yourself. Treat yourself to half-a-dozen dog licences.

When did YOU last visit your local Post Office? Perhaps you still think of it as a dreary old place, full of dreary old people queuing up to get their Old Age Pensions? Don't make us laugh!

Not that we of the G.P.O. can stop laughing, anyway! The modern Post Office is a real fun place, where, in bright, airy surroundings, with pictures on the wall, you can meet interesting people and enjoy the cheerful companionship of ordinary men and women like yourselves.

It's a club. But unlike most clubs, there's no charge for entry. Not yet, anyhow. The men and women of the Post Office are there to serve you with a cheerful smile and a ready joke to chase the blues away. The modern Post Office is a real fun place for real fun people.

Why not give it a whirl? Drop in at your "local" today. Join the new world of fun and adventure thousands are discovering for themselves. You'll enjoy it. And remember, the more stamps, postal orders, dog licences and other good things you buy, the more you'll be helping the Britain of Tomorrow.

[ADVT]

Poor old has-beens

"The Soviet Government," said a *Times* leader writer the other day, "has become hopelessly outdated and out of touch with contemporary movements at home and abroad."

So the Soviet Government is hopelessly outdated, is it? It has just imposed its will on the Czechs and Slovaks by force. And this is supposed to be hopelessly outdated in an age which, thanks to perverted science (a highly contemporary movement if ever there was one), has seen and will see force repeatedly and successfully applied on a scale undreamed of by the conquerors of the past.

So force is outdated. Treachery is outdated. War is outdated. Pain is outdated. Death is outdated. Evil itself is not only outdated but out of touch with contemporary movements at home and abroad.

That a writer, presumably intelligent, certainly literate and possibly able to influence the opinions of others, can believe these things is positively terrifying. If the Russian Communist leaders, as we are told day in day out, are now cowering in the Kremlin in a state of extreme terror here is some little comfort for them.

When Soviet tanks are on the Channel Coast, shall we still be telling ourselves that the Soviet Government is outdated and out of touch? As we are herded into camps for political re-education or worse, shall we still go on saying to each other, with a superior smile: "This is really too ridiculously outdated for words. I mean, it's quite pathetically out of touch with contemporary movements at home and abroad"?

Church news

Dr. Spacely-Trellis, the go-ahead Bishop of Bevindon, has suggested that a team of surgeons from the Medical School of the University should perform a heart-transplant operation on the High Altar of Bevindon Cathedral. This will be part of what he calls "a complete re-jigging of our religious productivity drive in the light of modern knowledge".

As well as the heart-transplant operation, a special all-secular service will feature (simultaneously) pop music by the Spirochaetes group, a happening, "Cybernetic Nudity," by the American Marylou Ogreburg Anti-Dance Company, and a solemn dedication of the new contraceptive vendomat machines to be installed in the People's Narthex.

There will also be a mass demonstration against the Greek Government, organised by popular revolutionary fun person and TV personality Gastriq Ali.

There have been some objections, mainly on doctrinal grounds, from reactionary elements in the diocese which somehow escaped the recent shake-out of redundant or under-productive clerical executives who failed to achieve work-norm targets.

But the Bishop is confident of dealing with any opposition. "Some of these reverend gentlemen may be socially useless," he stated yesterday, with a meaning laugh, "but their hearts are not."

Explosions

When you hear that the World Bank is to launch a world campaign for birth control does your heart leap up as if you beheld a rainbow in the sky? When you hear that the World Bank's loans of money to poor "underdeveloped" countries may be dependent on their taking steps under expert guidance to "curtail the population explosion" do you say to yourself: "How right! How true! How beautiful! How full of hope for humankind!"?

Or, unregenerate, do you mutter to yourself that if you were ruler of one of these countries you would feel inclined to tell the World Bank to keep its pills and coils, its statistics, its perversions and its money, and you would keep your people and do your best, with any outside help that was acceptable, to keep their souls as well as their bodies alive?

Do you even suspect—supreme heresy—that the real threat to the world is not that famous "population explosion"—people, however superfluous to the World Bank, are human beings, after all—but an explosion of aboriginal, inhuman evil?

Zero Minus Zero

by Jon Glasse Derkeley

A slim man in a rusty mackintosh, wearing heavily-rimmed, mud-spattered spectacles, moves slowly yet briskly about the municipal rubbish dump, dodging cameras, canvas chairs, trailing cables, dead cats, actors, all the paraphernalia of film-making on location. Every now and then he yawns and his head nods on his rust-corroded chest as if he is about to fall asleep. Sometimes, enigmatically, he does.

It is Jean-Paul Bourdon, the most controversial film director alive, the man who last year, with his controversial "De Gaulle is a Woman", won the World Boring Authority's award for the best film of the year. Now he is in England, in Stretchford in fact, making a new film, "Zero Minus Zero". Will it be a bigger yawn-maker still?

Actors, white, black, brown, a few painted in stripes, dodge amid the smoking rubbish. Snared by a tangle of old car-springs, a white girl stumbles and falls: Bourdon's eyes instantly flick open as he signals enigmatically to the controversially drooping camera crews. With a dull splash, a cameraman, yawning, falls in the mud and lies still, as a dozen hand-held cameras whirr at each other.

A group of typical Conservative women in flowered hats, some of them on fire, sit drinking tea at a large table on which is spread a disembowelled horse. A pop group, the Filthy Swine, try a few notes, break off, pour coloured poison into a guitar, watch Bourdon dimly with their mouths open, revealing orange peel teeth.

Why Stretchford? Why the Filthy Swine? Bourdon smiles. "All location is representation, a feeling that this is that, or one thing and another." Stretchford, he explains, is the most unpleasant place he has ever seen; the Filthy Swine are the most unpleasant and boring people he has ever met.

The purpose of his new film, then, is to expose the nastiness of bourgeois England? Bourdon smiles again, more controversially and enigmatically than ever, as a camera, coming in close, takes a long sequence of his slowly twitching face. The left lens of his spectacles cracks across.

"All purpose is immediacy. Function is representation. A film is a statement, an act, a state. The message is in the function. Life is what you make it. Time is money. The customer is always right . . ."

Like a wind from nowhere, the wind of change, the wind of the 20th century, his snores, enigmatic and controversial, stir the sparse acid-grass and rattle the mouldering metal on the rubbish-heaps. Mysteriously, a large wad of assorted bank-notes and dividend certificates falls from Bourdon's pocket and lies there on the ground as the camera moves in.

Alehouses of England

Many people (writes "Wayfarer") must have been intrigued by a recent reference by the Prime Minister (the Rt. Hon. Harold Wilson, M.P.) to "alehouse-gossip" by which, he said, a bogus financial scare had been created. Where, they ask, are these financial alehouses to be found? Couldn't they be smartened up and turned into tourist attractions, thus helping (to coin a much-needed phrase) Britain's vital tourist industry? Or, alternatively, shouldn't they be closed down, as a menace to Britain's economic revival?

Most of us, I think, would prefer to keep these picturesque old buildings just as they are now, a precious part of London's vanishing heritage. I know one such alehouse, not a thousand miles from Fleet Street, which is a real gem of its kind.

It has a thatched-roof with low eaves in which swallows seem to coo softly at all times of the year, even when December fog, a real "pea-souper" or "London Particular", as the speculators call it, comes down to shroud the cobbled lanes and invest the wharves and alley-ways with age-old mystery.

Once through the low doorway, with its ancient carved sign "Duck your nut", and the stranger will be met by a ruddy glow from the big open fireplace, a cheerful "Good day t'ye" from burly, baize-aproned Mine Host, and an open-hearted murmur of welcome from the currency speculators who sit on bench or in inglenook puffing their long clay-pipes and taking occasional swigs of ale, "the true and proper drink of Englishmen", from their pewter tankards.

Here the talk is all of exchange rates, and liquidity, and bullion, and the International Monetary Fund; and fascinating talk it is, full as a plum-pudding of the lore which was already old when Julius Caesar first trod these shores.

The low, growling voices, the flickering firelight, the crescent moon, often seen at midday in these parts, peeping in through the green bottle-glass windows, the traditional cry of "All's Well" from the Stock Exchange lamplighter on his rounds: all this induces a timeless, dreamlike feeling from which the unwary visitor may emerge in sudden panic; then, rushing through the strange twilight to the nearest telephone, wildly instruct his broker to unload everything he has . . .

Tunes of glory

The G.P.I. Television Network is often accused (by a vociferous minority of retired colonels and superannuated memsahibs) of being indifferent or even hostile to the British Army. It certainly made amends with yesterday evening's documentary "The Lads wi' the Needles and Thread", a stirring survey of the Royal Army Tailoring Corps.

With a forceful commentary written and spoken by the Corps' famous Commandant, Lt.-Gen. Sir Frederick Nidgett, this programme was a colourful evocation of a body of men who for sheer dash, élan, panache, brio, verve and flair must be second to few, if not most, of Britain's fighting men.

We saw parade ground scenes, with a stentorian Sergeant-major Cutter taking a squad of lapel-stitching "rookies" through their paces. There was the moving ceremonial of Coathanger Day, when in memory of an incident in the Boer War all members of the Corps wear outsize coathangers painted in the Corps colours of mauve and Nile green and adorned with bunches of holly, *inside* their jackets.

We saw seasoned Tailors on the assault course, cutting out, stitching and assembling pairs of trousers at the double under heavy fire; and by way of contrast, a sing-song in a typical Naafi canteen in the Home Counties with "You'd Be Far Better Off in a Home", a bombardon solo played by a veteran without once taking the cigarette out of his mouth.

Interspersed with these there were scenes from news reels showing the Corps ("the Grey Devils from East Ardsley Junction", as the baffled Germans used to call them) in action in the Second World War. Highlights were the mass-drops of trouser-presses to the Jugoslav partisans, and—from the dark days of 1942 when, at Rear H.Q. at Port Said, the Corps helped to hold Rommel's hordes at bay—Nidgett's amazing feat of organisation in withdrawing the bulk of his forces to Aden without loss.

As the Corps anthem, "Thimbles Awa," crashed out from massed pipes, drums, xylophones and viole da gamba, Gen. Nidgett delivered his peroration, bringing a lump, I should think, to the boots of the most arrant pacifist.

"What is the secret?" he asked, as a gleam of heroic light from nowhere lit up his knitted Tailoring Corps tie. "I will tell you. In a word, it is leadership, initiative, vision, guts, physical fitness, a sense of values, leadership, guts, initiative, vision, leadership. . . ."

Fall

A new book by John Gross, "The Rise and Fall of the Man of Letters", scarcely plumbs the depths to which some men of letters have now fallen. On Deadwater No. 3 Level, in the disused

Derbyshire lead-mine which is now his home, Julian Birdbath, last heir of Saintsbury and Gosse, smiles ruefully in the glimmering light of his storm-lantern over his own uncompleted manuscript "A Bookman Remembers".

With a plop, a toad climbs from a stagnant pool, slithers on to his mouldering desk and peers into his face. Birdbath, so inveterate, instinctive a man of letters is he still, at once begins to compare its face with that of a rival, hostile reviewer, long dead, and slowly quotes a line of Baudelaire aloud.

Echoes of his weak and nasal voice run eerily about the fluospar-encrusted walls, the sagging bookshelves loaded with mildewed, fungus-grown copies of *The Saturday Review, New Age, Horizon, John o' London's Weekly* and with review copies of forgotten books, books unimaginably unreadable, books unsaleable even on publication, books which even the rats reject and pig-farmers on the limestone uplands refuse to mix into their all-receiving swill.

Ruefully Birdbath remembers the days when men of letters were still powers in the land; the forms of great ones scarcely known—Lehmann, Connolly, Mortimer, Pritchett, Spender—loom before his mind's eye and seem to flicker on the cavern walls. Even the acrid snub of a Grigson would be welcome now.

How long since he last stood among his peers at even the humblest publisher's party? How long since even the most lamentable parcel of books for review on the literary page of the *Stretchford Clarion* was dropped down the mineshaft by a contemptuous postman with a shout of "4s. 6d. to pay"? How long since the last faint message from the fading world of letters reached his wax-stopped ears?

Yet as his fingers sink on to the rusting typewriter, like many an exile he dreams all will be regained. At some great literary gathering beyond the reach of time, where ponderous pipes are pointed at trembling young writers of promise, gold-rimmed glasses flash, port-thickened voices intone, Birdbath will come into his own again.

Convenient

At the World Council of Churches' "consultation on racism," the American Senator George McGovern said that if all other methods failed the Church must support resistance movements and revolutions to eliminate the "political or economic tyranny which makes racism possible."

What is "racism"? It is a term of supreme vagueness which can cover anything, as the user wishes, from systematic discrimination between races, such as exists in South Africa, to an instinctive preference for people of one's own kind, such as exists in every society in the world, capitalist or communist, tribal or centralised, tyrannical or libertarian.

There are people who are not prepared to admit a fact of life which, if not eternal, is likely to last until the Day of Judgment. That is why they have to maintain that discrimination between races is only made possible by political or economic tyranny.

What a godsend this is to professional revolutionaries of every kind! All they have to do, in order to enlist the support of liberals and idealists in subverting and overturning any established government on earth, is to insist it is a government which by its political or economic system is making racism possible.

A musical treat

It is not often that we have the privilege of hearing the Stretchford Municipal Symphony Orchestra in London. But last night's concert at the Sumerian Hall (writes CLIVE BOMBARDON, "Way of the World" Music Critic) fully justified this provincial orchestra's unusual reputation.

It might be argued that Sir Jim Gastropodi, their veteran conductor, was unwise to start the programme with "'Neath Stretchford Skies," a tone-poem by the little-known Stretchford-born composer Edward Phantomsby.

This rather banal, sub-Straussian work stretched, if the term may be forgiven, the orchestra's resources to the utmost. It is not often one sees, in a London concert-hall, a trombonist flinging down his instrument during a string passage, crawling furtively from the back of the platform and hurriedly snatching up a spare viola so as to give much-needed support to the string section.

The wood-wind playing, too, was noticeably ragged. In one tutti the top of one of the bassoons actually flew off into the stalls. The player's efforts to fill in the bassoon part vocally, though praise-worthy, were less than happy.

These faults of technique, resources and sheer bad luck were all magnified in the remaining work in the programme, Mahler's Eleventh Symphony ("the Interminable"), a dangerous choice for any conductor whose vital powers are beginning to flag.

One might have overlooked the series of snapped 'cello strings (and, in one case, even a snapped bow), the violent altercation, which occupied 245 bars of the slow movement, between the second flautist and one of the double basses, ending with the former's head firmly wedged in the latter's instrument, or the intermittent screams of a lady second violinist whose handbag a percussion player was furtively trying to draw towards him with a hook improvised from part of the tubular bells.

What really made me begin to doubt this orchestra's musicianship was their handling of the climax of the symphony, when Sir Jim, failing to turn over the page, went on conducting the closing bars over and over again, long after the orchestra had finished playing. Was it necessary for the bass tuba to guffaw quite so loudly?

All in all, an interesting evening.

Miracle

One of the most wonderful of all the wonderful achievements of the Labour Government has just been consummated. The mainly white electorate of Rhodesia has voted by a majority of 81 per cent. for the severance of all ties with the British Crown.

The white people of Rhodesia—discounting some of the South African elements—have always been just about the most fervently loyalist British people on earth. To convert such people, in a few years, into republicans is certainly no small feat.

If the Labour Government can do this, what can it *not* do? Or is its repertoire of miracles now exhausted? I am very much afraid it isn't.

Free moon offer

Today, conqueror of the Moon, Man steps out of the twilight of pre-history, the childhood of his race, into the full light of morning, and stands looking about him proudly, adult at last, on the threshold of the stars.

The money which Man has wasted in putting Man on the Moon, it has been estimated, would provide all the starving peasants of Asia with hot cooked dinners for the next 145,000 years.

Today, science calls the nations of the earth, still busy with their petty wars, their outmoded quarrels over equally irrelevant questions of politics, race and religion, to unite in a larger, nobler, universal task: the colonisation of the universe by Man himself.

If Man does not watch out, and stop meddling with what does not concern him, Man is going to have a very nasty accident—and then!

Cross out whichever of the above does not apply. Cross out the whole lot, if you prefer it.

Know your scripture

"Please provide facilities, Jesus commented, for infants of pre-school age to associate with me whenever feasible. They can play a relevant part in the life of the future world community" (from the Bevindon translation of the New Testament).

1969

Farewell

The news that Mme Alexandra David-Neel, the first European woman to enter Lhasa, had died in France, aged 100, set ringing in my mind not a bell but an enormous, intricately wrought bronze gong, accompanied by 30ft-long Tibetan monastery trumpets.

I remembered that summer before the war when I read her book, "Mystics and Magicians in Tibet," with its account of life in Tibetan monasteries; the festivals, devil-dances, exhibitions of butter sculpture; the annual psychic sports, when the monks would compete in levitation, in moving objects at a distance (or tele-kinesis, as it is now called), in the production of thought-forms and in the generation of supernatural body heat, when the competitors had to strip and sit naked in the snow all night, the monk who melted the largest patch of snow being the winner.

Then there were the graded courses of psychic exercises for anchorites, culminating in the "Dreadful Mystic Banquet," when the monk, with bell, thunderbolt and drum, summoned the demons to feast upon his sacrificial body.

There were the splendid ceremonials, when the great nobles and abbots of Tibet appeared in their ritual garments of silk, brocade and gold; at the New Year, there were the epileptic writhings and obscure pronouncements of the State Oracle before the assembled multitude.

All was unchanging ritual, an unchanging hierarchy accepted by all from high to low. Whether I believed every word—or even most of the words—of Mme David-Neel's highly wrought account, it seemed then—and still seems now—to portray a most satisfactory form of what is now boringly called social organisation.

Life in Tibet was hard, cold, uncomfortable even for the rich. The peasants were poor and unimaginably dirty. Yet they seemed always smiling. If they stank, they stank of happiness.

Now it has all gone (or perhaps, rightly regarded, from a Tibetan point of view, it is all eternally there). Now Mme David-Néel herself, after long years, has followed. My thanks to her. Apart from influencing my political ideas her book gave me for several nights a series of coloured dreams of such fantastic splendour that even now after 30 years they can flood my mind with wonder.

Need for compassion

"If Enoch Powell ever had a real friend who was Asian, African or West Indian," Mrs Eirene White told the Labour Party conference, "I just do not believe he could speak as he does. It is the measure of his failure in human relationships."

Yesterday Dr Heinz Kiosk, chief psychiatric adviser to the South-Eastern Gas Board, supported her view. Enoch Powell's speeches, he believed, were not to be taken in a political sense. As with so many delinquents and other disturbed people, they were "a cry for help," a projection of severe personality difficulties.

Instead of condemning Powell, we should regard him with

compassion, as a helpless victim of our society's distorted values. He had obviously suffered more than most from a reactionary educational system and from patriotic and militarist conditioning.

He offered to give Powell free psychiatric treatment in his Hampstead clinic, where he would be able, under medical supervision, to meet and make friends with the many Asians, Africans and West Indians kept there for experimental purposes.

If necessary, abreactive therapy could be used. Powell would be given an electric shock every time the image of a white person was projected on a screen, and offered chocolates or finely bound volumes of Herodotus whenever the images of coloured immigrants appeared.

After 10 years' treatment, Dr Kiosk thought, Powell might well acquire a normal, healthy, forward-looking dislike of his own race. If not, he would at least have been prevented for 10 vital years from trying to disturb, with his morbid, narcissistic fantasies, the present sane and orderly progress of Britain's social and political life.

Survey

Another traditional source of vulgar jokes is threatened. Housewives, says a survey conducted for that esteemed body, the National Dairy Council, are becoming more formal in their relations with milkmen. In London only 16 per cent. even know their milkman's name. But in the West Midlands the figure is 42 per cent., the highest in the country.

A "Way of the World" survey published today of council housing estates in the Stretchford area, conducted by a team of sociologists, some trained in karate, hardly supports these conclusions. But then the survey included the notorious Bog Lane Estate, which milkmen until recently visited only in pairs, or even threes, using special high-acceleration electric milk-floats for quick getaway.

Just over 81 per cent. of the housewives interviewed, many of them of gigantic size and terrifying appearance, claimed to know their milkmen's names, though of these 22 per cent. said they normally addressed them by names not their own (see Appendix B of the Survey, supplied under plain cover).

There was general agreement, however, that knowledge of a milkman's name was not necessarily an index of the degree of formality of the housewife's relationship with that milkman.

Blonde, attractive, mini-skirted, purple-faced, 17-stone Mrs J. Behemoth, 41, of Clement Attlee Way, summed up the position. "Some of the milkmen nowadays have such peculiar names—I had one only the other day who said he was called Léonidas Mfumbiro or something—that you can't even pronounce the names, let alone remember them.

"But who cares what their names are? Who cares what *your* name is, come to that," she added, making a sudden powerful grab at the interviewer, who fled screaming down the road, leaving part of his notebook in her gigantic hand.

Watch these shares!

Hippie Enterprises Ltd., launched yesterday, is one of the most promising new ventures of Nadirco, the giant commercial consortium whose word is life or death over large areas of England.

As well as the chairman, multi-millionaire Gordon Nadir, the board of directors includes several hippies: Swami Ron S. Bhattacharya, the only Indian holy man with a first-class degree in chartered accountancy, who owns a successful chain of yoga betting-shops in the Nerdley area; brilliant young disc jockey Jim Droolberg; millionaire anarchist badge manufacturer Norris Spivenham; millionaire hippie clothes designer Crispian Nidgett, bachelor son of Gen. "Tiger" Nidgett; and brilliant Kevin Frabb, formerly a director of documentary programmes on the GPI Television Network.

The new company intends to buy up islands, derelict country houses, disused churches, old folks' homes and other waste spaces for hippie settlements and run them as tourist attractions. Up-to-date factories, worked by the hippies themselves under expert supervision, will turn out exotic clothes, ready-soiled by a new, secret process, incense, souvenir slogans on sections of prefabricated wall, "Herbert Marcuse" anti-calendars and anti-Christmas cards, obscene and subversive newspapers, and so on, both for the home and export markets.

"I have an enormous admiration," Gordon Nadir said yesterday, "for these idealistic youngsters who want to opt out of our materialistic, money-mad society. I believe they have a great contribution to make to solving Britain's balance of payments problem and getting my economy right."

Your queries answered

by Clare Howitzer

Dear Clare Howitzer, I read in the paper where it says a woman had exchanged her two-year-old daughter for a second-hand record-player worth £3. This has caused a lot of argument in our home. My husband says the woman did not get value for money and should have held out for a record-player worth at least £6 10s.

As we have a son aged 32 and are thinking of exchanging him for a spin-drier, can you please advise?

Clare Howitzer replies: Relative values of goods and people fluctuate very rapidly. If you are exchanging your son, it is advisable to watch the market carefully. I know several wives who have recently exchanged their husbands or children for various goods and have been well and truly "sold a pup".

One friend exchanged her husband for a set of antique occasional tables, valued at £35. They turned out to be worth about 10s. Meanwhile, to her annoyance, she found that the woman who had taken over her husband had immediately exchanged him for a second-hand oil-fired central heating system, worth at least £200!

Keep out

A Mr. La Vey, a former American lion-tamer, head of the Church of Satan and occasional lecturer on sociology at the University of

San Francisco, is planning to start a branch of his church in England.

He has "a trim moustache, a goatee beard and a pair of plastic horns." His services are held in "a black ritual chamber with a scarlet ceiling. Nude, reclining women serve as altars, representing the flesh triumphant."

Mr. La Vey had better keep away from the Sowerby Bridge area, where Mrs. Elvira Mutcliffe, the Cleckheaton-born diseuse and devotee of solid pottery and eurhythmic dancing, has run her own highly successful coven for many years. Much respected in the neighbourhood and a total abstainer, she writes an occasional column on witchcraft in the local paper under the pseudonym "Mavis Demdike".

Mrs. Mutcliffe's coven meets every Tuesday at her semi-detached home, where a light meal of tea, potted meat sandwiches and assorted pastries is taken within the magic pentacle. On midsummer eve there is a special Witches' Sabbath picnic and infernal spelling bee in a wood near the J. S. Plugden Carbon Brush Factory, where Satan usually puts in an appearance for a few minutes and drinks a glass of non-alcoholic elderberry wine.

There is no nonsense about nude women either. Witches and warlocks wear close-fitting stockinet costumes for the ritual dancing, supplemented by mackintoshes and gumboots if the weather is wet. The Head Warlock, Cllr Albert Gogden, also wears a Trilby Hat of Invisibility.

"Foreigners like Mr. La Vey are not wanted in the West Riding," Mrs. Mutcliffe said yesterday. "He is the sort of person who gives black magic a bad name."

Talking point

In the country of the bald the one-haired man is king—Ralph Waldo Emerson.

Vandal notes

by "Supergoth"

With 27 telephone kiosks wrecked, 35 tombstones overturned, 53 inscriptions defaced, 167 ornamental shrubs uprooted and 746

windows broken (214 pts.), Bog Lane Wanderers are still hanging on to their commanding lead in the Stretchford Vandals' League this season.

Soup Hales Iconoclasts, with 191 pts., are still trailing second. But the "Connies", their go-ahead captain, Ron Gormley, told me yesterday, are going all out for bowling greens this week. In view of the high points yield for BGs under the new BVA rules this policy should undoubtedly pay rich dividends.

Breathing down the Connies' necks are Lampton Huns, with 187 pts., a team of real triers who have had a lot of bad luck this season. Last week, on a foggy evening, a group of them mistook one of their best destructionists, Len Fredds, for a statue on the patio of the new Income Tax Building in Cripps Road and destroyed him.

The funeral service at St. Attila's, attended by fans from all over the Midlands, was conducted by the Rev. Bruce Nethers, himself a keen practising vandal and a real friend and helpmeet to the lads. Thanks a million, Brucie Boy, and good hunting!

A Quiet Christmas

Christmas at Simpleham, though without the splendour of former years, when as many as 50 guests, including several Crowned Heads, would sit down to dinner, passed off pleasantly enough.

We had about a score of house guests—just a few old friends, country people like ourselves, one or two aged novelists or pianists, an eminent surgeon, a few admirals, a sprinkling of exiled Royalty. At the last moment old Picasso, a protégé of mine in my art student days in Paris, wired to say he could not come. In some scrape or other again, I suppose.

In these difficult times few guests bring their own servants. This is at least a relief for Venables, the butler, who at 90 is no longer up to dealing with the vicious faction brawls which in my father's day regularly broke out in the servants' hall and often resulted in multiple injuries and even death.

However, there were just enough players available for the traditional servants' football game after church on Christmas morning. This is played in the vast rooms and corridors of the deserted East Wing. There are no rules, but after an hour's play each player receives a traditional present of a gilded walnut.

After luncheon we rode, visited the Abbey ruins, listened to the Chaplain's traditional organ recital or tramped the waterlogged park, blazing away at nothing in particular.

At dinner, a traditional meal which lasts more than four hours, one of the roast geese exploded, showering the far end of the table with progressivist leaflets. Only one of the ex-Kings showed any alarm, polishing his monocle nervously for the rest of the evening.

On Boxing Day, I made up a party to visit the tenants, distributing traditional bicycles to the more deserving. A man from the local newspaper who tried to take photographs was seized by old Adam Strongitharm, the blacksmith and garage man, and would have been manhandled and even beheaded if I had not ordered his release. His photographic apparatus was, however, melted down and incorporated in an ornamental cast-iron dentist's chair Strongitharm is making in his random grim forge nearby.

By evening the guests, some of whom needed treatment for dislocated jaws, had gone, leaving us to talk quietly to ourselves about old times.

THE SEVENTIES

1970

Alternatives

Now it is Conservation Year. Suddenly the official talk is all of conservation, preservation, ecology, the quality of life, the environmental revolution: leaden words for the most important thing in all our material world.

The people who have been fighting for years for the beauty, seemliness and health of this country against technology, stupidity and greed, and have been called selfish, middle class, reactionary preservationist cranks for their pains, are suddenly seen to have been right after all.

Except that in the year 1970, being the sort of people they mostly are, they can't really be right, can they? "The environment," snaps the *New Statesman*, "is a socialist problem, not a preserve for well-meaning members of the middle class."

With these words, a large ferocious, dull-eyed and familiar-looking cat peeps out of what had seemed an attractively-patterned bag. The socialist way of saving the environment, if it means anything, means taking the environment—that is, in plain language, the land—into State ownership, so that its uses can be planned to the last detail and in equal shares for all.

It may be that this is indeed the only way in which this country in the long run can keep any of its beauty or even remain habitable at all. But whether we are socialists or not we should not delude ourselves that the England which would emerge from this environmental revolution would in any way resemble what we have known as England.

In that planned, departmentalised country, with its industrial areas, residential areas, leisure areas, amenity areas and all the rest, something of what Wordsworth thought of as "natural beauty" would remain (after all, it is now known to have social and educational value). It would remain; officially certificated, cold, dead and embalmed, its life and poetry gone.

"Queue here for the view." "Have you got your Solitude Voucher?" "National Wilderness No. 3. Property of the National Conservancy Board. Authorised Ecological Personnel Only."

An incorrigible, selfish, anti-social and thoroughly wicked voice whispers: rather than that, let England be ravaged from end to end, and perish.

A silly question

"At the end of the Second World War, news-reels showed the U.S. Marines, clean-cut and heroic, planting the flag on Iwo Jima. At the end of the 1960s they were on colour TV every night, burning villages in Vietnam" (from an article in the *Evening Standard*, "What 10 Years Did to America"). And what did the years do to Communist Russia, its news-reels and television? Did they start by showing clean-cut Red Army men planting the flag on Hitler's bunker and end with them causing students to burn themselves to death in Czechoslovakia?

If not, why not?

On the Ohm farm

"Young men interested in modern farming," says the Deputy President of the National Farmers' Union, "should have, or be capable of obtaining, at least four 'O' levels." There is no place in modern farming, he says, for the young man who cannot understand its increasingly sophisticated techniques.

One young hopeful recently presented himself to the gnarled, apple-cheeked agrotechnologist Seth Roentgen at the Ohm Farm, just as the sun had set o'er yonder hill, saying he wanted to be an agrotechnologist's administrative assistant.

Glancing at the lad's gaiters, his smock and wide-brimmed hat, at the straw dangling from his mouth and at his round, beaming, rosy face, Seth asked suspiciously, "How be thy nuclear physics then, young shaver? Do 'ee know about gas-cooled de-beaking units? Hast got thy B.Sc.?"

The youth shook his head. "Nay, maister," he replied with a carefree laugh. "But Oi can reap and sow, and plow and mow—and Oi've a strong back, an' willin' hands an'"—here he cast a longing look at buxom 18-year-old Hephzibah, old Seth's favourite daughter, Ph.D. (Heidelberg), and a ravishing sight in a mini-lab coat—"a lovin' heart——."

"Mebbe, mebbe," grumbled Seth, "but do 'ee know ought about inorganic chemistry? Electronics? Cost accountancy techniques?" The youth shook his head, aware of the contemptuous look in Hephzibah's sparkling black eyes.

"How many 'O' levels dost have?" she asked slyly. "'O' levels, young missy?" he replied, his honest brow creased in bewilderment. "What kind o' new-fangled tillage be they?"

With a bellow of rage Seth grabbed his portable flame-thrower and chased him back into the sunset. "The scallywag fair took me in," he confessed later to Hephzibah. "But not my little beauty, eh?"

The girl smiled complacently. "No, pa," she cooed, twining smooth, plump arms round the old man's withered neck. "One look at his hands was enough. All they danged ole callouses—and him pretendin' to be a farmer's boy!"

All done with mirrors

Suppose you are an "ordinary factory worker," making cars, or tea-trays, or nuts and bolts for cylindrical compensating turntables, or other vital products of an expanding economy.

You have been told, day in and day out, year after year, by politicians of all kinds, on television programmes and in newspapers, that this country is in a state of economic crisis. There is a nasty "trade gap" which has to be filled. There is a worrying "balance of payments" problem which must be solved.

The only way the country can "get the economy right," you have been told, now cajolingly, now in tones of severity and even anger, is for you to work harder and turn out more and better cars, tea-trays, nuts and bolts and so on.

But you, an ordinary factory worker, have not taken much notice of all this talk, on the whole. You have not worked harder. You have even asked for more money or, overcome by the sheer boredom of your ordinary factory work, have gone on strike from time to time, often for no very obvious reason.

This, you have been told, is absolutely disgraceful. What is more, if you persist in behaving like this the whole country and you with it will be ruined. But being an obstinate sort of person (and also noticing that the country, far from showing any signs of ruin, seemed to be bursting with money and luxuries) you have taken very little notice of that line of talk either.

Now, all of a sudden, though you have not been working harder, or refraining from strikes, or doing any of the things you have been told to do, you are informed by politicians, on television and in newspapers that "the economy is coming right," "the trade gap is narrowing," the "balance of payments" is looking much healthier and prosperity and happiness for all are round the corner.

What would you, an ordinary factory worker, think about all this? Would you think that since it seemed to make no difference to the "economy" whether you worked harder or not, the "economy" must be controlled by other factors you have not been told about?

Or would you think there was not much point in thinking—or voting—about such matters any further?

Chains and slavery

"Tell your husband not to be a fool and work like a slave. Milk should come out of larger herds than yours," was Mr Callaghan's celebrated advice to a Welsh farmer's wife.

Now a planning official advises farmers to turn land which is "unattractive for modern farming" into public parks and recreation areas, making a profit by charging entrance fees.

All sorts of powerful factors—large-scale, scientific agricultural methods, the demand for "leisure facilities" for townspeople, new food-marketing methods—are rapidly converging on the small farmers of this country to squeeze them out of existence.

These people are a remnant of a class traditionally independent, robust, hard-working, patriotic and conservative. Now they must either disappear or turn themselves into whole or part-time managers of amusement parks, dispensing, at first with natural shame, then with enthusiasm, cream-teas and souvenirs to leisure-maddened hordes whose urban, effete, servile, money-mad and empty attitudes they will very soon come to share.

What sort of a nation will it be which has none but this kind of people in it? How will it survive in a world which, however politicians may delude themselves or us, is growing rougher every day? Better to live like a slave than *be* a slave.

Don't miss this

"What did Wolfgang Amadeus Mozart do in the struggle for social justice in feudal, class-ridden 18th century Austria, even then ripe for take-over by the Nazis? What did he do to protest against the racialist horrors of the slave trade? What did he do to fight against the evils of organised religion?

"I'll tell you. Nothing! He just spent his time writing music and sucking up to the crowned heads of Europe. At one time he even worked for a reactionary clergyman, the Prince Archbishop of Salzburg—later, needless to say, one of Hitler's favourite haunts!

"It makes me sick. And when you see my film it'll make you a lot sicker."

Ron Fussell, the brilliant GPI television producer, was talking of his new film about the life and work of Mozart—which is to be shown on the network next week. As he spoke he danced brilliantly up and down, occasionally hacking at the furniture with an axe or setting his desk on fire in a frenzy of compassionate hatred.

In his own words, the film will really "put the boot in." Fussell makes no secret of his determination, at whatever cost—actually he's getting a special producer's fee of £150,000—to "shock viewers out of their complacency and make these wretched, boring little suburban shopkeepers sit up."

One highlight is a daring scene where Mozart, as a sexually precocious child prodigy, is dandled on the knee of Marie Antoinette, or Marie Theresa, or Catherine the Great or somebody. "Though dandling is not exactly the word for it," chuckled Ron.

Another controversial scene shows Mozart unconcernedly playing a piano sonata and having intercourse with his wife while
behind their backs Negroes are being beaten by white South
African sadists with steel billiard cues. "Mozart was very fond of
billiards," Ron explained, "and I believe that if white South
African billiard players had visited Austria this feeble racialist
time-server would not have had the guts to refuse to play with
them."

The GPI Network has installed a special unjammable switchboard to deal with the record number of protest calls expected.

Know your scripture

"If your national health dentures are not a perfect fit, Jesus
commented, discontinue wearing them, in due course applying for
a new upper or lower set; it will be better for you to play a relevant
part in the life of the community with half your teeth missing
rather than take up a backward-looking, anti-social attitude with a
complete set top and bottom" (from the Bevindon translation of the
New Testament).

Snores of protest

"The claimants also intend to show that unemployment or refusal
to work is often not their fault. They are victims of the 'structure of
our society' they say" (from a newspaper report about the Claimants' Union, a North London group for people who live on "social
security benefit").

Dr Heinz Kiosk, Chief Psychiatric Adviser to the White Fish
Authority, who has offered to give the new union his services for a
nominal fee, comments: "We are gradually getting rid of the
outmoded, unscientific idea that when a man refuses to work—or
refuses to do anything else for that matter—he is doing so of his
own free will. He is of course a helpless victim of the Establishment.

"A man who prefers to stay in bed all day rather than take a job
is uttering a muffled cry for help from beneath the bedclothes of
social discrimination. Every snore he emits is a criticism of our
unjust social system, all the more moving and cogent for its

underprivileged inarticulacy. It is high time we paid heed to that snoring message of protest.

"We are all guilty," he added, just when everybody was beginning to think he had for once forgotten to say it.

Up the Wandle

The ascent of the River Wandle, from its disemboguement into the Thames at Wandsworth to its source on the heights of Croydon is a journey seldom achieved, let alone attempted.

On a winter Sunday not long ago, with only a single companion and without native porters or any equipment apart from stout boots and a knapsack, I set out on this perilous journey.

Watched by a curious group of bystanders near the "Crane" public house (the base from which most previous explorers have started) the expedition set off beside the Wandle's dirty flood and was soon lost in the strangeness of South London.

A mysterious jumble of anachronisms: factories, some brand-new, some mouldering and half-derelict; a decayed, Pooterish villa overshadowed by an enormous towerblock; terraced cottages, some painted in the dull vermilion favoured in these parts; a child's face pressed to door-panels of many-coloured glass, changing at will the colours of the miniature park beside the stream.

Then a sewage-works; a whole suburb of semi-detached houses full of Sunday car-washers; another, larger park where dogs raced about and an old caretaker emerged slowly from a white-boarded house beside the already smaller, rippling but still filthy stream.

A caravan-site, with dirty-faced children and whippets, in the middle of a brand-new housing estate; a sinister, windowless villa surrounded by scrapyards and industrial waste beside rusty perambulator-infested water; a few pre-fabs peering from stunted trees.

So on to the mysterious source, which our maps—admittedly inaccurate—showed as an islanded lake in a small park on the confines of Croydon itself. It was already dusk when we reached it: gigantic cooling towers loomed ahead; a vast industrial plant, all twisting pipes and retorts of shining, iridescent aluminium, hummed and steamed strangely in the fading light; a single pensioner paced the wintry paths.

But the Wandle itself had disappeared down a concrete culvert full of nameless rubbish. There was no lake, no island, no bubbling spring in nereid-carved stone basin. There was only a solitary, inexplicable white-painted pillar with a locked door. But none of my keys would fit.

We stood for a moment in the deepening twilight, overcome by timeless mystery, then turned for home.

There are plans, I see, this being Conservation Year and all, to "clean up" parts of the Wandle, make it more acceptable to official ideas of tidy scheduled amenity.

Surely the genius of this London stream will resist the profanation, guarding its now-accustomed squalors, its effluent-poisoned waters, its mysterious urban poetry, as once it guarded its sparkling, rural, trout-filled pools in vain?

Reform

Moving the second reading of the Unwanted People Bill, Mr J. Computer-Smith (Lab., Soup Hales) said it was an urgent social measure designed to fill the gaps in the Abortion Act.

That wise and humane reform had already prevented thousands of unnecessary births. But it did not ease the predicament of parents (or single women) who might decide, after the birth of a child, that they did not want it after all.

Not everybody had a friend or neighbour they could give the baby to, and not everybody had the enterprise to leave it in a left luggage office or telephone kiosk where it would be found and later shown in a television programme.

Under the new Act, these at present underprivileged people would be able to take the child to a National Health hospital where it could be de-activated under proper medical supervision.

He realised that some doctors and nurses might refuse to co-operate. A clause in the Act would take care of such anti-social attitudes. It would provide that these misguided doctors and nurses, if they persisted, could themselves be disposed of by devitalisation.

When a Liberal member asked angrily why, in view of the menace of the population explosion, the Act applied in the first place only to children, Mr Computer-Smith said it was hoped eventually to extend it to the superfluous aged, to the socially unco-operative and indeed to all population units which could be shown by a majority vote to be unwanted (applause).

While the debate was in progress, a small number of people, mostly belonging to religious bodies, staged an ineffectual demonstration outside the Commons.

They were soon dispersed, as demonstration-space was required for 5,000 students, representing generous, idealistic, life-asserting Youth, who were protesting against the arrival in this country of a party of White South African croquet players.

Realm

"Does the desk, as a refuge, aid mental health?" "Are people afraid to clear out their desks?" "What rôle does the desk play in sex games in the office?" These, reports *New Society,* are some of the questions raised in a forthcoming book called "An Englishman's Desk is his Castle".

When I think of my own desk, a vast structure of mahogany whose remote corners I can hardly see in misty weather, these questions seem trivial and indeed improper.

This noble desk is not so much a refuge as a citadel. Sometimes, when the skies are clear, the world and all its multifarious activities can be seen spread out far below. Sometimes, when its topmost drawers and labyrinthine cupboards are wreathed in cloud, the desk seems to withdraw into itself and no sound can be heard in the intense, thought-heavy quiet but the distant creak of an expanding shelf and the low ripple of ink in profoundest wells.

The clearing out of such a desk, were it feasible, might well make people afraid. It is a good ten years since the last attempt, when a special desk force of archivists set to work on the task of exploring the desk and if possible separating the treasures of centuries from the accumulation, inevitable even here, of dross and trash.

Several of the explorers were never seen again, though for some days afterwards muffled knockings from distant, unidentifiable parts of the desk disturbed my concentration a little.

Others returned wild-eyed and half-demented, babbling of wonders: vast halls of verbiage glittering like many-coloured stalagmites in the feeble light of their lanterns; veins of gold and silver aphorisms; paragraphs of diamond, emerald, ruby and sapphire, interspersed with dull layers of slate and toadstone.

They spoke, too, of monsters; of blind, talking fish; even of unknown tribes which from the beginning of time had subsisted meagrely on stray thoughts fallen by chance through cracks in the immense structure. Whether in their case the desk had been an aid to mental health is a matter of opinion.

And what rôle, you may ask, does the desk play in sex games in the office? None. But there is room in the nearby waste-paper basket for those who ask impudent, vulgar, modish, pseudo-psychological questions.

Solid

A conference at Cavity House, the London headquarters of the Amalgamated Holeborers' Union, has instructed all holeborers to come out in sympathy with the striking town hall manual workers—transport drivers, including those supplying school meals, grave-diggers, dustmen and ambulance-men.

In a statement the general secretary, Mr Len Gollip, said: "Implementation of the decision will take immediate effect from forthwith."

Yesterday morning volunteer holeborers, including Gollip himself, were picketing London schools and snatching packets of sandwiches from children as they went in. One small girl whose sandwiches Mr. Gollip had militantly snatched burst into tears.

A teacher reproached Mr. Gollip, who replied: "These children, who are taking in their own meals, are technically strike-breakers. My union, which has declared its solidarity with the town hall workers, cannot and will not take cognisance of the age of those who by their intervention in the dispute at implementational and procedural level are acting by and large as enemies of the organised working class."

It has been suggested that if any householders are found emptying their own dustbins the holeborers should go and bore holes in them (that is, the dustbins). But some trade union logicians oppose this, arguing that such action would be a technical breach of the holeborers' own withdrawal of labour.

But all agree that if any people are reported digging their own graves the holeborers should go and fill them in.

158

Pretty wantons

"There is nothing really new about being young, rebellious, wanton or wanting to do experimental things," said Miss Jennie Lee, when she was asked why the "New Activities Committee" of the Arts Council should consider spending public money on people who experiment in such arts as rolling about in inflated plastic bags.

She is right of course. All that is new is the idea that people who may not be interested in these arts should be forced to help pay for them.

Is this good for the young experimenters themselves? They can't be blamed for taking the money. But the fact that they are patronised by the State and taken seriously by rather simple-minded people like Miss Lee makes them take themselves with unbecoming, irritating seriousness.

They soon learn to speak in modish jargon and chatter about new, experimental art-forms when all they are really busy with, most of the time, is Hobbies, recreating with modern materials and modern knowingness those "101 Things You Can Make on a Rainy Afternoon" of some Victorian Boys' Annual.

Nature notes

That esteemed body the Rareties Committee, which vets reports of rare immigrant birds, is concerned at reports of "lack of consideration for local private property" by some bird-watchers, which may jeopardise relations between local ornithologists and landowners.

"Redshank" writes: This is an increasingly serious problem in our part of the country. Only the other day I was standing in

Hundred Acre Bottom, peering through my glasses at a protuber-
ance on "Stogumber's Oak" which I took to be an early wryneck's
nest.

Suddenly a whole fleet of motor-coaches drew up behind me,
disgorging something like two hundred bird-watchers, who
immediately, to shouted words of command, formed up in line and
began tramping methodically across country, causing the entire
feathered population to rise screeching from their nests and flap
away in panic-stricken droves.

My remonstrances were met with threatening looks, coarse
laughter and the conversational small change of the new, urban
type of mass bird-watcher: "Move over, Dad"; "Get lost"; or even
"Drop dead."

One effect of this new kind of bird-watching is that the birds
themselves, formerly quite willing to be watched, are becoming
sullen and resentful, and are taking reprisals, not against the real
culprits, but against serious local practitioners of the art.

Not long ago Adam Broadcloth, a keen amateur ornithologist in
our village, was watching a female dotterel building her nest deep
in his thatched eaves when the normally timid bird suddenly
dropped the chewed tram-tickets from her beak, came close up to
him and gave him such a prolonged and searching stare that he
retired, blushing with embarrassment, to the shelter of the nearby
Chinese restaurant.

Is this the beginning of a new avian life-trend? An old saw, still
current wherever the country folk foregather in gun-room or four-
ale bar, provides a grim warning:

"Dunnot gaze too long on the black-backed shrike,
Or ee'll find a gurt eagle have snatched thy bike."

False colours

To be abused by Anthony Wedgwood Benn—one of the most
unreal-seeming politicians this country has produced since the end
of the War—is a high compliment for Enoch Powell by any
standards.

"The flag hoisted at Wolverhampton," says the so-called Minister of Technology, "is beginning to look like the one that fluttered
over Belsen and Dachau." It isn't. It is beginning to look, from

some angles, uncannily like the Union Jack. But should Benn, in any case, be prattling about flags?

There are some peculiar flags fluttering in his own vicinity (wasn't one of his most foolish day-dreams that one in which he imagined himself, as a victorious Socialist, entering London in triumph as Castro entered Havana?)

The party Benn belongs to has many factions and many flags. Some of these are already fluttering, others are ready to be surreptitiously hoisted when the moment comes. They include the fraudulent ensign of the United Nations; the Red Flag of Revolution (with or without the Hammer and Sickle); the White Flag of Surrender; and (in the last resort) the flags of the Communist death-camps of Siberia, which—and this is a point to notice—unlike the flags of Belsen and Dachau are fluttering still.

Never again!

howls Jack Moron

Bungrafta, *Thursday*

I do not cry easily. But today I watched as eleven men from Stretchford, in all their simple nobility, made a gallant, hopeless, foredoomed stand against Naked Evil, and I am not ashamed to say that hot tears ran down my face, mingling with gin and blood and sweat and tonic, to fall into the red laterite dust of this ancient, cruel African Continent.

All the cards were stacked against Stretchford United from the start. It was only yesterday that the team were released from the dreaded Bungrafta Central Gaol after President Ngrafta of Gombola himself had ordered all the charges trumped up against them to be squashed—an act that seemed at first one of wise statesmanship and simple justice, but which was to turn out far otherwise.

I watched with foreboding as our gallant lads limped on to the pitch at the gigantic £200 million Stadium of Ngrafta the Redeemer, yawning and rubbing their eyes, amid the yells, screams and curses of a million-strong hostile crowd, to face a star-studded team of Bungrafta Necromancers. And my forebodings were to be justified up to the hilt.

What is one to say about a match in which Stretchford had just about every low-down trick in the book flung at them—and then some? A match in which the referee himself—a notorious dwarf and astigmatic pervert—was so laughably biased that on more than one occasion I saw him actually threaten our players with a poison blowpipe loaded with deadly curare-tipped darts?

A match in which our opponents' goal was made to change shape or shifted out of the way by supernatural means whenever our boys looked like scoring? A match in which thought-forms—a speciality of the Gombolan witch-doctors—were unfairly used to confuse the Stretchford players, in particular goalkeeper Rasp, who at one point was so entranced by an enormous phantom plate of fish and chips that he let five easy shots past him in succession?

In the circumstances, I believe the final score—Bungrafta Necromancers 391; Stretchford United 0—represents a clear-cut moral victory for the visitors.

But in the name of international sport I say frankly and fearlessly, straight from the shoulder and with no punches pulled: NEVER AGAIN!

Election day, 1970

In the village of Simpleham yesterday, in the church hall—an ivy-grown Gothic structure built by my great-grandfather from Pugin's design, with roof-tiles of Cumberland slate donated by Ruskin himself—voting proceeded much as in any other part of the country.

As well as the sitting Tory, there was a Liberal and even a Socialist candidate in the Doomchester constituency. It is even possible that the still-overpowering presence of the great house, dreaming in the June haze beyond the wrought-iron gates and high walls of the park, failed to deter one or two of the more weak-minded electors from giving their vote to these subversive and atheistical candidates. These are strange times.

How differently things were done in my father's day! How well I remember the voters—all men, of course, for this was before the vote was so misguidedly given to women—how well I remember them, dressed in their Sunday best, holding their hats in their hands, shuffling down the dusty village street towards the polling booth in the shade of the great elms, watched by the beaming vicar, while the schoolmaster, also beaming, stood respectfully a little to one side.

Usually, I suppose, there was a Liberal candidate. But the only person in the village who ever voted for him was Godless Jack, a republican wheelwright, notorious for his oblong or even triangular wheels, an avid reader of Bradlaugh and Ingersoll. Repeatedly flung into the village pond by the loyal tenantry, he would take his revenge by sowing thistles in their cottage gardens or climbing on to their roofs at night and shouting "There is no God!" or "Property is Theft!" down the chimneys

Youth's rebellion

Rampton Enterprises, part of the vast Frabb Pop Consortium, is planning a gigantic pop festival at the old West Country town of Dorminster Newton next month. Half a dozen famous groups will be performing, including Ron Frabb's own Manic Depressives, the Bedbugs, the Filthy Swine, and from America the Spirochaetes and the Magic Bubonic Goitre.

More than three million young people are expected at the festival, and Mr Cliff Rampton, the man behind, under and in front of the idea, has asked the police to help by closing the area to other visitors and by evacuating the ordinary residents, if necessary demolishing their houses, and by banning all local activities not connected with the festival.

"Needless to say, we're having trouble from the fuddy duddy element," he said yesterday at a Press conference. "Some of these old killjoys are actually trying to get the festival banned. They'll do anything to stop young people enjoying themselves."

But Mr. Rampton has the support of Dr Spacely-Trellis, the go-ahead, youth-conscious Bishop of Bevindon, who said yesterday he intended to visit the festival himself, possibly with his own new secular religious pop group, Chocolate Meringue Narthex.

"The festival," he said, "will be an assertion of the uncorrupted ideals of Youth. It will be a relevant, meaningful gesture of protest against the false values of commercialism and exploitation in this day and age. No wonder every evil reactionary, racist and Powellite in the neighbourhood is against it. What we are witnessing is the long-expected puritan, Fascist backlash."

"Backlash, my foot," commented Rampton. "If it means I'm going to lose something like £500,000 clear profit, it's about time we did some lashing back against Fascism ourselves."

The Bishop, whose eyes had gone blank and had begun revolving rapidly, nodded agreement so vigorously that his Swedish-designed see-through mitre fell off and rolled on to a huge pile of £5 notes which happened to be lying in a corner.

Medical opinion

"Would you be more careful if it was you that got pregnant?" is the tasteful caption to a photograph of an apparently pregnant young man on a poster put out by the Health Education Council.

Medical opinion on the poster is divided. Dr John Henbane, one of "Way of the World's" top medical experts, said yesterday that he thought it decidedly dangerous, as it would lead many impressionable men to believe they really could become pregnant, with resulting pressure on the National Health Service.

"When I was a G.P. in the Midlands many years ago," he said, "I was continually having to deal with male patients who believed they were pregnant. One man of 60, a turntable-minder at a reversible deckchair factory, actually produced triplets—a boy and two girls—and brought them to my surgery, but I found, after carrying out tests, that they were merely Tibetan-type thought-forms which faded away after a few days, leaving the would-be parent inconsolable."

Dr Llewelyn Goth-Jones, Medical Officer of Health for Stretchford and a strong supporter of compulsory fluoridation, agreed that there were dangers in the poster. But he suggested that the Government should launch a massive campaign to persuade men that they would not become pregnant if they drank only fluoridated water.

Dr Goth-Jones, who is a brother-in-law of Mr Gordon Nadir and a director of one of the Nadir companies, Malebolge Chemicals, also thought that a more general belief in male pregnancy would stimulate the development of a new Pill to prevent it, thus helping Man in his onward march to the Millennium.

Happening

A writer, Jeremy Sandford, complains that at a private view of a "pop art" exhibition at the Tate Gallery, at 7.50 p.m. precisely, as the guests were "looking at the pictures or quietly talking among themselves," a bell suddenly clanged and uniformed attendants started shouting: "Come along then, let's have you! All out, all out! Time, gentlemen, please!"

What on earth is the man Sandford complaining about? Wasn't this incident itself "pop art," and of the highest order; a true "happening," designed to make the guests face long evaded reality and come to terms with their true though suppressed selves?

Wasn't it a densely actuated, relevant, coolly analytic ironical comment, tautly organised with dynamic multi-planar compositional control, on modern man's dilemma in a changing world without conventional landmarks, a world of existential flux, fragmentation, alienation?

Exquisite

"A contraceptive machine [sic] has been removed from the gents' toilet at Nottingham Polytechnic. And now students are meeting to discuss the ban," reports the *Nottingham Evening Post.*

"Mr Ron Hedley, the college director, declined to comment. . . . In the students' union newspaper, just out, union official John Ferber writes: 'If one had to choose one problem that most threatened the future of mankind today it is that of not being able to control the increases in the birthrate. Mr Director, you fail as an adult and as a person responsible for young adults if you fail to appreciate. . . .' "

There is more of this homily, which combines scientism, pomposity and humbug to a degree unusual even today. Has there ever been a time before this in the history of the world when young adults felt they had to justify their ancient, traditional pastimes by lecturing their elders on the future of mankind?

A graded land

That strangely-named body the Countryside Commission is to spend £18,000 in three years on a research project for a "nationally accepted standard for assessing the importance of landscape" in this country.

How will the researchers set about their grotesque labours? Will they stand at different viewpoints, at different seasons and times of the day, awarding marks for this line of hillside and that curve of river bank, that colour of autumn wood or heather moor, until they have established an Official Scale of Natural Beauty?

Will every landscape, every loved and familiar scene which fails to reach a certain point on that graduated scale (the point to be adjusted according to supply and demand, cost-effectiveness, leisure availability and other relevant factors) be declared officially redundant and available for exploitation and destruction?

The scientific spirit, which cannot leave anything alone and aspires to draw the whole universe of objects, people, ideas and even feelings into its own dull, inhuman empire, was certain, sooner or later, to cast its screwed-up, calculating eyes on the splendour in the grass and the glory in the flower.

Boring notes

by "Narcolept"

Aficionados of the yawn game have a real treat in store this Yuletide Season—such a feast of boredom that merely to think about it sets the pulses beating more slowly and the eyelids drooping, while the shoulder muscles begin seizing up with those good old fibrositis symptoms which however familiar remain ever new!

One highlight for catalepsy fans is the seven-day series of six-hour Christmas lectures at Turgis Hill Town Hall. Visiting speaker this year is Ron Stupor, the Australian boring maestro, holder of five inter-galactic medals. His subjects include "Plywood through the Ages", "Some Unusual Oil-fired Central Heating Systems" and "Aspects of the Anti-Apartheid Movement in Tasmania".

For many the zenith of this year's Noël will be the Boring Day Charity Contest at Harringay between Grant Coma Jr., America's reigning trance champion, and Czechoslovakia's mighty Antonin Bvorak. All proceeds go to a most worthy cause, the Sunset Home for Retired Bores at Redhill, Surrey.

On the lighter side, of course, there'll be parties and dances galore. One occasion I've marked in my Bore's Diary as a must is the Annual Fancy Dress Ball of the British Boring Board of Control at Lethargy Hall. Most of the top brass of the boring world will be rotating in stately measures and rumour the hundred-headed hath it that this year there will be a high-powered contingent of bores from the Outer Planets, Neptune included!

Goodbye for now, fans! And good boring.

Seasonal

Christmas in Stretchford. Along Victoria Road, "the city's main shopping artery and spending cynosure of the North Midlands" (to quote the official guide), the many-coloured Christmas lights blaze and twinkle overhead in patterns which good judges believe are at least as hideous and tasteless as any in the past 25 years.

On the pavements, glistening with a thin seasonal mud, the merry shoppers shove and jostle, occasionally forcing one more weak or undersized than the rest to his knees in a confusion of anguish and burst parcels.

The mammoth Nadirco Superstore is packed to the doors in all departments. In the toy department Father Christmas, a burly man whose luxuriant side-burns peep out from behind his snowy beard, warring with it as his habitual squinting, ruffianly expression wars with his temporary benevolence, distributes toys guaranteed to disintegrate within minutes, often with painful results.

Above the hubbub cries and groans can be heard from the nearby sports department where, as a special Christmas attraction, old age pensioners are allowed a free turn on the artificial ski run.

Further from the city centre, where Halibut Bridge Street

crosses the evil-steaming, polluted River Stretch, big blue chauffered cars convey the wives of important businessmen to their lighted mansions in Hokewell Wood or Lampton-on-Hoke, scattering pedestrians before them like withered leaves, their thin cries lost in the roar of engines.

In Sadcake Park at twilight, as the huge red sun sinks behind the trees, a last sex maniac wheels his bicycle along the wintry paths, or stops, fingering his madman's cut-away collar, to stare long and intently across the ice-bound lake.

Mystery intruder

Royston Fotheringhay, alias Lt. Col. the Rev. and Hon. Rollo Taskerville-Vavasour DSO, alias Prince Otto of Krampf-Frolstein-Lotenburg, alias Jim Fruitcliffe, 35, of no fixed address, described as a consulting ecologist, was accused at Nerdley magistrates' court yesterday of demanding money with menaces.

"Mr. X", 45, stated to be a wealthy man with an attractive blonde wife and two swimming pools, said that Fotheringhay, a well-dressed man with a public school accent, approached him when he was lunching with his secretary, "Miss Y", in his private lay-by on the Soup Hales by-pass. After some casual conversation about pollution, radio-active effluent, the danger of the melting of the polar ice-caps, and related topics, Fotheringhay offered to deal with his environmental problems for a fee of £5,000 spot cash, followed by yearly payments of £1,250 plus a retainer of an amount to be negotiated later.

When "Mr. X" demurred, Fotheringhay threatened to run a six-lane motorway through him and plant him all over with regimented conifers. He also threatened to tell his wife, "Mrs. X", of his association with "Miss Y" and "make his life an ecological hell on earth".

"Mr. X" informed the police, who arranged that he whould leave a packet of heavily polluted £5 notes in the middle of Numb Lane Roundabout, a well-known local eyesore. When Fotheringhay arrived to collect it he was arrested.

Denying the charges, Fotheringhay said he was a man of independent means with a distinguished war record, who had made it his life's work to travel round the country helping people who seemed to be having trouble with the environment. "Mr. X's" behaviour had been an eye-opener to him and had impaired his faith in human nature.

Dr. F. Gestaltvogel, 51, consultant psychiatrist at Nerdley General Hospital, said that apart from believing himself to be a nature reserve Fotheringhay was a perfectly normal, well-adjusted member of society. As it happened, he had a vacancy for an experimental subject in his own abreactive clinic and would be glad to take charge of the accused immediately.

Binding Fotheringhay over, the chairman, Dr Ellis Goth-Jones, 62, said the problem of the environment explosion was one of the most urgent facing mankind today. But that was no excuse to taking the law into one's own hands. A spirit of tolerance and "give and take" was needed. But he doubted whether charges for admission to museums and art galleries would prove to be the answer.

Used car bargains

Boggs Yobbo Convertible 1967. Perfect condition. Owner going abroad owing to decimalisation. 45,000m. on clock; fully rust-treated chassis; four wheels (two missing); crack-treated windows; spare gear-box; interesting steering-column with plenty of "give"; suet-pudding wedged in accelerator. £250 or near offer. Tel. Bevindon 4457.

14-cylinder Ombra Mai-Fu 1948, 700 c.c. Formerly driven by racing-driver Ettore Ossabuco in 1956 Le Mans Grand Prix and at Silverstone, Shelsley Walsh, North Circular Road, South Bank Car Park, etc. A superb job for the real motorist. Tel. Turgis Hill 3029.

Porphyrogenitus Sedan 1919. Custom-built fittings, jewelled

speaking-tube, stained-glass partition, roomy passenger section with log fires, billiard hall, servants' quarters, children's photographic dark room, sunken garden with lily pond, etc. Suit large-scale immigrant smuggler. A bargain at £45,000. Tel. Angsworth 4062.

Boggs Oaf Saloon 1964. Magenta bodywork; Nile green flash; plastic leopard-skin upholstery and headrests, slightly soiled; intact collection of battery-operated mascots in rear window; nodding devil, Spanish doll with mantilla, skeleton drinking Babycham, poodle vomiting, etc., etc., all in working order. Tel. Brassgrove Park 5591 or nearest police station.

Writing on the wall

A law just announced in Cuba provides penalties ranging from six months to two years' forced labour in "rehabilitation centres" for what Dr. Castro calls "loafers, bums and parasites". It decrees that all males between 17 and 60 have a "social duty" to work on a systematic daily basis unless they are attending an "approved" school.

Hippies, yippies, yappies of the West, squatters, lotus-eaters, sham artists, anarchist clowns, denizens of the "underground" whether innocent or corrupt, members of the "alternative society" likewise and all those Leftist verbalisers (sometimes the same people) who have praised Castro's Cuba as a prefiguration of paradise on earth and a model for ourselves: take note.

Round the salerooms

An *art nouveau* deckchair made in 1906 for Grand Duke Vsevolod of Russia by Wilhelm Krebs, in gilded cedar wood inlaid with semi-precious stones, with coverings of purple and gold Indian silk, a bronze and gold lectern and built-in central heating with solid gold pipes, was knocked down at Gotheby's for £7,000.

A Staffordshire syndicate of businessmen paid £2,500 for "Kevin", a rare plastic gnome by Mulligan, 25-feet-high and incorporating a treadle-operated windmill and vultures' bird bath.

A mirror (cracked), formerly in the collection of the late Viscountess Shalott and believed to have magical properties, was knocked down for £3,000 after some spirited bidding.

A solid gold medallion, four feet in diameter, struck by the late Alderman Jabez Foodbotham for the Bradford Arts Festival in 1922, showing the Alderman receiving the homage of various symbolic figures representing Music, Poetry, Woolcombing, Trade Journalism, Peace, War, Local Government, Deference, etc., failed to realise its reserve and disappeared into a chasm which suddenly opened in the floor as a supernatural voice pronounced a curse on Gotheby's salerooms.

Retreat

An international conference on "Man-made Memories" in London is to include discussions ranging from "TTL, MOS and MNOS techniques to SLAM micro-circuits, optical and bubble domains and the developments of glass devices."

I have always been more interested in bubble domains than in TTL, MOS, MNOS and SLAM myself. For those who find real life (as it is often called) rather too much for them at times a bubble domain makes an ideal retreat where soul and body can be restored.

The bubble domain at Simpleham is one of the best-known in the country. My father, a keen amateur natural philosopher (or scientist, as I suppose it would be called nowadays), had it blown to his own design from a special kind of soap, producing bubbles of very high tensile strength, which he had himself developed in his private laboratory.

The bubble domain is now more than 50 years old but is just as sound and serviceable as ever. A circular stairway leads from one end of the long gallery to the interior of the great iridescent dome, which is furnished with a few simple Bokhara rugs, armchairs, a small table and a tantalus.

I love to sit there on a sunny day, watching the shifting colours on the bubble's surface, and through them the images, upside down, of course, and strangely curved, of some passing footman, librarian or lowing Jersey strayed from the Home Farm into the green glades of the park. As I watch I sink gradually, as in a feather-bed, into a mysterious, calm, blissful condition of semi-trance.

Yet for all that (how can I deny it?) I am a child of my own destructive, vandal times. Sometimes I start awake with a sudden impulse to stretch out a finger and with one jab explode the shining bubble domain in a shower of many-coloured droplets.

What on earth would happen then?

1971

Explosion

Dr Llewelyn Goth-Jones, the popular Medical Officer of Health for Stretchford, has welcomed the Government's report on population with an enthusiasm almost amounting to dementia praecox.

At an emergency meeting of the City Public Health Committee, called at his own urgent request, he demanded that Stretchford give an example to the country by immediately setting up 2,000 new family planning clinics throughout the city, that is, approximately one for every 300 people, as well as a 24-hour mobile corps of "contraceptive wardens" with what he called "statutory powers of persuasion" over the public.

He also suggested using the weapon of ridicule to deter couples from having children. People should get into the habit, he said, of laughing and pointing derisively at anyone they saw accompanied by more than one child (an occasional kick would not come amiss, either); teachers should encourage pupils who belonged to large families to feel shame at their own existence and anger at their parents for having brought them into the world: these and other methods would go far, in the long run, towards solving Britain's population problems.

As an expert, Dr Goth-Jones got a respectful hearing. As well as being Medical Officer, he is a director of Malebolge Chemicals, a subsidiary of Nadirco which manufactures hundreds of millions of contraceptive pills and other devices yearly.

He is also a director of the new Nadirco sex supermarket chain, with branches throughout the West Midlands; runs a popular network of abortion clinics (with supporting air and taxi services) in the Stretchford area; and has a controlling interest in an educational cinema at Nerdley which is now showing a film of women having intercourse with Alsatian dogs, horses and computers.

Yet one councillor at the meeting (evidently malevolent, half-witted or both) actually had the nerve to say he thought it odd that Dr Goth-Jones, while advocating non-stop sex, practical, cerebral or voyeuristic, for all, should so strongly condemn the natural result of that activity.

The Medical Officer of Health rose from his seat. "That is a typical example," he said, controlling himself with difficulty, "of the spite and envy of repressed middle age at the new, joyous and above all life-affirming and life-creating sexual freedom of youth today.

"Reactionary! Fascist! Racist!" he yelled, his eyes beginning to revolve like burning contraceptive pills. "I only wish I had you in my sterilisation clinic," he went on. "My assistant, Dr Jill Grese—one of a pioneering medical family—would know exactly what to do with you."

Sunt lacrimae

The news of Herr Ulbricht's resignation as First Secretary of the East German Communist party, though not altogether unexpected, has brought sadness to Mrs Dutt-Pauker, the Hampstead thinker —sadness and long, long memories of youth.

The two first met in Barcelona in 1937, in the heady days of the Spanish Civil War. They were immediately drawn together by a mutual interest in the techniques of conspiracy and purges, secret police methods and the running of concentration camps.

Though 20 years parted them in age, passion bloomed swiftly under the velvet, star-throbbing night skies of Spain. Their parting, when it came at the behest of the Party, which assigned both to other, distant tasks, was as agonising as it must be to all lovers. But it was borne with Marxist fortitude.

There are those who have seen a resemblance to Ulbricht in Mrs Dutt-Pauker's daughter Deirdre; and an even more striking resemblance in Deirdre's four-year-old, bearded, baleful-eyed Maoist demonstrator son Bert Brecht Mao Che Odinga.

Let them be left

Environmentalists, conservationists, anti-pollutionists: the dull, pseudo-scientific words, endlessly repeated—imports, like so much else, from future-crazed America—can arouse in certain moods a perverse rage to build oil-refineries and cement-works all over Dartmoor.

The latest thing to come to their notice, I read, is the view from railway carriage windows, on the outskirts of cities. They say these squalid breakers' yards, heaps of scrap, derelict industrial sites, overgrown back gardens, half-scorched cuttings are eyesores. They must be cleaned up as soon as possible.

To the official mind, the mind which has invented national parks and conservation areas and areas of outstanding natural beauty, the mind which measures the colours of the Spring and assesses Wastwater and Ludlow by an index of aesthetic value, they are simply eyesores and that is all. To people who casually look out of railway carriage windows they may seem quite otherwise.

They are miniature wildernesses, places that men have made, certainly, but places which have the pathos of all things that have once been used but are now neglected and abandoned: tangled garden-plots, rusting springs, shattered bricks, shards, books sodden by the rain and, blistered by the sun, lumps of newspaper that no one will ever read again.

The train, held up by signals, slows down in the summer heat; the wondering eye looks through the glass into those suburban jungles and finds there, as in childhood, a mysterious poetry. Who knows what strange flowers—moly, nepenthes—may grow among that unloved, grimy undergrowth?

Perhaps it is as well this has not occurred to the official mind. Wouldn't it wish to institutionalise this sense of wonder, to incorporate it into its official system: tidy up almost all the eyesores in its own image but leave, for recreational purposes, a few Protected Areas of Designated Suburban Railway Squalor?

Nothing new

The five-day congress of the Czechoslovak Communist party is over. Dr Husak, re-elected as leader for a further five years with the new title of Secretary-General, has done everything his Russian masters expected of him, even virtually eating his own words in public.

The man who, when the Russian and satellite forces invaded Czechoslovakia in 1968 spoke of a "tragic misunderstanding" now says he is grateful for the invasion. The only explanation he can give for the undeniable fact that the majority of his countrymen condemned the invasion is that they were victims of "mass psychosis". And the assembled Czechoslovak Communist party applauded him for saying so.

Husak is doing neither more nor less than a Communist leader must do in such circumstances. Truth is not bourgeois truth (or bourgeois attempts to approximate to the truth); it is what agrees with the current purpose of the party.

Make no mistake; we have our Husaks here, and our obedient party men; the whole apparatus of tyranny and lies in embryo. The British Communist party has been commended for refusing to send delegates to the Czechoslovak congress on the ground that the proceedings would be subject to censorship.

That is the line at present. But does anyone think that if circumstances required it the British Communist party would not find men to play the game of Husak here with dishonesty as abject and absolute?

The people's revenge

Shrewd political observers in Britain believe that the infamous Tory Government, already shaken to its foundations by the scorn and hatred of the exploited workers, may be finally overthrown by its latest measure of class-discrimination, a proposal to charge for admission to museums and art galleries.

Yesterday a crowd estimated to be over a million strong demonstrated outside the British Museum, most of whose treasures, stolen from the people over the centuries, are kept locked away for the delectation of the Tory aristocrats and their flunkeys. A fiery speech by Andrew Faulds, the beloved poet of the people who is known as "the Lord Byron of the 20th century", was cheered to the echo.

A small group of journalists wearing the hated boys' death's head brigade uniform of the official Government organ, *The Daily Telegraph,* and including the notorious Government hack, spy and police informer Lord Peter Simple, were recognised as they arrogantly tried to shoulder their way through the crowd, and narrowly escaped a lynching.

Fortunately for these gentry, the attention of the workers was diverted by the appearance of a jewelled coach carrying priceless paintings looted from the Tate Gallery and bound for the gilded mansion of a notorious art-collecting grandee, the Duke of Eccles. The guards were swiftly overpowered and in a sudden reverent hush, punctuated by gasps of art-appreciation, the Jackson Pollocks, Mondrians, Kandinskis and other masterpieces were shared out among the rightful owners.

Serious disturbances are reported from other parts of the country. In the Windermere bauxite-mining area, thousands of tough miners, veterans of a score of cultural hunger-marches, wept as they called on Sir Anthony Blunt, the much-loved Socialist art-historian and darling of the people, to take the lead in overthrowing the tyrants in Whitehall.

Troops, including élite formations of the dreaded mobile art gallery attendants' corps, have now been drafted to this and other areas, including the Ilfracombe Coalfield, and there is every sign that the climax, which will blow the lid off the seething volcano of revolution, cannot be long delayed.

(Dutt-Pauker Azerbaijani News Agency.)

Under the leaves

For all my dislike of Hampstead thinkers and their thoughts, I have lived in Hampstead twice myself. I too have walked her winding streets and lanes and peered into her umbrageous gardens where rich progressive ladies sit under the trees and plan to overwhelm South Africa with blood and fire.

I too have tramped her noted heath in all weathers and listened darkling as groups of Indian economics students, among the most gifted bores in the world, passed nattering like clouds of flies with many a fine-wrought gesture of dissent.

I have hated Hampstead for her Left-wingery, but I have loved her for her strange, secret, leafy soul. Nowhere in London are green thoughts so green, especially in a rainy June, when the grass grows high in her innumerable gardens tamed or wild.

As "Wayfarer" says in his book "Afoot in London" (in the chapter called "Hampstead Heritage"), "a man may walk with stick and knapsack, map and compass a livelong summer's day from Archway to Finchley Road Underground Station, and so be he can read a map and have an eye for country, need scarce once put foot on tarmac."

I have often thought of trying this out, following the hidden, half-overgrown paths between garden fences, sometimes crossing the gardens themselves or even passing through houses when no other way seems open.

What adventures I might have in those damp and leafy solitudes! "Wayfarer," in the book I have mentioned, says there are parts of Hampstead which have never been fully explored; in one densely-wooded stretch, between the garden of Mrs Dutt-Pauker's Queen Anne house Marxmount and the Heath, there is a tribe of Left-wing pygmies of cannibal habits and strong views on racial integration.

That would be among the least of the perils I might have to face as I pushed on through the dense foliage or paused to eat my bread and cheese by some gay flowerbed, watched by indignant progressive eyes from a book-lined study or seized and dragged indoors to take part in a discussion on comprehensive education and the need for Socialist play-groups.

Tourist trap

One landowner who seems not to have been present at Lord Montagu's seminar at Beaulieu on "the management of country parks, historic houses and castles" is Lord Mountwarlock, whose historic house in Leicestershire is often called in the travel brochures "The Stately Home that is Different."

I should have thought the eight-foot-tall, Cyclops-eyed Earl would have had a lot to contribute to the discussions. Mountwarlock Park, with its fabulous monsters, Deadly Upas Tree, 18th century artificial volcano and bottomless pit believed to communicate directly with the Infernal Regions, draws thousands of visitors during the season. Many find it literally impossible to get away.

An innovation this year is a Mediaeval Banquet, where for a mere £2 a head visitors can sit at the historic table in the Great Banqueting Hall under which Cardinal Umfravile was murdered by Fulke the Red in 1292. There they can gorge themselves silly on peacock stuffed with red mullet, honey, tinfoil and minced wild boar's trotters while the estate harpies—a particularly disgusting breed—swoop down and try to snatch the food in their filthy talons amid delighted screams and cries of "Get away, you nasty thing!"

Phantomsby the major domo, one of the few practising werewolves still left in the Midlands, is in overall charge. He has fixed the next Mediaeval Banquet, by manipulating the calendar, for the night of the next full Moon. As he told me yesterday, with an infectious smile which revealed his large gleaming white incisors, he thinks it may be the most successful banquet yet.

Can I help you?

by "Genuflex"

"My elder brother Eric, who is in holy orders and also holds medical and dental degrees, joined the police force some 10 years ago and has just been promoted detective-sergeant. Soon afterwards, through the death of a cousin, he succeeded to the baronetcy.

"When writing, how should I address him, as he is a stickler in such matters?" (Mostyn Sheep-Harris, Loughborough).

"GENUFLEX" replies: "'The Rev. Det.-Sgt. Dr. Sir Eric Sheep-Harris, Bt., DD, MD, LDS' is the correct form. Should your brother be appointed a Privy Councillor, join the Navy, Army or Air Force, or make a pilgrimage to Mecca, please write to me again."

Mystery intruder

Mrs Brenda O'Gourke, 46, housewife, of Termite Road, Nerdley, was accused at Nerdley magistrates' court yesterday of dishonestly handling 51 pork pies, the property of the Nadirco Fooderama in Effluent Road.

Chief Pork Pie Section Leader Mr Kevin Stentorian, 35, said that while watching his section on the closed circuit television screen he saw Mrs O'Gourke methodically levering off the upper casings, or "lids," as they were technically called, of a large number of pork pies with an outsize nailfile. She appeared to be checking the contents, occasionally writing in an outsize notebook.

When he questioned her Mrs O'Gourke said she was conducting an independent survey of the contents of Nadirco pork pies. There was no knowing what you might find in them nowadays. One friend of hers had recently found a hairnet, part of an alarm-clock and what seemed to be the incisor-tooth of a badger; another had found a long, rambling letter, possibly an appeal for help from someone who had been at one time imprisoned in the pie, for what reason she could not say.

Told her remarks were defamatory, accused became abusive and the police were sent for. Cautioned by Sgt J. Mackenzie, 38, of Nerdley Special Branch, Mrs O'Gourke tried to climb into one of the pies, damaging part of the main casing, or "side," and was arrested.

Giving evidence, Dr F. Gestaltvogel, 51, consultant psychiatrist at Nerdley General Hospital, said he had examined Mrs O'Gourke. Apart from disturbance in her sense of spatial relations, particularly where pastry was concerned, and a morbid horror of string, she was a perfectly normal member of society. He believed she would benefit from membership of a sensory contact group; failing this, euthanasia by a variety of methods was always available at his own clinic.

Binding Mrs O'Gourke over, the chairman, Dr Ellis Goth-Jones, 62, said that in view of her previous good conduct he would deal leniently with her. But he must emphasise the duty every member of our society owed to great national trading groups like the Nadirco Organisation.

He believed that many of the urgent problems of society—such as pornography, subsidence on motorways, the generation gap, racial discrimination and a growing disillusionment with politics—stemmed from a basic failure of respect. But he did not think a referendum on the Common Market was necessarily the answer.

Triumphs of reason

"All but a handful of fanatics, Irish earls or dowager ladies, with ample private means and time on their hands, now recognise that the great mass of people are not unduly concerned, one way or the other, over 'charters for queers,' four-letter words, nudes, profanity or dirty postcards so long as checks are kept on prices and unemployment."

This passage comes from the Annual Report of the National Secular Society, whose "Distinguished Members' Panel" (*sic*) includes Michael Foot, MP, Brigid Brophy, Baroness Wootton, Lord Willis and George Melly.

The Society was founded in 1866 by Charles Bradlaugh. He and his fellow-Victorian secularists, however basically silly they may have been, at least thought themselves serious and high-minded people. What would they have thought of the cheap, vulgar, frivolous stuff their heirs are dealing in today?

They may well have had an equally patronising and contemptuous attitude towards the working classes. But they would have hoped, in however misguided a way, to improve them.

If they had thought that after a century the working classes might come to be totally uninterested in anything except money (as the National Secular Society seems insultingly to think), they would have deplored the fact, not giggled over it. If they were honest, they might even have had doubts about helping to rob the working classes of their morality and religion for such an end.

Hand-out

"In late 1919 more than nine-tenths of the Soviet Union was occupied by the British, Americans, anti-Bolsheviks, White Russians and their allies. Lenin and Trotsky were fighting for their lives in the remnants of their country around Moscow. More than 13 million Russian men, women and children died from starvation, disease and armed force during the Allied Intervention and the Civil War it did so much to bolster."

This is an extract from the BBC's publicity hand-out for a television programme, "The Forgotten War." I can say nothing of the actual programme, which may, for all I know, give a reasonably fair account. But for sheer bias and partisanship the hand-out could hardly go further. That it merely repeats the accepted myths about this period of Russian history is no excuse. Isn't it one of the the supposed functions of the BBC to educate, to "make people think," as the Leftists say?

Who would imagine from this hand-out that the White Russians, anti-Bolsheviks and their allies were fighting in 1919 to defend the legitimate government of Russia against Lenin and Trotsky, who by conspiracy and terror had usurped power in "their" country?

Who could have imagined then that for their defence of that legitimate government against the Bolsheviks, the allies, including Britain, could be accused by a British Broadcasting Corporation 50 years later of having practically *caused* the suffering and death of 13 million Russians?

And who would guess from this hand-out that if the allied intervention in Russia had succeeded (as, given determination and realisation of what was at stake, it would have done) the subsequent history of Russia, Europe and the world would have been immeasurably happier?

Is this your problem?

By Clare Howitzer

Dear Clare Howitzer—I live on a very "with-it" council estate where all the other wives seem to have husbands who make love to them all the time. Most of them, I gather, rush back from work every day in the lunch-time—or even several times a day in tea-breaks—for this purpose.

My own husband, Jim, who works in a local turntable factory, seems to be the "odd man out." Now the other wives are beginning to laugh at me, particularly my neighbour, a blonde of 50 who has taken to standing on the roof every lunch-time in seductive postures, wearing a bouffant hair-do and "see-through" nightie and shouting about sex, etc., in a sing-song voice.

When I told Jim about this the other day he stayed at the factory all night. He has now been sacked for assembling more than 4,000 unwanted turntables. Is there something wrong with us? (Mrs L. Tropes, Nerdley).

Clare Howitzer replies: This is a problem which is facing more and more husbands and wives who find they cannot cope with the

Sexual Revolution in this permissive day and age, when it is becoming more and more difficult to reconcile the claims of booming productivity, full employment and the "leisure explosion" with meaningful relationships in the context of traditional marriage.

If all else fails, and your husband cannot understand your difficulties, I suggest you join your local group of Women's Liberation urban guerillas on a part-time basis.

Science corner

Has Nature's Ultimate Secret—regularly discovered in the science columns of Sunday newspapers every week—been unearthed again? A team of biologists working in Stretchford University's prestigious Nadir Institute under the redoubtable Prof. Ron Hardware believe they have stumbled on a genetic secret which could not merely revolutionise human life in a matter of seconds but even force many scientific journalists to look elsewhere for their subject-matter in future.

Briefly (and in non-technical language) it has been found that at sub-enzymic level the well-known "G" effect of metabolised cromagnonose on the genetic structure of the average unhealthy human body does not operate uniformly, as has hitherto been thought.

There is a "retardation factor"—Hardware calls it "lag"—which in certain conditions—at temperatures exceeding 4 million degrees centigrade, for instance—can slow down the ageing process and even reverse it—*but only for periods of less than 5 millionths of a second.*

The problem, as Hardware and his team see it, is to "universalise" this process, thus realising the age-old dream of human immortality. The snag, as always, is lack of money—and the obstructive attitude of our still backward-looking social system, conventionally-minded scientists included.

"All we need," says Hardware, "is a few thousand billion pounds, a laboratory in which temperatures equivalent to those in the interior of an exploding supernova can be created and a few hundred million human experimental subjects—and Bob's your uncle!"

It doesn't seem a big price to pay. But once again it looks as though Government timidity and professional jealousy will combine to smother at birth one more boon which Science is only too anxious to place in Man's hands for good or ill.

Haggard's journal

Dec. 22, 1771: Fog. Obadiah Horseworthy blown to pieces while trying to turn lead into gold. Spent a.m. evicting Blind Benjamin and enclosg. common land for mine own use, An unusual event occurred in p.m., viz. the appearance of my wife whom I had not seen since I flung a pease pddg. at her last Michaelmas. She informed me that her brother Daniel sends word he is coming tomorrow to spend Christmas with us. This threw me into apoplexy as the man is a canting Dissenter, but I cannot refuse him as I owe him 30,000 sovs. Drank a vat of punch to recover.

Dec. 23: Storms. Spat on elderly Jew in a.m. Evicted Crippled Simon and Deaf Peter, also re-evicted Blind Benjamin who was lodging with Deaf Peter. Brother Daniel arrived in p.m. but I was unable to greet him as I was lying insensible in the fireplace. When I recovered he told me that if I drank anything more he would be compelled to call for his 30,000 sovs. for the good of my soul. ITEM: To physick £0 0s 0½d.

Dec. 24: Snow. Shot unusual crippled poacher in a.m. Evicted Halfwitted William. While chasing a fleeing tenant I fell into a snowdrift and to restore myself pulled forth a flask of brandy, only to find Daniel had filled it with barley water. The rage for drink so possessed me I was fain to ask the Rector for something, but the canting dog gave me nettle wine. ITEM: To emetics £0 0s 0¾d.

Dec. 25: Today being that feast most sacred to all men, viz.

Quarter Day, I was out early evicting Palsied Peter, Granny Turnip and Blind Benjamin, who had moved in with Granny Turnip. Granny Turnip snivelled "Did I not know what day it was," to which I replied "Rent Day," which caused me much mirth. On returning home was nauseated to see jugs of barley water on the table for dinner, whereupon I hit upon an ingenious Device, pouring a pint of laudanum into Daniel's jug. Halfway through dinner, he collapsed insensible and I then made merry with six botts. of Madeira, a pint of brandy and three maidservants. ITEM: To gift for wife, one groat.

1972

Fallen majesty

There is bad news from Manchester. For nearly a hundred years now salon quartets and trios have provided the music at receptions in the imposing Town Hall of the fabled city by the Irwell. Now (the miserable and unconvincing excuse is "shortage of money") they are to be replaced by a tape-recorder.

What the situation is at other Town Halls I cannot say. When Alderman Foodbotham, the 25-stone, crag-visaged, iron-watch-chained, grim-booted perpetual chairman of the Bradford City Tramways and Fine Arts Committee, was Lord Mayor (1906-1927, with an interregnum in 1924, the chaotic "Year of the Four Lord Mayors"), he used his own household musicians from his titanic mansion "Green Garth," on Cleckheaton Moor, for all important receptions.

The great alderman scorned string and woodwind players ("fancy fiddlers and penny-whistling whipper-snappers") and the band consisted entirely of brass and a large percussion section, with one exception—sometimes commented on in behind-hand whispers by the bolder councillors—a young lady harpist, Miss

Brenda Travis, who without obvious qualifications held a secretarial post in the Parks Department.

The players, drawn from the alderman's gardeners, chauffeurs, body-guards and handymen, were of varying degrees of skill but were anxious to please their master and made amends by always playing as loudly as they could; this made it impossible to tell whether Miss Travis was really playing at all, but as all agreed, the graceful movements of her bare arms made this musically and aesthetically irrelevant.

What with the strange uncoordinated uproar of the band, now buzzing, now droning, now braying discordantly as it crashed its way through "Selection: Maritana" or "A Bradford Rhapsody" (Delius, arr. Rimmer); the mad shouting of the guests, as they vainly tried to make themselves heard above the din, and the majestic sight of Alderman Foodbotham himself presiding mountainously over all, nobody who was ever privileged to attend one of these receptions will ever forget it.

Nowadays . . . but it is best not to think of such things.

Private sector

What, many keen trade union dogmatists and lovers of protocol are asking, is the position of this column's own small private coal mine in the present strike? Will the age-old tradition of continuous working be maintained? Will the National Union of Mineworkers try to interfere?

Situated in a remote, hilly part of the column, Rawsthorpe Bridge Main is in most ways a model of what a colliery should be. It is worked on a shift system by 14 men and an aged winder who operates the historic brass-bound cage specially made for this pit by the Fafnir Engineering Company in 1885. Annual production averages 150 tons.

When not at the coalface, the miners spend their time squatting on their heels against walls with their whippets and lurchers beside them; sitting in big tubs of scalding hot water before beautifully blackleaded kitchen ranges and having their backs scrubbed by their wives; breeding racing pigeons; playing brass instruments, mainly tubas, in a desultory way; marching through the grimy, cobbled streets at their weekly galas, carrying beautifully worked banners and singing Welsh hymns; or getting drunk on Saturdays at the Miners' Arms.

They are intensely conservative and to judge from the zeal with which they touch their caps on those rare occasions when Bennett, my chauffeur, drives me slowly through the village in the purple Daimler, they are as loyal and contented as any mine owner could wish.

Industrial disputes are unknown, except for the yearly ritual strike, greatly enjoyed by all, which lasts for 24 hours and culminates in a traditional siege of the home of the popular works manager, Mr Brayshaw, followed by a tremendous ham-and-egg tea with parkin, fruit salad and outsize meat pies.

The fact that nothing in this unique coalfield ever seems to change in any way, and that the miners, their wives and children and even their dogs and racing pigeons never get any older has been commented on unfavourably by visiting officials of the National Coal Board.

But I am glad to say there is nothing whatever they can do about it.

People and parties

Dropping into a delightful party given by Pippa Dreadberg, the brilliant attractive novelist wife of brilliant avant-garde playwright, painter, TV personality and self-publicist Neville Dreadberg (drools REX HICKFIELD), I found she had brought off a real coup which will make swinging London's rival party-givers emerald green with envy.

Guest of honour was a real-life, genuine, 24-carat high-ranking officer of the IRA Provisionals, fresh from Belfast, where I hear he's gratifyingly high on the wanted list!

He's Brig. Seán MacGuffog, a fast, amusing talker who had everyone crowding round for a glimpse of the amusing sub-machine-gun he always carries with him.

Later on, at Pippa's insistence, he produced a lot of wires and alarm-clocks and batteries and sticks of gelignite and things and showed how to wire up a bomb.

"Do let's have an explosion—just a little one," begged brilliant model girl and autobiographer Giselle Frabazon, and the Brigadier, whose Irish charm simply oozes in gallons from his cordite-stained finger-tips, obliged with an amusing bang which had fellow-guests like brilliant actor Mike Tove, brilliant footbal-ler-sculptor Ken Valve, brilliant young architect Crispin Spasholm, brilliant art historian Dr Rex Weak and brilliant Tory progressive MP Jeremy Cardhouse rolling about in convulsions.

"Brigadier, I love you," breathed Pippa, as she planted a kiss on the IRA leader's cheek, drawing a flood of what sounded like poetic endearments in his native tongue as I dropped heavily and obtrusively out.

Threshold of hell

"The lowering of the grievance threshold is a feature of our society," says a writer in the *Observer* on the existing laws against "racial discrimination," the attempt, so far foiled, to bring in a law against "sexual discrimination" and the proposal—even more preposterous, if possible—for a law against "age discrimination."

"The lowering of the grievance threshold"—translated into English, what does this painful jargon mean? It means that ours is a society in which envy, spite, discontent and petty-mindedness are growing daily, and are being encouraged to grow daily by every means open to publicists and politicians.

The normal, unselfconscious relation of one human being with another human being, whether of different race, sex or age, is being systematically distorted and perverted. In the name of an unattainable equality, the individual man, woman and even child is being turned into a member of a category, a militant group moved not by human love but by inhuman malice and hatred.

What would our society be like if this process reached its ultimate though fortunately unattainable conclusion, in which every single person saw himself as a victim of discrimination by some other person? What will our society be like if the process continues, as at present, unabated and unopposed?

Chess problem

Reports from Australia suggest that the world champion chess player Boris Spassky of Russia and the American challenger Bobby Fischer are "limbering up for their contest like a couple of heavyweight boxers."

There is a contrast, possibly significant, between their training methods. Spassky's is said to include roadwork and weight-lifting, whereas Fischer is merely consuming enormous quantities of steak and apple-juice.

Does this emphasis on physical strength reflect an increasing tendency to violence in chess, already noticeable at humbler levels of the game?

At a recent Stretchford chess tournament the final match between Ron Ghoules (Nerdley) and Stan Hammercake (Soup Hales) was marred by what the *Stretchford Clarion* called "a disturbing plethora of ugly incidents."

When, after 14 moves, Ghoules, using a variation of Ballcock's Knight Sacrifice Gambit, forced Hammercake's Queen into a corner, the attitude of the crowd, who had been catcalling and throwing toilet rolls from the beginning of the game, became so offensive that the Nerdley man, leaping from his seat, seized a small spectator at random and stuffed him up a convenient chimney.

Hammercake immediately appealed under Rule 86B, whereupon a mob of spectators ran on to the board, displacing or knocking over several pieces, and the match was abandoned amid what the *Clarion's* Chess Correspondent called "scenes reminiscent of the notorious saturnalia of Ancient Rome.

"It is right, indeed essential," he added, "that chess players should keep physically fit. But to use their physical strength, however justifiably, in the course of play, is to introduce an element into chess which will eventually make the game distinguishable from Rugby League football only by its greater violence."

For your bookshelf

Thanks to the painstaking efforts of scholars, authors and publishers, more and more lids are being removed, as the saying is, from the façade of Victorian respectability. We gaze, horrified yet delighted, into the seething maelstrom of vice and perversion revealed below.

A new contribution to the work of demolition—perhaps the most sensational yet—has just appeared. It is "The Diaries of Arthur Sadcake" (edited by Julian Birdbath and published by Viper and Bugloss at £3·50, with an introduction by Dr Heinz Kiosk).

Arthur Sadcake, son of the Alderman Joseph Sadcake who gave his name to Stretchford's largest open space, lovely, sex-maniac-haunted Sadcake Park, inherited the family carbon brush manufacturing firm on his father's death in 1861 and ran it with conspicuous success until his own death at the end of the century.

He married young, and, as was the custom in Victorian times, fathered 47 children, including two sets of twins and one of triplets. He was an Alderman and a munificent patron of charity. His obituary in the *Stretchford Clarion* refers to the "unbending rectitude, the fervent piety, the insistence on absolute purity in word and deed" of "this distinguished son of Stretchford who might well be taken as an outstanding model and an arbiter of the moral law for all who come after."

His diaries, discovered by a literary agent at the back of a chimney when the Sadcake family mansion at Hokewell was being demolished last year, tell a very different story.

When first discovered, says Dr Kiosk, the diaries seemed disappointing—a somewhat banal and wholly blameless account of courtship, marriage, the birth of children, illnesses, deaths, tours in Switzerland, Italy and Norway, the unchanging routine of a Victorian factory and home.

But skilled editorial work, allied to the new publishing techniques of interlinear insertion and deformative cryptography, soon produced a very different picture.

From beneath the stiff Victorian frock coat there emerged a fascinating monster: Sadcake the transvestite (he used to dress up once a week in women's clothes, then visit working-class areas to press Lesbian attentions on barmaids, hoping—and in this he was seldom disappointed—to satisfy his masochistic tendencies by being beaten up); Sadcake the foot-fetishist, the egg-cup-fetishist, the homosexual sadist, even the cannibal (there is an account of his cooking and eating an Irish housemaid which has a curiously modern ring): this apparent pillar of Victorian society was in fact a psychopathic all-rounder who, if he suddenly appeared today among the feeble and degenerate modern sex-maniacs in the park which bears his name would put them to panic-stricken flight.

That this book will be a best-seller goes without saying. But Viper and Bugloss are not a firm to rest on their laurels. They believe, and rightly, that the chimneys of many a demolished Victorian mansion will yet yield treasures of scholarship and profit which will not only shed fresh light on Victorian hypocrisy but will make Sadcake's Diaries read like the journals of Samuel Smiles.

Move over, Dad

The decision that bishops of the Church of England should retire compulsorily at the age of 70 has the support of Dr Spaceley-Trellis, the go-ahead Bishop of Bevindon, who still has some years to go.

But he has another even more-far-reaching proposal, which he outlined in a sermon not long ago: that God has served his time and should be compulsorily retired in the near future.

"This is above all an age for Youth," Dr Trellis said, "and never has Youth been so clear-eyed, so compassionate and so committed as it is today.

"Progressive theologians have felt for some time that the present God lacks social awareness; he has failed to give a clear lead, for instance, on the problem of racialism. When has he stood up and been counted with the rest of us on the question of South Africa or Portugal?

"He is out of touch with current trends. His attitudes on such vital matters as housing, censorship, the sexual revolution, drug addiction, the environment and, above all, the Women's Liberation Movement have been unsatisfactory, to say the least.

"Altogether he gives the impression that he is far too pre-occupied with outmoded eternal matters—often tinged with elitism—which mean little or nothing to the average man and woman of today.

"It is high time he retired and made way for a younger man."

Boom

A big oil field has been discovered 100 miles north-east of the Shetlands, capable of producing 15 million metric tons a year. A pipeline is to be laid to the Shetlands, where the oil companies are already setting up their bases and complex installations.

It may seem perverse not to join in the cheering at this "boost to the economy." Yet there are probably many more people than the oilmen and the economists suspect who, far from cheering, will simply give a groan of helpless anguish. Of these strange people I am one.

Why should we be glad to know that those remote, austere and beautiful northern islands are going to be transformed? Why should we be glad at the imminent destruction of a "way of life" in many ways infinitely superior to our own; a life still lived by a hardy, brave, loyal and neighbourly people, scarcely touched as yet by our urban philosophy of cleverness and greed?

A new industry

There are spokesmen (self-appointed or otherwise) of the Church of England who seem determined to drag that church down to a level so far beneath contempt that there is simply no word to describe it.

Of the setting-up by the people who call themselves the "Family Planning Association," of a "contraceptive and sex information stall" at a "pop festival" at Reading, a local Anglican curate says he was "favourably impressed."

He also says that he and other Anglican clergy were "deeply annoyed" by suggestions that it was encouraging promiscuity.

Whether it was encouraging "promiscuity" or not (and many people who talk about these matters seem uncertain of the true meaning of the word), that is not the main ground for objecting to it.

What is called (by this time surely with unnecessary coyness) "family planning" is now big business. It is a huge, continually expanding industry employing countless numbers of research workers, salesmen and propagandists, even though some of the latter may be unpaid.

Many of these people, no doubt, sincerely believe that what they are doing is in the national interest, even in the interest of all mankind. They cannot see that what they are serving is a branch of industry—the systematic application of commercial technology to the hitherto scarcely exploited field of sexual love.

As such it is essentially inhuman and amoral. It substitutes statistics, cold calculation and ultimately scientific control for the natural relation—however brief and animal—of one human being with another. And even if it were absolutely certain (as it is not and never can be) that its "population policy" would save the world in some hypothetical future from destruction it would still be totally and profoundly wrong for living people now.

At the butts

There are a few bright spots (writes "BLAZEAWAY") to enliven the general dismal tale from the moors this year. Grouse themselves have been in short supply, though a party on Lord Burntalmond's moors in Sutherland bagged 14,602 brace on the Glorious Twelfth itself.

Landowners who have had the foresight to stock their moors with other game as well as grouse have generally had the last laugh. On one North Riding moor a record bag of 2,470 brace of Left-wing students was secured, as well as 662 brace of ecologists and 75 brace of social scientists.

Once again this year Au Petit Coin Anthropophage, the trendy West End restaurant which specialises in New Guinea dishes, had student flambé (specially flown from Yorkshire) on the menu on the evening of the Twelfth, though few people seemed to be ordering it, preferring no doubt to stick to more familiar delicacies.

Boring notes

by "Narcolept"

Pity the poor British Boring Board of Control and its hard-working president, Sir Herbert Trance! The kerfuffle over who shall and who shall not compete in this year's Global Boring Contests at Harringay is threatening to turn one of the highlights of the boring scene into an all-time shambles which will make the Second World War look like a vicarage tea-party!

It's no longer a question of introducing politics into the yawn game. It's a question of politics taking over our much-loved sport altogether!

There are the African countries which have threatened to boycott the contests if the Rhodesian multi-racial boring team is allowed to compete. There are the Arab countries who won't compete if the Israeli No. 1 seed, Shloime ben Chloroform, appears. And who can imagine a global boring battle without "Glorious Shloime," a yawnmaker of galactic ranking, arguably one of the greatest bores who ever lived?

There is a question-mark, too, over the appearance of Czechoslovakia's premier drowse-maestro, Antonin Bvorak. It seems he's not altogether in favour with the present rulers of the country which has given us so many world-ranking coma merchants of recent years.

Then there is the demand from the Emerald Isle that both the Official and Provisional IRA shall be represented. Admittedly the Irish, who have lagged behind so long in the boring field, are now beginning to catch up at last. But there are limits! Most aficionados of the yawn game will agree with me, I imagine, that explosions and boredom simply do not go together.

And now, to cap everything, the "Women's Lib" movement are threatening to picket the stadium because of alleged discrimination against women bores! If I were the Powers that Be, I'd almost be inclined to welcome them inside to see what they could do against the pick of the world's masculine yawnmakers!

Judging from recent form the Fair Sex might give some of us quite a surprise!

Film notes

The new Piledriver Films offering, "Wittgenstein and the Mad Ecologist from Outer Space," now showing at the Odium Cinema in the Haymarket, has all the ingredients of horror, suspense, terror, suspense and horror we expect from its talented director, Brian Hohenzollern.

Aficionados may even notice that some of the props used in "Wittgenstein and the Curse of the Pharaohs" do duty again in this new epic, notably a giant cobweb-hung, vampire-infested grandfather clock which last appeared in the lounge of a Transylvanian castle but is now converted for use as a mobile coffin operated by remote control to run up and down the motorways seizing and trapping its terrified victims.

Once again the domino-playing, banana-guzzling sage of Cambridge, played by Bruce Braganza, is pitted against an incarnation of pure evil in the shape of Dr Karl Abyss (Stan Bourbon Parma), a mad ecologist who has developed a deadly laser-operated gas capable of boring the whole population of the world to death in ten minutes, thereby (as Wittgenstein points out in a thrilling conference-scene at the United Nations) "ending life on this planet as we know it."

Helped by his blonde, violet-eyed, mini-skirted girl assistant (Kay Wittelsbach) and by a new character, bluff, blarney-crazed Maj. Patrick MacSeedy of the IRA Dental Corps (Ken Capet), Wittgenstein is soon on the track of the secret formula and after a thrill-packed chase which takes him to Transylvania, Ancient Egypt and the unicorn-haunted recesses of Cannock Chase, he finally runs Dr Abyss to earth in a sinister South London underwater supermarket.

I will not spoil your enjoyment by revealing the totally expected twists of the denouement.

Music by that grand old team Ted Hapsburg and Bing Karageorgevitch. Historical advice by Dean J. Angevin. Costumes and fashion research by Marylou Romanoff, Tracy Cantacuzene and Shirley Porphyrogenitus.

Self-defeating

The Prime Minister speaks of the prospect of unsurpassed prosperity for this country if the economy can be made stable through a voluntary prices and incomes policy.

What kind of prosperity does he mean? A larger and larger production and consumption of material goods, of course. What else has any politician of any party, in or out of office, talked about for the last 20 years and more?

Apart from anything else, this is self-defeating. If you tell people for 20 years and more that in effect the only thing that matters is the ability to acquire more and more money to obtain more and more goods, should you be surprised when it turns out that they have learnt the lesson too well? Should you be surprised that individually and sectionally all they do is demand more money?

In former times you might have appealed to their patriotism, their instinct to sacrifice themselves for the common good, their sense of justice. Now all you have to appeal to is their sense of calculation, which is supposed to tell them that if they agree to make do with less money now they will get more money later on in an unsurpassably prosperous country of the future.

What is there here to inspire men to change their hearts, their attitudes, their acts?

Winter scene

By a dank and dripping beech-wood the shooters' cars, mushroom-coloured or dull green (and the occasional fluorescent two-tone of peacock blue and puce, with leopard-skin upholstery) are drawn up by the roadside.

The men with dogs and shotguns stand about helplessly, knowing that no creature larger than an insect now lives in these suburban woods through whose leafless boughs a line of bunga-lows—"Bide-a-Wee," "Spinoza Holme," "Tregastel," "Kafkacote" —can be seen not far away.

Yet shooting there must be, since it is for that the men and dogs have left the blue-flickering television screen, the peppermints and colour supplements, the oil-fired central heating this winter afternoon.

A shot rings out, startling in the gathering dusk. It is a near miss on a nodding dachshund, electrically operated, in the rear window of a tomato-red saloon. The owner, incensed, though in a ritual fashion only, raises his gun and with a single lucky shot demolishes a dangling skeleton and a Babycham gazelle.

The shoot goes on till only a lighthouse-like bust of Churchill with a huge cigar, the end electrically glowing, remains, spared perhaps by ancestral piety.

Winter twilight is coming down, coldly and sadly. With no words spoken, a burly man, by his looks an antique-dealer, brings out a baize-covered collapsible card-table from the boot of his bullet-chipped car, sets it up on the beech-mast covered floor of a selected glade. Another brings out folding-chairs and soon, as drops of rain fall without human agency and light gusts of wind occasionally waft the playing cards from the table, a ritual game of Solo Whist is in full swing.

A young policeman in his panda-car drives past. City-bred and new to this neighbourhood he speculates idly on the card-players in the wood. Welsh nationalists? Ecologists wanted on a dozen charges? Master-criminals planning a £2 million bank robbery? The crew of a flying saucer? A feeling of helplessness comes over him, as he drives on, noticing with a townsman's bewildered irritation the telltale badger's sett in the telephone-kiosk by the leaf-clogged stream.

1973

Up to date

"The principal defect of the industrial way of life, with its ethos of expansion, is that it is not sustainable. Its termination within the lifetime of someone born today is inevitable." This is the basic message of "Blueprint for Survival," published by *The Ecologist* magazine, organ of what must, I'm afraid, itself be called the "ecology industry."

Readers of this column will know that it has also been the basic message of the column from time immemorial. It is amusing, in a way, to find that it has now passed from the hands of cranks, misfits, reactionaries and handloom-weavers and become the property—and since we live in an expanding industrial society, the quite valuable property—of perfectly serious, respectable people.

Since these people are mainly scientists, they believe that every "problem" has a "solution"; even this one. So they propose various remedial measures—a deliberate slowing down of "growth"; decentralisation; population control and so on.

There are two objections to this view. One: with the nature of mankind as it is now, these measures could not possibly be put into effect. Two: an attempt to put them into effect, though doomed to failure, would involve the imposition of a universal tyranny more merciless than any yet imagined. We should have the worst of both worlds.

What then is the "solution?" Is it not possible that within the terms of what scientists think of as reality there is no solution?

Process

A plan to run a motorway close to the city of Winchester; a gigantic scheme for an airport, industrial complex and road system which will obliterate a whole slice of the coast of Essex: a plan to flood mysterious Otmoor and build another motorway through the pleasant countryside of North Oxfordshire; a plan to turn the road through the beautiful hills and meadows of the northern Lake District, from Penrith to West Cumberland, into a great industrial highway; these are merely some of the more outstanding moves to be observed at present in the process by which our country is being turned into something which, when the process is complete, will no longer be recognisable as England.

All these threatened places, Winchester and Foulness, Otmoor and the Lake District, have their tireless defenders of course. These will not admit defeat even where, as in the case of the horror in the Lake District, the so-called Ministry of the Environment has actually approved the outrage.

What is the use, some people may say, of protesting and again protesting? The cause is lost. You will only make yourselves unhappy. Learn to love, as engineers and businessmen and politicians do, the roaring new roads; the rending scream of jet airliners: the landscapes of steel and concrete, of money and power objectified.

The answer is that these things are ugly, evil and inhuman in themselves. We should have to fight against them even though we knew the cause was hopeless. What else, after all, can decent people do?

With the Nodules

Before every public holiday those well-known traffic-jam fans Harry and Janet Nodule, of Brassgrove Park, discuss where they are likely to find the best hold-ups.

This time the usually united pair had quite a tiff on the Saturday over where they should drive on "Spring Holiday" Sunday. Harry said he had a hunch that Kent would be the best part to make for, with a good chance of hold-ups on the roads leading to the seaside.

But Janet said she had had a dream in which a man "dressed in a sort of AA uniform, only made of sort of gold cloth, and with sort of wings sprouting from his shoulders," had revealed to her that there would be "a really wonderful jam" on the way to the Lake District, somewhere in Lancashire.

"It was ever so vivid, Harry," said Janet, "and if we aren't going to miss it, I think we ought to start off straight away." What might be described as the front part of her head got all screwed up and she began to snivel.

But Harry was adamant. "You and your dreams," he said scornfully. "Just like a woman! I prefer to go by facts, statistics of former holidays and so on, as supplied in *Traffic Jam*, the magazine for all traffic jam fans. That's the way to get results."

It might have turned into quite a nasty scene. But in the end, realising that, as Harry said, life was too short to quarrel and traffic jams all too few, they compromised and made for the Norfolk Broads, where they were lucky enough to find a three-mile jam on the A17.

Thus marital harmony was restored. "Thank you for a lovely day, Harry," said Janet, as they reached home tired but happy and a curious, stretching effect appeared on the lower part of her head.

But she became rather quiet and thoughtful next day when Harry tactlessly read out a piece in the paper about a wonderful four-mile hold-up in Lancashire.

"They say dreams go by opposites," said Harry, fingering the top of his head where it comes to a marked point. "Anyhow, roll on August Bank Holiday! Perhaps you'll dream about that AA man again."

Mystery chaos bid

Yesterday saw yet another sensational development in the breathlessly unfolding drama of Stretchford United's wonder goalkeeper Albert Rasp, who let through 1,107 goals last season, comfortably breaking his own record.

Rasp is not merely unmarried and without any blonde, attractive, mini-skirted dolly girl-friends. Last week he stupefied the world by neither announcing a romance with a glamorous airhostess nor leaving for a secret hide-out in Spain's glamorous Costa Brava.

Now the mystery surrounding Rasp has deepened to desperate, twilight tones. A horde of reporters and photographers finally ran the star to earth yesterday in the serve-yourself refreshment centre in Stretchford's lovely, sex-maniac-haunted Sadcake Park.

The wonder goalkeeper was seated by himself in a corner of the deserted cafe, trying to suck Seven Up through a broken straw and staring into the interior of one of his football boots, which he had placed on the table for convenience of observation.

Later a team of "Way of the World" research workers took a survey of a cross-section of average men and women.

"Disgraceful," was the comment of 46-year-old housewife Mrs L. Glottis, of Thelwall Road, Gnomesall Heath. "If Rasp has no glamorous girl-friend or even a drab, work-worn wife he can desert, what right has he to play football or pontificate on matters he knows nothing about?"

Tracylou Hornet, 20, an attractive blonde secretary at a well-known toothbrush-hire agency in Nerdley, commented: "Good luck to Rasp, I say. We have long ago thrown outmoded Victorian conventions like marriage, children and all that into the dustbin. Today, unlimited sex is the birthright of everyone."

And Mr J. S. Duttcliffe, 52, a carbon brush welder and member of the Soup Hales Urban District Council said: "To complain that we are bringing politics into sport is sheer hypocrisy. It is the racists of South Africa, Rhodesia and Portugal who have brought politics into sport, and vice versa, by their fiendish policies of discrimination."

A new explosion

Officials of the so-called Department of the Environment are planning methods of saving archaeological sites from being obliterated by motorways and office blocks. Up to 800 new jobs in archaeology, with (of course) 15 regional centres to co-ordinate the work, are planned.

But the solution proposed by Dr John Goodmound, head of the Archaeology Department at Nerdley University, still seems the best.

Realising that motorways and office blocks must come first, while at the same time more and more archaeologists must be trained and given work to do ("the archaeology explosion") Dr Goodmound suggested the creation of a "pool" of artificial archaeological sites which could be moved about the country as required.

Archaeologists could thus conduct "digs" to their hearts' content while not getting in the way of our vital economic progress.

Dr Goodmound constructed a "pilot prototype" or "mock-up" of an artificial site, complete with bones, flints, masonry and prehistoric relics in appropriate layers, not far from Soup Hales.

Unfortunately he could not resist the temptation of immediately digging it up himself. While he was doing so, a new motorway suddenly bore down on him and an office-block suddenly began to rise near by. He only just got out of the way in time.

Dee Bladder's diary

Monday: Am I losing my grip? Was examining an old bandsman's euphonium in one of those fearfully smart new Chelsea junk shops (thought it might be just the thing to put in one of my downstairs loos, with the aspidistras, amusing old miners' lamps, old Singer sewing-machines (not later than 1925, of course), late Coptic mummy-cases and those lovely old tin advertisements for ink and pork pies and bicycles and things they used to have nailed on the walls of workers' cottages), when I got my fingers stuck between the valves (I think they're called) of the instrument, and none of the assistants, helpful as they were, could get it out.

Does one send for the fire brigade on these occasions? Or does one just hope some knowledgeable friend will come along, like Michael Parkinson, or dear Jon Glasse-Derkeley, or Ron Frabb, or Rex Weak, or Norman Mailer, or what's his name, that marvellous up-and-coming footballer-publisher, Christopher Brunette (oh dear, I think I must be rambling), or Lennie Bruce (forget, he's dead: yes, I *am* rambling)?

Or does one just pay up, and jump in a taxi, euphonium and all, and go to Père Pemphigus, that marvellous new place in Croydon where you can tuck into a Basque Fish and Sago Pudding Mornay as good as any I've ever had in New Orleans . . .

On the move

A government report recommends that 31,500 civil servants should be "dispersed" from London and "re-settled" in other places which may not necessarily want them and where they may not necessarily want to go.

Is this only a beginning? Will the figures rise till millions of these unlucky people are on the move (once dispersed, what is to stop them being dispersed over and over again?); till the late Herr Hitler's interesting scheme for transferring the whole population of Holland to the Urals will begin to look like—now wait for it, please—a vicarage wine and cheese party?

It is impossible not to feel sorry for these pitiful hordes of involuntary nomads as they stand wringing their ink-stained hands by the roadside; or hobble along, wheeling the pathetic equipment of their trade—filing cabinets, in and out trays, tea-making apparatus, swivel-chairs (Grade III), hat-stands, desks and wastepaper baskets—piled high in wheelbarrows, derelict prams or make-shift carts.

Moved on by the police from the road verges where they try in vain to set up temporary offices to deal with the allocation of school meal vouchers; jeered at by children; pelted with stones and offal by local hooligans unoccupied between football matches: their lot will be a hard one indeed.

Will many of them gradually sink into the mass of travelling people, distinguishable from the rest (and no doubt shunned) by the boredom of their unending talk of bygone administrative triumphs in "the office"; making at best a pitiful living by cutting up their desks into clothes pegs and trying to sell them, with a few battered old electric kettles and "lucky white papers" from door to fierce housewife's door?

Basic rights

A writer in the *Evening Standard* the other day renewed the old complaint about the extreme sexual deprivation suffered by prisoners in gaol and suggested that they be allowed private visits from their wives or girl-friends to "prevent them becoming homosexual."

A homosexual reader at once wrote in to suggest that as homosexual prisoners suffered equal deprivation—as well as persecution from heterosexual fellow prisoners and warders—they should be given equivalent facilities.

Dr Heinz Kiosk, the eminent psychopenologist and chief psychiatric adviser to the Eccles Cake and Garibaldi Biscuit Council, urged at a recent seminar that prison authorities should go much further than this and be obliged to provide facilities for every kind of sexual practice conceivable.

Some of these practices (see Krafft-Ebing's collected works, edited with introduction and notes by Dr Kiosk himself and Dr Melisande Fischbein) require elaborate and expensive equipment.

To those who objected that rate-payers might not be willing to pay for all this, Dr Kiosk replied: "It is one way in which these so-called rate-payers can make amends for the persecution of these so-called "criminals" by our unjust consumer-orientated society.

"And not only the ordinary rate-payers," he shouted hastily, as Dr Llewelyn Goth-Jones, the medical officer of health for Stretchford, who is a director of a new chain of "sex aid factories," a Nadirco subsidiary, just opened in the Midlands, rose to his feet to support him, "WE ARE ALL GUILTY."

Logical

In Durham, where there is a strike of ambulance-drivers, a woman, seriously injured when knocked down by a van, had to be taken to hospital by an ambulance crew of volunteers.

Pickets, it is reported, jeered them as they left for the hospital with the patient and jeered them again when they arrived there.

That is the level to which some people in England have now sunk. But disgusting as such behaviour is, is it altogether surprising? The English people have been told for years now by public men, by industrialists and by the politicians of successive Governments, told over and over again, day and night, that the only thing in the world that matters is economic growth, raising their "standard of living": in other words, getting more money.

Is it surprising that they behave accordingly? That ordinary human decency, even of the most elementary kind, seems to them irrelevant and out of date when the great principle of their life is in question?

This outbreak of evil—and that is the plain word for it—is only at a comparatively early stage. But it is spreading rapidly. We shall know that it has reached its logical fulfilment when lifeboatmen, striking for higher emoluments, take a few moments off from watching a strip-tease show to go and jeer at the ineffectual efforts of amateur boatmen to rescue drowning children from the sea.

Christmas reading

A coffee table book to end all coffee table books comes out this year from Nadirbooks, the publishing subsidiary of the Nadirco Consortium. It costs £760·75 and is called "Coffee Table," by Julian Nadir. It is in fact a coffee table, complete with electric percolator, cups, saucers, spoons, electro-plated bowl for polychromatic sugar crystals and all other accessories.

"Coffee Table" has been awarded this year's Nadir Book Prize, worth £10,000, for the best book by a new author. One member of the judging committee, the critic Julian Birdbath, dissented from the general view, pedantically asking how "Coffee Table," which includes no words or other literary material, could be considered a book at all.

He was forcibly ejected by the other committee members, including top-ranking playright Neville Dreadberg, top-ranking footballer-sculptor Ken Valve and top-ranking model and TV personality Giselle de Frabazon, sustaining minor contusions and damage to his spectacles and ball-point pen, but was not detained in hospital.

A paperback version of "Coffee Table" is also available at £153·50. It has a tendency to bend and collapse, and, when soaked with leaking coffee, to disintegrate altogether into soggy lumps of cardboard. It is described as "a good Christmas buy for old age pensioners and others of limited means."

Wanderers

It is now being suggested that Kohoutek's Comet, far from appearing in the sky as the brilliant awe-inspiring prodigy foretold by most astronomers, may turn out to be a very feeble luminary indeed, scarcely visible to the naked eye.

Some astronomers (whether out of professional jealousy I cannot say) are even hinting that this comet may have already broken up and will therefore not be visible at all.

Let us hope they are wrong. Meanwhile there are disquieting telepathic reports from the "Way of the World" space-vehicle "Don Carlos and the Holy Alliance V," now on a routine tour of the solar system, that a bedraggled, dimly-lit celestial object claiming to be a comet of Czech nationality, was encountered yesterday near the Outermost Ring of Saturn.

It asked for political asylum and was taken on board to await instructions from columnar headquarters.

The message may turn out to have been garbled in transmission. But should this object turn out to be Kohoutek's Comet it will either have to be released at some distant point in space or brought back in due course to the column itself.

The trouble is that we already have several comets and it will not be easy for technical reasons to accommodate any more. There are complex orbital arrangements to be considered, for one thing.

I myself keep a small personal comet, a very beautiful one with a fine iridescent tail, in one of the drawers of my desk. I take it out and play with it sometimes when I am feeling depressed, allowing it to make several orbits of my study before returning it to its box of amethyst and jade.

I find this very soothing and can recommend it to sufferers from melancholia.

Coming shortly

A state visit to this country by President Ngrafta of Gombola (formerly Gomboland) is long overdue. The Redeemer, who knows England well (he is the only African Head of State who as well as being a highly qualified witchdoctor holds a degree from the London School of Economics) has often said he is anxious to come here. But the Foreign Office is suspected of stalling.

This would not be altogether surprising. Dr. Ngrafta, a sophisticated man who combines a stern sense of his own importance with magical powers and a keen sense of humour, would certainly expect to be received here with all the pomp and ceremony befitting a world statesman.

But thanks to his mastery of the techniques of producing thought-forms and mass-hallucinations he is quite capable, if necessary, of providing for his own reception, and on a scale which, as the saying is, beggars description.

Imagine a combination of Alexander's progress through Persepolis, the inauguration of the Emperor Nero, the coronations of (say) Charlemagne, Montezuma, Tchaka and Tsar Alexander II and a magnified Nuremburg Rally, and you may get some faint idea of the stupendous yet insubstantial pageant—itself dissolving, fading and continually changing shape—which London would witness.

Amid the thunderous cheers of millions of wraiths and zombies selected from the dead of all the nations of the earth, the procession moves slowly down Whitehall in unnatural African sunlight. Now the full complement of bands of the Royal Navy, the Army and the Air Force, supplemented by Foden's No. 1 Works Band in phantasmic form, booms forth the Gombolan anthem (arr. Rimmer); now strange, exotic melodies, seeming at once to tinkle from the sky and rise as emanations from the earth itself, sound from massed dulcimers played by Abyssinian maids, accompanied by the BBC Symphony Orchestra, augmented by 10,000 extra 'cellos and conducted by Gustav Mahler.

Even with a thought the wrack dislimns, leaving Dr. Ngrafta alone, illuminated by a single specially-designed shaft of sunlight shining through a rift in the suddenly grey London clouds. . . .

Nor is this all. With the simulacra of elephants, lions, hippopotami and other illegally imported animals pacing along amid the dwarfs, eunuchs and houris in the President's retinue, and with a single roc (a notable Gombolan contribution to the Wildlife Conservation movement) flying overhead, the quarantine authorities would have their hands full.

Yes, it is quite a problem. But it cannot wait for ever.

1974

Breakers ahead?

Lord Rothschild's Central Policy Review Staff—an important agency of the planning industry—has made a recommendation of great interest to another key British industry—race relations.

It has suggested that the Community Relations Commission and the Race Relations Board should merge. This has naturally caused concern at Ethnic House, the £45 million London headquarters of the industry.

What directors of the big race relations firms are asking is whether there is a move towards outright nationalisation. Many of them, who would get the plum jobs in that event, may welcome the prospect.

But others, judging from the experience of other nationalised industries, believe it would result in a fall in output, labour troubles and above all a slowing-down of the export drive which is doing such splendid work by introducing British race relations "know-how" into underdeveloped countries where the race relations industry was hitherto virtually unknown.

And what of the small men, the little race relations factories dotted up and down the country, often employing only a handful of operatives with out-of-date plant, but doing their level best for the spread of race-consciousness nevertheless?

One managing director in the Midlands, who inherited a small family race relations business from his father only a few months ago, was apprehensive. "It will mean ruin," he told a "Way of the World" reporter, a multiracial lump visibly working in his throat.

"What will become of our workers if they are made redundant by amalgamation?" He gestured towards a shed where a group of ageing discrimination testers could be seen closely watching a Pakistani who was trying to order a pint of draught Guinness from a hard-faced White landlord in a cardboard "mock-up" saloon bar.

"It's the only life these chaps know, the only work they understand. Race relations is in their blood. Above all, they're craftsmen. Are they to be chucked on the industrial scrap-heap, with nothing but fading memories of past multiracial triumphs to cheer their declining years?"

Teething troubles

Is Mr McGahey (or Micheál Mac Eachaidh, as I pedantically prefer to spell his name) a Tory forgery? The answer is; not exactly.

Some time ago, at a high level columnar conference, the idea of constructing a portable, all-purposes British Communist leader was discussed. After some hesitation (previous constructs of Tory, Labour and Liberal politicians, in various shapes, now moving about and apparently breathing and talking, have not proved very satisfactory) I gave my consent to the project and roughed out a preliminary sketch and guidelines.

The first papier-maché "mock-ups" produced by the columnar workshops, under the expert supervision of Mr Hargreaves, the popular works manager, were interesting and even impressive.

I was particularly taken with a model called "Len Moth," an angular figure with steel-rimmed spectacles, a face deeply trenched with Marxist lines of dialectic and trouser-ends permanently secured with bicycle clips—the very pattern of an old-style English Communist.

Although "Moth" appealed to the romantic side of my nature, I soon realised he would not do. He was, though I dislike the term, out of date, and, though waterproofed, liable to disintegrate in wet weather.

Various other "mock-ups" were submitted to me: "Abe Bummaree," "Jim Grasp," "Jack Tosh." All had their points, but had to be rejected for various reasons, such as Bummaree's ingenious, self-renewing inbuilt halitosis. When "Grasp," a square ginger-bearded figure, was activated to make a speech on the wrongs of the workers, his voice, owing to some technical fault, got out of control, growing louder and louder and causing widespread panic until he blew a fuse and exploded.

It was, as the saying is, "back to the drawing board." In a flash of inspiration I realised that no model would be really satisfactory unless he was of Scots "birth" and Irish descent and possessed, under a harsh, fanatical exterior, a certain lovable and endearing quality.

The rest followed. We were as Mr Hargreaves said, "in business." Within weeks a "viable" model had been produced. "Mick McGahey," Tory asset and Wilson's bane, was born. The world knows the rest.

Perhaps

"All the independent African countries are now agreed and determined to liberate Southern Africa through armed struggle no matter how long it takes and no matter how much suffering it inflicts on human life."

This statement is reported to have been made by Mr John Malecela, the Foreign Minister of Tanzania, at a banquet in honour of the Foreign Minister of Great Britain, Sir Alec Douglas-Home.

Sir Alec's reaction is not stated. Had he "made an excuse and left" as some old-fashioned people may think he should have done, this would certainly have come to light, in the shape of a "diplomatic incident."

So presumably he didn't. Perhaps his thoughts were on other matters, and he didn't hear the remark. Perhaps he thought it was a "sick" joke ("Dear me, I don't think I shall ever understand the African sense of humour"). Perhaps his thoughts strayed to the past and in his half-dreaming state he imagined he was listening to a strangely distorted parody of a speech by the late Herr Hitler. Perhaps he was asleep.

Perhaps we shall never know. Perhaps it is just as well.

Another silly question

Every year, every week, every day, huge numbers of cruel experiments on animals are carried out in research laboratories in this country, some in the interest, real or supposed, of medical science, some in the interest of various industries. It is happening as I write this, it is happening as you read it.

When people (I mean, of course, "a vociferous minority of cranks and luddite reactionaries who love animals and therefore hate the human race") ask if all this cruelty is really necessary, they are often asked sarcastically if they imagine scientists do it for fun.

Few, if any, scientists, I imagine, consciously do so. But people who advocate flogging for crimes of violence are invariably reminded that things are not as simple as they think. At a deeper level there are bad psychological effects (it is a cherished belief of "armchair psychiatrists") not only on those who are flogged but on those who order and carry out the flogging.

If this is so, what must be the psychological effect of continually torturing animals on scientists who spend their working days in their laboratories in this manner, and then, perhaps, take off their overalls and go home to their loving wives and families just like anybody else?

Afoot in London

By "Wayfarer"

I see that a troupe of Whirling Dervishes from Turkey is now performing in London with great success. But how many Londoners, even those who think they know our beloved city well, realise that there is an old-established Whirling Dervish colony to be

found tucked away behind a furniture store in humdrum Turgis Hill High Street, in South London?

The origin of the colony, like most things, is lost in the immemorial mists of antiquity. But many historians believe these Whirling Dervishes are the descendants of a party attached to the Arab armies invading France who got cut off from the main body after the Battle of Poitiers (732) and somehow found their way to England, perhaps crossing the Channel as illegal immigrants.

By the time of the Norman Conquest they were well established around Turgis Hill, then a remote, densely-wooded wilderness with little to remind them of their native deserts except the absence of coal-mines. A pipe-roll of 1291 shows them paying a nominal sum of three groats a year for the right to whirl. That they were an object of curiosity to the charcoal-burners of the neighbourhood and of suspicion to the monks of the newly-founded Turgis Abbey is apparent from a reference in the "B Text" of "Piers Plowman."

Their right to whirl in perpetuity was granted by Henry VIII at the time of the Dissolution of the Monasteries, rescinded by Mary I and restored by Elizabeth, but on condition that they restricted their whirling activities to their own neighbourhood.

Dr Johnson and Boswell watched a display of whirling in 1770, the doctor remarking characteristically: "Sir, he would be a man of narrow mind and lethargic temper who would not wish to emulate these prodigious circumvolutions." Thus exhorted, Boswell attempted to whirl, but to the Doctor's amusement immediately fell to the ground.

By the beginning of the 19th century the Dervishes were already beginning to feel the effects of the Industrial Revolution and the decline of the colony was hastened by the departure of a detachment of young Dervishes who volunteered for the Turkish Army in the Crimean War, later settling in Anatolia.

When Carlyle visited the Dervishes in 1867 they were already only a pitiful remnant, with such slowed-down rotation that the philosopher unkindly called them "a combogulous sect of enfeebled turbinators which the Time-Spirit (ha!) hath spewed expectoratingly forth."

At the time of the First World War the Dervishes, by then reduced to a single family, endured some mild persecution as reputed "Turkish spies," until T. E. Lawrence (of Arabia) made representations on their behalf in high quarters. Attempts to incorporate them in some of C. B. Cochran's musical shows came to nothing, and in the Second World War the colony was taken over temporarily by a REME workshop and all whirling ceased "for the duration."

Today only a single aged Dervish, Mr S. Habibullah, remains. He can be persuaded to whirl, though only very slowly, for a small fee.

How to get there: 184B bus from Aldwych to Turgis Hill High Street. Turn sharp left at Gringe's Furniturama, left again at the Chez Diane Coffeerama, and ring bell marked "Press" at No. 18 Kandahar Road.

On the Ohm Farm

Midsummer on the Ohm Farm! At this crown of the year, what intimations of immortal technology, what synthetized ecstasies and panagnostic longings haunt the agrotechnical, neopastoral scene!

A heat haze, chemical-compounded, deadly to everything that breathes, shimmers on the boundless plain which stretches on every side to what, if it could be seen, might be called the horizon. Here and there, as you watch through protective goggles, a glint of metal appears as the sun strikes, indicating the electrified barbedwire fencing which separates the various experimental areas: the semi-automated pig centre, the 40-foot beet-processing compound, the nuclear-operated bovine forcing sheds.

Far off appear (or is it a mirage, born of some memory of angel infancy?) the dazzling white shapes of the administrative buildings. There gnarled Old Seth Roentgen and his devoted team of research scientists watch the flickering dials on the control consoles and programme the computers which will show, in millionths of a second, the current rate of broiler-egg production, the broiler-calf fattening indices or ratios of lamb-hormone-injection.

A line from Arnold's "Scholar-Gipsy," written, perhaps, on just such a midsummer day as this, comes into the mind unbidden: "Go, for they call you, shepherd, from the hill."

And sure enough there emerges from an electronically operated manhole not far off, the figure of Bert Fischbein the shepherd, muffled in protective clothing. Geiger-counter in hand, he makes his way carefully through the light, poisoned breeze, to where his flock of giant, 60-uddered experimental ewes bleat plaintive thunder in their aluminium cotes.

Central issue

"What the country needs," says some Liberal politician or other, "is a 'revolt of the Centre.'" Is it? What we must first do, before any revolting begins, is to define this so-called "Centre."

The fact is that during the last 20 years or so a semantic shift has occurred by which what was formerly the moderate Left has come to be called the "Centre," while what was formerly the Centre, patriotic, firm for law and order, moral standards and so on, has come to be called the "Right" or the "Lunatic Fringe."

What is now called the "Centre," whether it is nominally Liberal, Conservative or Labour, is simply the liberal consensus, liberal with a small "l."

It is the body of opinion which favours "power-sharing," multi-racialism and the anti-discrimination industry in general, sanctions against Rhodesia, moderate "permissiveness," selective disapproval for certain foreign governments, internationalism and so on and so forth. It feeds on clichés and meaningless formulae of goodwill and fairness, which it greatly prefers to taking a straight look at what the enemies of this country, internal and external, are really up to, and acting accordingly.

This "Centre" is supposed to represent the opinion of all "ordinary, sensible people." But, as anyone who has talked to any number of real people, as opposed to abstractions, will know, it does not represent them at all. Far from it.

What need has this fallacious, cosy and essentially fraudulent "Centre" for revolt? It is in all the seats of power now. What the country needs is a revolt against it, which will put back the genuine Centre there instead.

Let them eat roads

Anybody who travels about England will notice how quite large tracts of it are beginning to look like battlefields of the First World War, with churned-up earth, water-filled craters, uprooted trees, partly demolished buildings and other signs of bombardment by heavy artillery.

What is happening, of course, is that, as huge notice-boards proudly declare, motorways, or roads linking existing or projected motorways, are being constructed, or existing main roads are being "improved to motorway standard."

It is possible that many of these schemes, which are very expensive for the public and very profitable for the contractors, will never be completed, because the money to pay for them will run out before they are. It is also possible that these great highways are being built to carry traffic which, if they *are* completed, will not be there to use them.

Meanwhile the face of England is destroyed; large stretches of fertile land which could, and not long ago did, produce large quantities of food, are sterilised. No matter; the process goes on; evidently it is impossible to stop it; it has become, except for those who profit by it, its own object and needs no other.

We may end up fighting for scraps in a barren land littered with bits of abandoned motorways, spoil-heaps and craters; but who are we to complain?

Haggard's journal

July 13, 1774. Josh. Black to be hanged for stealg. a lamb. In p.m., whilst pursuing a wounded poacher towards Long Bottom I encountered an alrmg. sight, viz., sevl. villagers in a state of undress hurlg. balls at each other and wavg. wooden staves in the air. Thinkg. this to be preparation for a further Papist Rebellion, I give them a blast from my fowlg. piece, when one ran to me begng. me not to fire, as they were but practisg. for a game of Cricket against Soup Hales.

July 14, 1774. Mist. Bart. Thisby d. from Seethg. of the Pipes. To Nerdley to see Josh. Black hanged, he owg. me £0 0s. 0¼d, for which I forgave him. In p.m. dined with my neighbour Sir Josh. Faggott. Upon my recountg. my experience with the Cricketers, Sir

Josh. wagered me 500 sovs. that Soup Hales would defeat Stretchford in the match tomorrow.

July 15, 1774. Drizzle. Eli Grunge d. from a surfeit of pease
puddg. Up early and to Long Bottom for the Cricket. Soup Hales
batted first, and achieved 130 notches, chiefly owing to Sir Josh's
son, whom nobody would bowl out, for fear of offendg. one of the
gentry. His inngs. only terminated when he put his foot in a rabbit
hole in the middle of the pitch, and was carried away with a
sprained ankle.

When Stretchford batted, they soon made 129 notches for the
loss of only three men, and it seemed certain I must win my wager.
But at a signal from Sir Josh. his son was carried to the wicket to
bowl, despite his injury, whereupon the Stretchford batsmen
cringed and touched their forelocks and surrendered themselves
without the ball strikg. the wicket, so that they lost by one run and
I went home 500 sov. the poorer, ventg. my wrath by horsewhippg.
a Methody preacher whom I met on the road. ITEM: To horsewhip
£0 0s 1½d.

Tilt

An American news photographer who tried to take a picture of ex-
President Nixon in his wheel chair in a hospital corridor reports
that Mr Nixon's face became distorted with rage and he yelled:
"You Goddam son of a bitch!" The photographer says he was so
shocked that he failed to take a picture before an attendant
hurried Mr Nixon away.

I asked Jack Moron, the eminent journalist, what he thought
about this. His first comment cannot, I am afraid, be reproduced in
a column intended for family reading by the fireside. Had this
sensitive American heard it, he would have fainted.

But after the great man (we were in a well-known Fleet Street
bar at the time) had emptied at a gulp a large glass of dark yellow
liquid and called for more, he declared, in more moderate language, that the news photographer was a ——disgrace to his
profession.

There was no place in it for shrinking wayside flowers, he went
on (I am obliged to paraphrase). A photographer who was shocked
by Mr Nixon should sell his cameras and take up collecting
porcelain teasets.

What, I asked, would Moron himself have done in the circumstances? He fixed me with a bloodshot eye, half rose from his chair, thought better of it, sat down again and said he would have rebuked the ex-President in suitable language, knocked the attendant unconscious and then, circling the wheel chair, taken pictures of Mr Nixon from every possible angle until his film ran out.

He would then have filed a sensational story telling how the ex-President had tried to run him over with his wheel chair and, finding this impossible, summoned a band of thugs to his aid, only to see them knocked unconscious in their turn.

"Nixon Wheel Chair Assault Bid Mystery Chaos," he murmured to himself, rising to his feet before slumping heavily to the ground.

Tell me a story

A Miss (or Mrs) Mann, who runs something called the Children's Rights Workshop (Book Project), complains in a letter to a magazine, *Books for Your Children,* of bias in children's books.

"Most books for children," she says, "are about boys. Girls hardly appear, or if they do they practically always take second place and do less interesting things. We know that girls are just as active and independent as boys and that women do go out to work . . . sit down with the newspaper, drive cars and enjoy themselves as much as men.

"And what about men? Does Dad always have to come home with a briefcase and smoking a pipe? Dads do wash up sometimes —in fact 81 per cent of them do it regularly." (Consider, by the way, the ghastly "survey" which must have yielded this figure and the kind of mind which accepts it as significant).

"And where is the rest of the world in children's bookland? Where are the working class, Black people, the handicapped, travelling people, the children with one parent or none? . . . We live in a rich and varied multi-racial society. Why is so much of it left out of children's books?"

All right, all right. Help is on the way. Deirdre Dutt-Pauker, brilliant daughter of the well-known Hampstead thinker, and herself the mother of a brilliant, bearded activist little son, has written a brilliant children's book which should meet all these objections and more.

It is Mum who comes home from her work (sitting down with newspapers, as a matter of fact) with a briefcase, smoking a pipe, to find Dad, who is Black and handicapped (he has webbed feet, the result of racial discrimination) busy at the sink trying to wash up some travelling people who happened to be travelling past their home that afternoon.

Mum is a bit put out at first because she hoped Dad would have washed up the piles of crockery instead. She goes out again to drive a car and have a look at the rich, multi-racial society all around.

Calming down, she comes back, still puffing away at her pipe, to find that Dad has gone off with the travelling people and that their two kids, Rudi, the girl and Judy, the boy, have been rowing about whether they have one parent, two parents or none. . . .

It is a rich, multi-racial slice of real working-class life, as opposed to the class-ridden, sexist, racist fantasies which pass as children's books today. When I add that the richly multi-racial illustrations are by Pippa Dreadberg, brilliant wife of brilliant Left-wing playwright, critic, designer and self-publicist Neville Dreadberg, I need say no more.

A word of sense

"A Religion That Makes Sense." This announcement on behalf of some sect or other, glimpsed on a poster, made me wonder what sort of people it would appeal to. One might think that "making sense" was the very last thing a religion would be required to do.

But it is not a bad definition of the kind of religion advocated by such people as the go-ahead Bishop of Bevindon, Dr Spaceley-Trellis: a religion which "moves with the times"; a religion which is expressed not in the language of the Authorised Version but in the language of public notices and census forms ("Do nothing with this

Space until you are told what to do with it)"; a religion which "works"; a religion, in fact, which not merely renders unto Caesar the things which are Caesar's but includes itself among them.

No wonder people are turning to demonolatry. At least it doesn't make sense.

1975

At Marxmount

You might imagine that Mrs Dutt-Pauker, the Hampstead thinker, and her family would be welcoming this New Year with quiet or even noisy satisfaction. After all, there is a fair chance that all she has striven for through so many devoted years, all her hopes for this country, may come to fulfilment in 1975.

But apart from the shadow cast by the death of Mrs Dutt-Pauker's distant kinsmon Palme Dutt, so long the *eminence grise* of British progressive thought, ideological rifts in the family have been widening lately.

Things came to a head on Christmas Day (or "the Winter Festival of Labour," as they prefer to call it) when the family gathered round the "Dialectical Tree," all hung with chocolate grenades in silver paper and topped with a glowing red star, in the big drawing-room at Marxmount, for the distribution of presents.

Mrs Dutt-Pauker's daughter Deirdre and her husband, Leftist television documentary producer John Armature, were delighted with their leather-bound set of Stalin's Collected Essays on Philology. But Deirdre's bearded six-year-old activist son Bert Brecht Mao Che Odinga began screaming even before he had opened the first of his gifts, a set of model African terrorists.

Efforts by Dr Pixie Dutt-Pauker, over for the party from Stretchford University, where she heads the Department of Protestology, to calm the lad were in vain. Yelling that he wanted some real live terrorists, not rotten little bourgeois-type toys, he rounded on her and accused her of revisionism, formalism and "green" neocolonialist constructivism in a speech which lasted for over half an hour (with standing ovation from himself).

Eventually Gjoq, the giant Albanian Maoist au pair girl, who had watched the scene with a grim smile, holding her own present, a marzipan sub-machine gun, under her arm, led Bert from the room.

Soon afterwards an explosion from the distant day-nursery showed that the pair, who had been storing gelignite and detonators for weeks for the great occasion, were celebrating enjoyably in their own way.

Stands to Reason

The Solicitor-General's ruling that people should not be prevented from seeking public posts or penalised in any way merely because they may have broken the law once or twice in the past will be welcomed by all decent, progressive people.

Dr Heinz Kiosk, the well-known social psychologist and chief psychiatric adviser to the National Eccles Cake Institute, told reporters yesterday: "This is a step in the right direction, though a pitifully halting one.

"What is important is to break down, once and for all, the invidious distinction between 'criminals' and 'the law', a significant aspect of the social violence inherent in our unjust, consumerised society.

"Is there any reason, for instance, why the Lord Chief Justice, while continuing to discharge his present duties, whatever they may be, should not be on probation or serving a suspended sentence, or even actually be in jail?

"Alternatively, is there any reason why a convicted terrorist should not at the same time serve as a circuit judge? Such an arrangement, apart from social considerations, would ease the energy crisis, since the same man could plant bombs while travelling from court to court, thus saving valuable petrol.

"If he should be so unfortunate as to blow up his own court and himself with one of his own bombs, this would at any rate bring home to him the fact that he is essentially guilty. WE ARE ALL GUILTY," added Dr Kiosk hastily, as frenzied reporters rushed for the doors, hurled themselves through windows or tried vainly to escape by climbing up the walls.

Among the squatters

By Doreen Gaggs

I've just been talking to some of the big group of squatters who've occupied Hokewell Manor, a big Regency house in its own grounds which formerly belonged to the proud-lineaged Lestrange-Haggard family but is now encircled by the Stretchford Conurbation.

The squat was organised by the Department of Theoretical and Applied Squatting at Stretchford University, part of Dr Pixie Dutt-Pauker's prestigious Department of Social Protestology. The squatters were supplied by Rentacrowd, the mammoth mob-supplying consortium, which has a section dealing with orders for small, specialised groups, human, semi-automated or mixed.

Hokewell Manor was just about to be opened by the Corporation Welfare Department at a centre for homeless families, so the squatters moved in just in the nick of time.

"I mean like we're here to make a statement about the plight of the homeless in an alienated society," said Jim, the leader, a gentle, raucous-voiced 19-year-old who's had a varied career (after leaving university he tried to go back there but found it too alienated).

"I mean like we're here to make a statement about the plight of the homeless in an alienated society," put in Jim, a raucous, gentle-voiced knee-length-haired 18-year-old. All the men squatters are called Jim and all the girls are called Jill. As there are about fifty of them this might make for confusion in some circumstances. But here, in this relaxed, infectious, youthful atmosphere of protest it somehow doesn't seem to matter.

"I mean like we're here to make a statement about the plight of the homeless in an alienated society," explained Jill, a fair-haired, rather jerky girl who plays a microbiotic guitar and is trying to recycle baked bean tins all over the place. "It's ecology," she added.

"As this house was just due to open it's all properly painted and wired for electricity and that, so it seems just the right place for our statement," said another squatter, Jill, a dark-haired girl with staring eyes who is recycling saucepans and takes a lot of interest in the environment.

Twenty-year-old Jim, another "drop-out" from university who has played the bicycle-wheel in a West Indian steel-band and is recycling door-knobs, and 55-year-old Jill, a recycled student who believes even ecology to be alienated, both told me as I left, speaking in unison, that they were all there to make a statement about the plight of the homeless in an alienated society.

Whatever you may think of these dedicated youngsters you've got to admit they are ready to defy conformity and think for themselves.

Norman the Good

12 March, 2015

One of our national characteristics which still persists in the age of Socialist Monarchy is a love of dogs. So it is only natural that King Norman and his family should keep one. Indeed if it were not for this he would long ago have been overthrown by a Council Palace Revolution.

The Royal fox-terrier, Spot, is an elderly, obese, balding and malodorous animal of indeterminate sex, but makes up for this in popular estimation by its greed and its habit of biting Princess Tracy, the younger and more unpopular of Queen Doreen's daughters, whenever it sees her.

Spot also gains popularity for the Socialist Royal Family on ceremonial occasions (as an economy measure, it also has to do duty as mascot for the Royal Socialist Anti-Nuclear Air Force) by being able, on the order "Die for the Socialist King," to roll over ponderously on its back, slowly waving its paws in the air like a monstrous beetle.

It is too infirm to get on to its feet again and has to be helped by Brass-Stair-Rod-in-Waiting, who is invariably bitten for his pains, to the delighted cheers of the crowd.

Republicans, of whom there are a few even in Good King

Norman's Golden Days, are putting out rumours that Spot has in fact been "put to sleep" and its carcase sold to a Chinese restaurant, and that the creature shown in photographs of the Socialist Royal Family is a stuffed replica.

The other day, to scotch these rumours, King Norman asked Duke Len of Erdington, the black sheep of the Socialist Royal Family, to take Spot for a walk in the Council Palace Garden of Plastic Gnomes at Bevindon, which is of course open to the public.

Instead the Duke made straight for a nearby public house, the Quantity Surveyors' Arms, where his close friend Miss Gwenda Briggs, 21, works as a barmaid. There he not only drank several bottles of light ale himself but gave some to Spot. The dog lapped it up greedily, then instantly went into a coma.

The Duke laughingly carried the animal back to the Council Palace, where the Queen Gran, thinking it was dead, upbraided him and repeatedly struck him with her iron-tipped outsize handbag. She was mollified only when Spot, suddenly regaining consciousness, bit the Duke, King Norman, Queen Doreen, Prince Barry, Princess Shirley, her husband Duke Ron of Brownhills and Baby Cindy in rapid succession.

That Sunday the French newspapers carried a headline: "LE DUC D'ERDINGTON, MOUTON NOIR ALCOOLIQUE DE LA FAMILLE ROYALE SOCIALISTE D'ANGLETERRE, EST-IL SADISTE?"

On a visit

Mr Roy Jenkins, the Home Secretary, has paid a visit to Brixton, to see how the multi-racial society is coming along there. When I first read about this, one of my gigantic, never-to-be-painted Victorian Royal Academy historical paintings immediately came into my mind's eye, complete with dusty gilt frame and all: "Roy Jenkins Talking with Race Relations Operatives at Brixton," perhaps, or "Roy Jenkins at Tulse Hill Comprehensive School."

But after reading the report more carefully, I think a lighter medium would be more suitable—a delicate aquarelle, perhaps, of pale greens, mauves and grey half-tones, the details no more than suggested, sketched in with a few faint lines against a background of palest pink wash.

"There is a very substantial problem of urban social deprivation, but I don't feel any sense of hopelessness," said Mr Jenkins. "I don't know what the solution is or I would not be here."

That must have gone down well with the people of all colours who actually *are* there all the time. "But," went on Mr Jenkins, rising to a terrific climax of liberal wetness, "I believe it requires an effort on the part of people of all origins to overcome these problems in an atmosphere of constructive tolerance."

Yes.

Warning

Certain student unions at British universities are "adopting" Ulster internees. This is part of an "anti-internment" campaign initiated at a recent conference of the so-called National Union of Students.

Steve Parry, the union's Communist secretary, denies that the campaign implies support for the IRA. As well as opposing internment, he says, it calls for the withdrawal of troops to barracks, leading to an eventual withdrawal from Ulster, and the introduction of a Bill of Civil Rights for Ireland. These are measures which, curiously enough, are also advocated by the IRA—an odd coincidence. But Mr Parry says that Protestant extremists will also be "adopted."

Progressive people who may wish to adopt one or more internees (and why should the privilege be confined to students?) should be careful. Last year Mrs Dutt-Pauker, the well-known Hampstead thinker, offered to adopt a released internee.

The ex-internee arrived in Hampstead two days later. To the horror of the whole Dutt-Pauker family he proved to be a Protestant extremist, Tommy McGroan, a fierce-looking character who stamped up the drive of Marxmount unabashed by the splendour of its flower-beds and cedared lawns to greet its Marxist chatelaine at the door with a raucous, heavily back-vowelled shout of "Up King Billy!"

He was followed next day by his wife and ten ferocious, red-headed children, and the whole family quickly installed themselves in parts of the former servants' wing not already occupied by Chilean Marxist refugees. Not that they kept to their own quarters for long.

A non-stop, open-ended dialogue on political activism (with practical demonstrations by McGroan) followed. Had not Bert Brecht Mao Che Odinga, Deirdre's bearded Maoist child, himself a notable activist, hit on the idea of boring the McGroans off the premises by non-stop reading of Stalin's Collected Works, they would probably be there to this day.

Keep out!

People ask me why it is that Dr Kissinger, in his continual circling of the globe, has never set foot in this column. The reason, of course, is that the prodigious prestidigitating Doctor was declared a prohibited immigrant some years ago.

But only last month, it is suspected, Dr Kissinger, on one of his orbiting journeys, may have flown over a remote mountainous corner of the column on his way from somewhere to somewhere else. At any rate reports reached the capital later, signalled by heliograph, that the sky had been darkened for 10 minutes, as though by a partial eclipse of the sun, while hordes of frogs of a species hitherto unknown in that region, invaded peasants' cottages and even tried, vainly of course, to enter a church.

The columnar defence forces were alerted and a squadron of balloons, accompanied by a few Blériot Mark II bi-planes, was immediately sent up. They were unable to intercept the Doctor (if it was indeed he), and the intruding aircraft made its escape at high speed over the frontier into the neutral territory of Latest Wills.

Ancient wrongs

A large group of men, women and children describing themselves as Aztecs suddenly occupied a public reference library in Victoria Road, Nerdley (Staffs) yesterday afternoon, seizing several elderly men as hostages as they drowsed over copies of the *International Computer Annual* and the *British Journal of Banausics*. So far they have defied all efforts to persuade them to leave.

The group, who wear feathered headgear, leather jackets, jeans and gym shoes decorated with Aztec ideograms, claim to be descended from the Aztec colonists who according to tradition occupied parts of the great Midland forest in the Dark Ages, after crossing the Atlantic in stone boats. They believe that one of these colonies occupied the site of the present library.

"We claim this territory as inalienably Aztec for ever," stated Aztec leader Royston Vibes, 27, a ninth-year sociology student at Nerdley University whose home is in South Shields. "We also demand payment of a lump sum in compensation for the wrong done to our forefathers, as well as free heating, lighting, water, sewerage services, cooking facilities and supplies of food and drink in perpetuity."

"As Aztecs," added Fred Tove, 35, another sociology student, "we condemn this unjust consumerised society and demand the release of the Shrewsbury Two, an end to internment in Ireland and the withdrawal of British troops from Ulster."

So far the authorities have taken no action to dislodge the group, though Insp. J. R. Inkwell, 41, of Nerdley Special Branch, has warned the Aztec leaders that human sacrifice, particularly on the scale practised by their forebears, is illegal in this country.

On the motoring front

At a meeting of leaders of the militant Motorists' Liberation Front yesterday, J. Bonington Jagworth, chief of the MLF, highly praised a financier who, finding the entrance to his garage blocked by a Rover, drove his own Jensen Interceptor into it and was fined for causing damage.

Jagworth, though a Boggs Super-Oaf man himself, holds that the owner of a Jensen Interceptor has "inalienable rights" over less powerful cars. He suggested that the Financier be awarded the Order of the Golden Crankshaft, the MLF's highest honour.

Not for the first time, Royston Cylinder, leader of the so-called "Young Turks" in the MLF, demurred. In a quiet but closely

reasoned speech he argued, "with respect," that Jagworth's attitude not only "smacked of élitism" but revealed "inherent contradictions" in his mental transmission system.

In the present automobilist situation, he went on, the correct line to take was the fundamental equality of all cars, whether they were Jensen Interceptors, Boggs Super-Oafs or even Nibbs Snail three-wheelers. Only thus could a united front of motorists be brought into being.

In spite of Jagworth's frowns, his empurpling face and furious gulping of "BGA" from his personal silver-mounted hub-cap, there were a few murmurs of agreement from some of the delegates at this implied challenge to the Leader's authority.

Is an ideological rift developing in the MLF? Cylinder has frequently declared his absolute loyalty to his Chief. But his pale, fanatic's face, with its deep-sunk lines of dialectic, to say nothing of the small red booklet he keeps clipped to his log-book, suggest that he may have certain plans of his own.

The meeting broke up with the fervent singing of "Windscreen-wipers of My Soul," the MLF anthem, composed by the Rev. John Goodwheel. But Jagworth, still frowning angrily, could be heard to mutter "Reds in the Inspection Pits," as he topped up his hub-cap again.

For analysis

"A crowd estimated at 50,000 filled New York's Central Park yesterday to celebrate the end of wars in Vietnam and Cambodia. Organised by a coalition of peace groups, the crowds heard calls for new policies to make future Vietnams impossible. And Joan Baez, the peace activist, describing the orphan airlift as 'an awful sham,' urged that they be returned to Indo-China" (news report).

It would take up too much space to analyse in detail what makes this passage so peculiarly nauseating. But to cut it short, there is, firstly, the spectacle of 50,000 people in America—who can say what proportion of fools, duped idealists or plain traitors this crowd contained?—gathering to "celebrate" what amounts to a great defeat for their own country and a further step towards its projected enslavement.

Secondly: the "calls for new policies to make future Vietnams impossible," that is, policies of surrender, conditional at first, finally unconditional, to the advance of Communism—and whether it is always called "Communism" or not is irrelevant —over the whole world.

Thirdly, we have the spectacle of one of the most nauseating and characteristic figures of our Western decadence—a "peace activist," and a rich "showbiz" one at that, urging the return of orphans to Indo-China, where they would have to live under the monstrous system Miss Baez has helped, in her silly little "showbiz" way, to impose there.

I would urge that she and all the other Baezes and Fondas and Redgraves of the West be sent to Indo-China themselves, were it not that the Communists themselves would soon find them propaganda work to do elsewhere. Better to employ American space-technology for a useful purpose; the construction of a giant "multiphase" rocket into which all these people could be crammed and blasted off in the general direction of Alpha Centauri.

Can I help you?

Dear Clare Howitzer—Both Freddine, my husband (I mean my man, of course) and myself are keen members of our local Women's Lib Workshop, where we spend every evening, when we are not experimenting with multimedia encounter group techniques, trying to think of new ways in which women are being discriminated against.

We are now very nearly running out of material and there are periods of silence, punctuated by fits of coughing and sneezing (obviously of psychosomatic origin) which are getting on everybody's nerves. Last night Freddine fairly put his foot in it by saying that men ought to have the right to be Lesbians, otherwise they should stop doing equal shares of the washing-up as a meaningful gesture of dissent.

Later, on the way back to our commune (we are certified bisexual squatters) we nearly came to blows when I tried to enter a "men's" public lavatory and Freddine shouted that if I said just once more that Women had the Right to Choose he would reassume his original name of Fred and demand the right to stop wearing children's clothes and spend his evenings in the local pub in future.

Is he turning into a fascist, racist, chauvinist reactionary? I am at my wits' end. (Greer Pilchard, Turgis Hill, London).

Clare Howitzer replies: You must remember, Greer, that you are not alone. There are thousands of liberated women facing the same problem. As your letter suggests that you can read and write, why not write a best-seller about your personal struggle? Although you may think the market for books about Women's Lib has already been cornered, and the field thoroughly worked out, I believe there is still big money to be made if you set about it the right way.

If you will write to me again, enclosing s.a.e., I can recommend a good publicity agent.

Operation moderation

Gen. Sir Frederick Nidgett, the veteran war hero and distinguished public servant who has been called "Britain's man of bone and iron," is said to be planning to form a "private army" which will go into action immediately in what are known as "certain eventualities."

When I called on the "Tiger" at his rhododendron-infested Godalming home yesterday, I found a state of very tight security. A small, bald, elderly man with steel-rimmed spectacles whom I felt I had met before somewhere (the Western Desert? Arakan? The British Museum Reading Room?) opened the door and gave me as keen a scrutiny as extreme presbyopia allowed before showing me into the General's study.

"Take a pew," said the great man instantly, half turning from a large map-table on which he was moving pins, flags, dice, obsolete coins and miniature liqueur bottles in a purposeful, dynamic way.

I sat down. He stood opposite me now, hands behind his back, still straight as a ramrod, the piercing blue eyes in the teak-like face staring into space as compellingly as ever.

"It's all tremendously hush-hush as yet," he said. "I expect you've gathered that already." I nodded. "As I see it," he went on, emphasising his points with the jabbing forefinger which once struck terror into Jerry and Eyetie alike, "as I see it, the whole shooting-match boils down to this. The moderates have got to take a hand.

"Your average moderate is a pretty moderate sort of chap. Are you with me so far?" I nodded. "What he lacks is *positive* moderation. What he needs is moderate stiffening. That's where my show comes in. I'm going to call it the Moderate Commando Force—'Modcomforce' for short.

"These are early days yet. But offers of help from moderates all over the country are pouring in like a dog's breakfast. Soon I'll have a body of moderates, with moderate guts, initiative, vision, leadership and, above all, sheer moderate physical and mental fitness, ready to go anywhere at any time and do anything in moderation.

"Your common or garden Briton may be a bit of a grouser, a scrimshanker, even a bit of a bolshie and a bit of a leadswinger. But at heart he's a moderate. Give him the real moderate lead he's waiting for and he'll hit inflation—with all its attendant ills—for six and give it a moderate kick in the right place that'll keep it bouncing for a fortnight.

"Now is the time for all good men not only to come to the aid of the party but to stand up and be counted. You pays your penny and takes your choice. What you lose on the swings you lose on the roundabouts. Any questions?" he suddenly barked in a voice which nearly had me out of my seat and standing at attention.

A smile seemed to hover for an instant about his knitted Tailoring Corps tie, as he held out a firm hand. "Remember," he said, "softly softly catchee monkey. And now good morning to you, and cracking good moderate hunting, whoever I may be."

Funeral

Dublin (or Baile Atha Cliath, as the late Eamonn de Valera would have preferred it to be called), though a city of funerals, of black-clad figures forever shuffling through its streets in tribute to some national hero, can never have seen a funeral like his.

It was a symbolic funeral. De Valera died in extreme old age at the very moment when that old dream which occupied all his active life—the dream of an independent Irish nation—has turned to a squalid, fantastic and thoroughly up-to-date nightmare. He fought and killed, but he did not plant bombs to kill without discrimination.

Did he know before his death that everything he dreamed—and it was not ignoble, that dream of an Ireland of small communities, Irish-speaking, Catholic, traditional, standing apart from the modern world—had failed and gone to ruin; that the Irish Republic is now less "Irish," more cosmopolitan, more assimilated to un-Gaelic modernity than it was at its foundation?

It is said that de Valera once declared he would rather have an Ireland Gaelic-speaking and poor than an Ireland rich but speaking the language of the English oppressor. In this he was wholly consistent. Language is the one supreme, unchallengeable symbol of nationality, and without the Irish language Ireland at best can be only half a nation.

What does that mean to most Irish people now? How many citizens of the Republic, how many who followed in de Valera's funeral procession, know that his funeral was also the funeral of his dream?

Beyond our ken

Mrs Thatcher's suggestion that Conservative members of trades unions should learn their union rules and beat the Leftists at their own game has caused some amusement in the Amalgamated Holeborers' Union, particularly in its Office of Dogmatics and Rule Book Exegesis.

The AHU Rule Book, a volume of more than 2,000 pages closely printed in double columns, is about as long as the Bible, the Koran, the Book of Mormon and "War and Peace" combined.

There are also The Commentaries, which have accumulated since the time of the Soup Hales Martyrs, transported to Nerdley in 1821 for forming an illegal combination. They are now about the same length as the Rule Book itself.

It is unlikely, to say the least, that any member of AHU would be a Tory voter or that he would be allowed to go on boring holes (the union operates a closed, indeed bolted, chained and double-locked shop) if he were discovered to be one.

But even if he escaped detection, the chances of his mastering the Rules and Commentaries are so slight as to be virtually non-existent. In complexity and subtlety, it has been well said, they make the writings of Wittgenstein seem like a vicarage tea-party.

Only the learned doctors of the Office of Dogmatics itself, a hereditary caste descended from Habakkuk Luggage (1779-1890), a radical schoolmaster in the West Midlands, are capable of grappling with problems which exist (or do not exist) at the very extremities of human thought.

Central

In a report just published the trustees of the National Gallery suggest that it may be unwise to honour a great artist with an exhibition of all his best works under one roof, where they may be threatened not merely with attacks by solitary madmen or fanatics, as in former times, but by fully organised, up-to-date, politically-motivated terrorists.

Reg Fork, "Way of the World" Art Critic, comments: One great British living artist whose masterpieces could be collected and exhibited under one roof with perfect confidence is John Gasby. A big retrospective exhibition of his work is long overdue.

Gasby, now 40, started as a leader of the "rubbishist" school. His first major works were in fact huge collections of rubbish, spreading over several acres. Some examples, such as his masterpiece "Rubbish Dump IV," exhibited at an open air show near Nerdley in 1960, incorporated derelict buildings, with people living inside them.

In his second, or "destructivist" period, Gasby worked on a smaller scale, producing more densely concentrated junk-collections which included powerful steel springs and other devices, ensuring that any vandal who attacked them would regret it.

His later works of this period are not only "destructivist" but "aggressivist," that is, they do not wait to be attacked when they sense a hostile presence, but "come out fighting with everything they've got, baldheaded and with no holds barred" ("Gasby: Catalogue Raisonné," by Julian Glasse-Derkeley, 1969).

In the work he is doing now Gasby emerges as the first purely "terrorist" artist. His oeuvre, minatory, exuding an impacted "fear," chaos-orientated yet firmly directionated both in function and image, smashing (as in his huge, cast-iron "Handbag," 1974), planally yet with a glottal, otiose tonality through our imploded consciousness, can now be seen as massively and hermeneutically central to the art of our time.

Norman the Good
28 May, 2115

In Good King Norman's Golden Time, everybody without exception is a member of a trade union. King Norman himself is not merely a member of the Association of Monarchical Workers and Allied Trades but is *ex officio* general secretary of the union and Father of the Chapel of the Bevindon Council Palace Branch.

He is also, in his capacity as Assistant Supervisor, Rationing (Dried Fruits) at the local food office, a member of the National Union of Public Executives. This situation has long been a matter of dispute between the two unions, and Fred Carapace, the energetic general secretary of NUPE, has several times threatened to direct his members to withdraw their labour unless King Norman agrees to merge AMWAT with the larger union.

This King Norman cannot do, for two reasons. First, the separate existence of AMWAT is guaranteed by the Socialist constitution, and second, the Queen Gran has threatened to hit both King Norman and Mr Carapace over the head with her stubby umbrella ("and that'll be just a first instalment") if the King shows any signs of weakening.

This is only one of King Norman's union troubles. AMWAT is, of course, a closed shop to which every member of the Socialist Royal Family must belong, but Duke Len of Erdington for a long time held out against this before he grumblingly agreed to join.

His persistent lateness in paying his dues and absence even from mandatory meetings are a matter of public concern, and at the last meeting he attended he spent the whole four hours swigging fortified light ale and noisily munching onion-flavoured potato crisps, finally slumping unconscious to the ground.

The Duke is, from the union's point of view, "a right pain in the neck" (Queen Doreen's phrase) in more ways than one. At the last meeting of the Bevindon Council Palace Chapel there was a heated discussion as to whether Miss Tracy Binns, 26, the blonde Canvey Island coiffeuse (she runs the Chez Elaine Coffeurama) who is the latest in the Duke's endless succession of mistresses, should or should not be a member of AMWAT.

King Norman, whose sense of duty to the union overrode his concern for moral standards, argued that she should be in membership because she was an Allied Trade. But the Queen Gran, raising her handbag threateningly and using expressions which cannot be printed in a column intended for family reading, declared she was "adamantly opposed." At the moment a Royal Socialist deadlock reigns.

Provincial news

"Way Of The World" Reporter

Allegations that members of the Stretchford Municipal Symphony Orchestra were permanently drunk during their recent tour of Belgian coastal resorts have caused seething anger in the orchestra and a violent public controversy which shows no signs of abating.

It was Mr Fred Klopstock, the orchestra's managing director (he is also manager of Stretchford United football club and sometimes seems to find it difficult to separate the two rôles), who sparked off the controversy when he alleged that even the lady harpist, Miss Kay Gristle, had been "under the influence" during a four-hour performance of Mahler's Symphony No. 13 ("the Intolerable") in Ostend.

It was, he said, "a beer-stain on Stretchford's musical reputation and a travesty of what was intended to be a triumphant tour 'showing the flag' as a prelude to a big export drive of Stretchford-made trombones to Belgium. Now those high hopes lie in mocking ashes. It is a tragedy for English football."

Members of the orchestra themselves tell a different story. "Considering," said tympanist Len Gosparrow, 47, "that we were put up, often six to a room, in low-grade boarding-houses and that we got hardly anything to eat during the whole tour except when some kind Belgians threw us the odd 'croque-Monsieur' and watched us scramble for it, it's not surprising we looked drunk.

"Look, chum," put in principal 'cellist Frank Trambe, 62, "you try playing Mahler's bleeding No. 13 on an empty stomach, with your 'cello barely held together with string and rubber bands, and with old Gastropodi, our conductor, 81, falling off his rostrum from sheer fatigue every few bars and see how sober *you'd* look."

That went home.

Changing times

Local government affairs are much in the news. Some people seem to think there are too many local government officials and that they are overpaid.

Things were certainly different in the days of Alderman Food-botham, the 25-stone, crag-visaged, grim-booted, iron-watch-chained perpetual chairman of the Bradford City Tramways and Fine Arts Committee, and for many years Lord Mayor.

There must be people still living who remember the local government hiring fairs which were held every Monday morning in Town Hall Square, in the shadow of the vast smoke-blackened building with its bell-booming towers piercing the rainy skies (and indeed, as some believed, actually precipitating the rain.

People used to take their children to the hiring fair for a treat. Long lines of would-be local government officials, or "servants" as they were called, stood waiting on the greasy cobbles, some in thread-bare serge suits, some in patched mackintoshes hardly concealing the meagre woollen vests and long under-pants which, with split yet pathetically polished boots, barely served to cover their nakedness, yet all without exception wearing the regulation bowler-hat, however holed, brimless, charred or even bandaged it might be.

There was a long gasp from the crowd and the passing trams stilled their bells in awe as the Great Alderman himself, wearing his chain of office, emerged from the Town Hall with his entourage. Then he would go along the lines of waiting men, occasionally stopping to poke a likely-looking young accountant in the shanks with his stick, or peer into an open mouth, or address a stern yet kindly word to some veteran ledger-clerk or departmental sub-head who had known better days.

Sometimes a desperate applicant for work would sink to his knees in supplication ("Purgatrovd, Sir, widower, Sir; eighteen children and a drunken aunt to support"). The great man was unmoved. His duty to the City was all. Only the best men were taken on.

At last the choice was made. The lucky few were bidden to report next day at 6 a.m. to start work on the basic salary of 14s. 6d. for a 75-hour week; the rest shuffled away in the rain, some in quiet despair, a few with angry gestures, dashing bowler hats or false teeth to the ground.

Men stood to attention, women curtsied, children watched round-eyed as the Alderman, with measured tread, his entourage at a respectful distance, slowly strode up the mighty, rain-glistening steps of the Town Hall and passed through the lofty Gothic portals.

1976

The right to know

Mr Harold Wilson is reported to have become angry when questioned about the number of SAS men who have allegedly been sent to Northern Ireland, and to have spoken of "criminal misrepresentation of the facts." He should be ashamed rather than angry. In a democracy the people have the right to know full details of all military dispositions made on their behalf.

To set the people's minds at rest—and also to anticipate revelations from any Leftist "group of journalists" who may be interested and to help members of the IRA and terrorists in general—I can state authoritatively that *only one* SAS man has been sent over.

His name is Sgt. Ron Marzipan, 65, and his Army number is 17WP27600279. He is 5ft. 2in. tall, of slim build, dyed hair receding, drawn features, blue serge suit, grey trilby hat with stained band, mole on left shoulder blade, furtive manner, frayed gym shoes, one sock holed at heel, West Midland accent.

Like all members of the dreaded force to which he belongs, Sgt. Marzipan is skilled in slow-motion karate, living off the country, "holing up" at bus stops and other key-points and in all the latest techniques of counter-insurgency. He collects cigarette-butts and is a stylish but inaccurate darts-player.

His home address (at which his wife, Brenda, 62, and his brother-in-law, Len Hamster, 76, are now living) is 482 Haldane Way, Nerdley (Staffs). He reached Ulster last Friday and can be found most days, during opening hours, at the Finn MacCoul Bar and Off-Licence, 473 Klopstock Road, Croydonards, Edg-warehamilton, Co. Down.

Further details on request.

Mystery chaos bid

"Way of the World" Reporter

The moving scenes at Heathrow when the Concorde took off for its flight to Bahrein were also enacted in less fortunate parts of the country:

In the Stretchford conurbation, crowds estimated at 100,000, many of them weeping and carrying portable television sets, rushed about the streets or climbed rooftops in the vain hope of catching a glimpse of the great machine even at a distance of more than a hundred miles. One man, wearing a white sheet and a beaked cardboard head-dress, leaped from a seventh-storey window, yelling: "I'm a Concorde" and according to eye witnesses, glided to the ground unharmed.

At Stretchford Airport, which is normally avoided by aircraft because of subsidence on the weed-grown, baked-bean-tin-littered

runways, a crowd estimated at 110,000 watched as Paul Ohm, the well-known Edgbaston amateur technologist, wheeled his own home-made Concorde on to the famous No. 2 Runway, scene of so many dramatic events in aviation history.

Ohm, who believes everybody should help Britain by building his own Concorde, gave a cheery thumbs-up sign as he climbed on to the flight-deck, followed by civic dignitaries, co-pilot Air Marshal (formerly Group Captain) "Jumbo" Goth-Jones of the Stretchford County Borough Air Force, and glamorous blonde air-hostess Cheryl Toast, 18, wearing a nine-piece off-white narcocryl uniform with turquoise revers cut on the bias and Concorde-shaped wedge-heeled sandals so high that her head, with bouffant hair-do, had to be accommodated in a special "bulge," as it is technically called, in the roof.

As the only reporter allowed on the flight-deck I watched, fascinated, as Ohm manipulated the gleaming instrument-panel with over 2,000 levers, buttons and dials, five manuals and 12 supersonic hydrants, while Cheryl rapidly served, over and over again, a meal fit for the gods—smoked salmon, iced Yorkshire pudding, smoked cigars in aspic, light ale, champagne, what you will.

We could hear the crowd cheering behind us as they reeled back, choking enthusiastically, from the black fantastically evil-smelling smoke pouring from the sixteen mighty bunsenised exhausts.

We waited, tense and relaxed, as the needle on the cough-meter climbed steadily towards "Cough One." Ohm gave another thumbs-up sign. "It is a time for greatness," he stated calmly. We were earthborne!

Tomorrow: Through the "Cough" Barrier.

It must not be

A man has been sent to prison for 12 months for selling large quantities of obscene magazines and films. This is a sad let-down for those who believe that pornography has therapeutic value.

One cannot help feeling sorry for those earnest-looking people, soberly dressed and bearing the obvious marks of intellectual distinction, we must all have seen standing about in little groups outside therapeutic cinemas, discussing the social and historical significance and therapeutic value of the film—"Afternoon Teas of Lust," perhaps, or "Boiling Virgins"—they have just been watching.

Notebooks are brought out, textbooks consulted, many a weighty argument is put forward, only to be confuted by a weightier.

"But surely the Emperor Heliogabalus—"In a masturbatory situation—" "Yes, but it's a question of hermeneutics—" "Dr Kenneth Tynan has argued—" "Exegesis, my foot—the spatio-temporal significance of the scene where—."

Sometimes the learned throng will become so excited by their discussion that some policeman, who has been watching them with a tolerant smile, may eventually say (respectfully, of course, and with full knowledge that he cannot match even one of them in learning or intellectual depth): "Come along, ladies and gentlemen, don't you think you'd all be more comfortable in your libraries at home?"

Are such people to be deprived not merely of therapeutic but of intellectual nourishment?

Trouble at Marxmount

There has long been an ideological rift in the Dutt-Pauker family. Mrs Dutt-Pauker herself and her daughter Deirdre support the Soviet Russian line, whereas Deirdre's bearded activist little son, Bert Brecht Mao Che Odinga and Gjoq, the Albanian au pair girl, owe ideological allegiance to Peking.

The other day yells of anger were heard coming from the nursery wing at Marxmount, the Hampstead thinker's mansion beside the Heath. Going to investigate, Deirdre found that a secondary rift had opened up. Bert had not only accused Gjoq of supporting the discredited Chinese leader Teng Hsiao-ping but also of "capitalist roading" and favouring "Khrushchev's goulash paradise."

The hot-tempered Albanian girl had put him across her knee and given him a sound spanking, only to be called a "neo-revisionist dwarf" and "adventurist" monster. Deirdre rebuked Gjoq for her reactionary methods of punishment, whereupon the Maoist pair, temporarily united, turned on her and drove her out with shouts of "running dog of the Kremlin imperialist clique!"

They then returned to their own dispute, Bert hastily scrawling a "big character" message on the day-nursery wall which unfortunately cannot be reproduced in a column intended for family reading by the fireside.

Nature Diary

by "Redshank"

I see that road safety experts are trying to devise a more efficient type of crash helmet and are studying the woodpecker, which as everyone knows can hammer away with its beak for hours without apparent harm to its skull.

Any human being who tried to do this, Dr Genge, our local sawbones, tells me, would finish up with a severe headache, if not concussion. Quite a few local bird-watchers and ornithologists have tried it as an experiment, which accounts for the large number of people one sees staggering about in a dazed condition, bumping into trees or collapsing in thatched bus-shelters.

Woodpeckers are probably more common here than in most parts of England, and the concerted noise they make on a fine spring day—perhaps a hundred of them at a time—is so loud that a lot of us have taken to wearing ear-plugs.

However, the woodpecker, with his gay plumage, his harsh yet melodious call and his keen sense of humour (rare among birds) is a popular creature. In his cottage down Grumb Lane way Old Fred Clegg, a former school-master, keeps an unusually large green woodpecker, Jim, as a pet and seems not to mind having holes drilled into his few bits of furniture.

Worried by possible damage to Jim's skull and brain-centres (if any) from his incessant pecking, Old Fred has designed a small crash helmet for his pet, though what effect it has on the rare occasions when he can persuade the bird to wear it I cannot say.

When I last passed that way I noticed that Fred (he was handicrafts instructor at Old Miss Blethers's Dame School), had built a small motorcycle for Jim and was out in his garden trying to teach him to ride it (wearing his crash helmet, of course, as the law demands). In the fine March weather with a nip in the air and clouds hurrying in all directions in a pale blue sky, it made a real picture, redolent of the old English ways of our forefathers which still linger on if you know where to look for them.

Farewell

Valedictory messages to Mr Harold Wilson on his retirement have been pouring into the columnar premises in such enormous quantities during the last two days that at one stage even our changeless routine—the tradition of uncounted ages—seemed threatened.

However, our works manager, Mr Hargreaves, tells me that he and his loyal operatives have now "broken the back" of the problem, and processing in the sheds is back to normal. I have space to quote only three—a fair sample—of the messages we have received:

"Farewell, a long farewell to all thy greatness. Farewell, thou art too dear for my possessing. Ae fond kiss, and then we sever" (from "All at the Oxford Dictionary of Quotations").

"Si monumentum requiris, circumspice" (from "146 retired schoolteachers, Nerdley").

"Wilson! You shall be flung like a discarded, broken puppet of capitalism, on a tit for tat basis, on the dust-heap of history" (from "The 12,000-strong workers, herdsmen and creative intelligentsia of the North-North-Eastern Roumelian People's Republic," c/o Box 4369).

I add a reminiscence of my own. One day in the early Twenties I was driving my Hispano-Suiza somewhere near Huddersfield, possibly on the way to Chatsworth, with my mechanic, T. E. Lawrence (a bit of a mystery man, as I recall), in the passenger-seat.

Suddenly we came to a level-crossing, one of the old hand-operated kind. As I pulled up, a barefoot lad of six or so, poorly but decently dressed, with well-brushed silver hair and smoking a briar pipe, dashed forward and opened the gate.

"A smart lad that. Should go far," I remarked, flinging the boy a half-crown which he caught with remarkable dexterity, at the same time knuckling his forehead, as I drove on. But Lawrence, whose thoughts, as often, seemed far away, made no reply, and until long afterwards I thought no more of the incident.

What the papers say

In a thoughtful leader the *Feudal Times* and *Reactionary Herald* discusses what it calls "tasteless and inept" parallels which some readers have tried to draw between the situation of the rebellious colonies in North America and that of Mr Ian Smith's Government in Rhodesia.

"It has been suggested that in the event of Cuban forces invading the so-called United States of America—now a distinct possibility—this organ would at once 'change its tune' and, dropping its demand for the rebels' return to their British allegiance, call loudly on the Government to help our 'kith and kin.'

"Nothing could be further from the truth. In the first place the stock of the North American colonists has by this time become so greatly diluted by alien elements that it is doubtful whether they can now claim any considerable degree of kinship with us.

"In the second place, the Cubans are themselves, properly speaking, rebellious subjects of the Spanish Empire. This organ has never acknowledged that their so-called independence (brought about, ironically enough, through aggression by the North American colonists themselves in the disgraceful episode of the so-called 'Hispano-American War' at the close of the last century) has or can have any legitimate basis.

"To complicate matters yet further, Cuba itself, as many will recall, was a possession of the British Crown during the years 1762 and 1763, after which it was returned to Spain in exchange for the territory called Florida—a settlement which not all of us, whatever the subsequent course of events, thought judicious at the time.

"Far from being a disaster, an invasion of the rebel North American colonies by rebel Cuban forces might prove a blessing in disguise, a catalyst, making possible a general settlement between the British and Spanish Governments, by which all the rebels concerned, of whatever persuasion, would return to their respective allegiances—a most happy conclusion to a long-standing and until now seemingly intractable problem."

A goodly heritage

The English Tourist Board is hoping to attract American visitors to selected parts of the country which have associations with the United States. "American Heritage Trails" will be marked with special signposts directing tourists to such places as Plymouth, whence the Mayflower sailed, and Alnwick (the second Duke of Northumberland is said to have been an honorary member of the Mohawk tribe).

"WAYFARER" writes: It is to be hoped the Tourist Board will include No. 56 Savannah Road, off Boggis Hill High Street in North London. Here, behind an ordinary-looking sex shop, can be found the only Southern Slave Plantation still left in England (or for that matter anywhere else).

The plantation was founded in the mid-18th century, owing to an administrative muddle in Bristol and the misdirection of a small consignment of slaves bound for America to what was then the sleepy hamlet of Boggis Hill, where they became, through a series of coincidences, the property of a local eccentric, Elihu Jones, evidently a man of suggestible nature.

A fine white porticoed Colonial-style house was soon erected and filled with chandeliers, rocking-chairs, brass spittoons and other appurtenances. But since it proved impossible to grow cotton the slaves, who in any case, when another administrative muddle was revealed, turned out to be Scotsmen from Glasgow, had a very easy time of it, lounging about the fields, eating imported sweet corn, fried chicken and molasses, drinking a mixture of mint julep, brandy and bourbon, and composing spirituals, said to be of indifferent merit, none of which, perhaps fortunately, have survived.

The advent of American independence seems to have made little difference to the Jones Estate, but as the 19th century advanced and London closed round, its area gradually contracted until only one small cotton field remained. In the American Civil War, Elihu Jones III declared for the Confederates and made himself Colonel, but in spite of denunciations by John Bright, who urged unemployed Lancashire cotton operatives to occupy the plantation, it was left alone.

At the end of the war, the slaves were nominally freed, but to their former owner's disgust they refused to leave. Their numbers were gradually thinned by alcoholic poisoning, cirrhosis of the liver, fried chicken pox and other traditional scourges.

Today all that remains of the Jones Plantation is the house in Savannah Road, which still has one decaying column and part of a verandah, where the present Col. Elihu Jones, aged 86, lives with the last freed slave, Mr. Angus McGeikie, 127, who may be heard on summer evenings, as the sun goes down over the Boggis Hill branch of the North-Eastern Gas Board showrooms, crooning his favourite spiritual, "I belong tae Glasgae", vainly trying to accompany himself on a stringless banjo.

How to Get There: Apply to the English Tourist Board.

Mystery

Mr. Hugh Scanlon, president of the Engineering Workers, asks why newspapers, instead of interfering in union elections, do not expose the role of international financial speculators who threaten "the democratic fabric of our nation.

"At their whim the value of the pound is slashed, threatening the international trade on which this country depends, while they make off with their ill-gotten gains. Like some disgusting carrion crows these un-elected money barons hover over our society."

Now Mr. Scanlon may not be a reliable authority on electoral practices or on democratic fabrics. But in suggesting that some attention might be paid to the activities of international financial speculators he may be speaking for many more people, of all shades of opinion, than he supposes.

Here is a mystery. It is not so much a matter of carrion crows, of the un-elected money barons of Communist legend, making off with their bulging bags of ill-gotten gains, as of demi-gods who conduct their unintelligible operations in the clouds above our heads, remote, supernal, not to be questioned.

Politicians like Mr. Healey tell the people of this country that these mysterious operations, by affecting the value of the pound, affect the lives of all. But they do not tell us how these operations are carried out; by whom; or for what purpose, temporary or ultimate.

Not only do politicians fail to answer these questions; they seem to assume it will never occur to anybody to ask them. If, as appears, the questions are of such importance, isn't this a false and even dangerous assumption?

Norman the Good

26 May 2116

The strike (or lock-out) at the Council Palace at Bevindon New Town is growing in complexity. To put it as briefly as possible, the dispute arose yesterday when King Norman, who is, of course, *ex officio* general secretary of the Association of Monarchical Workers and Allied Trades and Father of the Chapel of the Council Palace Branch, agreed to work overtime at the local food office, where he is an Assistant Supervisor, Rationing (Dried Fruits).

This meant that when the new Gombolan Ambassador, a nephew of Dr Ngrafta, the 115-year-old President of Gombola, arrived in the State Double-Decker Bus to present his credentials, the only Royal Personage available to receive him was Duke Len of Erdington (Queen Doreen and the Queen Gran were busy at the laundromat, Princess Shirley was working in her boutique at Harold Wood and the other members of the Socialist Royal Family were occupied in various ways).

The Duke, as it happened, was drinking light ale in the lounge and chatting easily with his current mistress, Miss Tracy Binns, 26, the blonde Canvey Island coiffeuse, when the Ambassador arrived. Confusion followed as Miss Binns ran into the dinette to hide and the Duke, rising easily to his feet to greet the Ambassador, slumped easily to the ground.

When Queen Doreen and the Queen Gran returned with their bags of washing, they found that the Ambassador had flung his credentials on the floor and driven off in a huff, declaring that a rupture of diplomatic relations or a demand for an extra £450 million in aid, or both, would follow this affront to the dignity of his country.

The two Royal Socialist ladies immediately announced that they would withdraw their labour with effect from forthwith. Duke Len, who was now smiling foolishly, was forced to do likewise after the Queen Gran, wielding her stubby umbrella and outsize handbag, had chased Miss Binns, whose claim to be a member of AMWAT has never been ratified, off the premises.

When King Norman arrived home late in the evening he found his way barred by the Queen Gran herself, constituting one of the most formidable picket lines in the history of the Trade Union movement. An unofficial strike had been declared and our Socialist Monarch, feebly protesting that this was in breach of Rule 489 (a) in the AMWAT rule book, was nonetheless forced to spend an uncomfortable night in the leaking Royal Socialist Caravan, which is parked in the palace garden.

Today the Queen Gran, who has appointed herself head of the unofficial strike committee, stated that there was no light to be seen at either end of the Royal Socialist Trade Union tunnel at this moment in time.

Time Machine

"It is necessary to be insensitive or very Left-wing not to feel deeply moved by the tragedy of white Rhodesia, by the mad, grim battle to move the time machine back half a century" (*Evening Standard*).

Time machines, as readers of science fiction know, are tricky things. In the Middle East the State of Israel might be said to be fighting a mad, grim battle to move the time machine back two thousand years.

What sort of battle with the time machine are we fighting in our own country, where all the clocks which have not stopped show different times?

Norman the Good

4 June 2116

There have been further developments in the strike (or lock-out) at the Council Palace at Bevindon New Town.

For the past week the Queen Gran, armed with her stubby umbrella and outsize handbag, has maintained a personal picket-line barring King Norman's entry to the Palace. He has been forced to live in the leaking and insanitary Royal Socialist Caravan in the Palace garden and has been unable to enter the Palace even during the Queen Gran's rare periods of sleep, when she stretches out her considerable bulk across the doorway.

King Norman, in his capacity of Assistant Supervisor, Rationing (Dried Fruits) at the local food office, is also a member of the National Union of Public Executives, whose energetic secretary, Mr Fred Carapace, is threatening to bring out his own members "in sympathy," whether with the Queen Gran or the King is not clear.

Yesterday the King, who had had nothing to eat for several days except for a packet of onion-flavoured potato crisps which Duke Len of Erdington surreptitiously threw down to him from an upper window, went to a local consumerama and bought a deep-frozen individual fruit pie (gooseberry flavour) manufactured at the State Individual Fruit Pie Factory at Nerdley and date-stamped "Eat before August 11, 1984."

Suffering stomach pains soon afterwards the King tried (vainly) to summon a junior medical executive officer, Dr S. Nashtrapati, from the near-by Barbara Castle Memorial Hospital.

All these actions soon became known to the Queen Gran, who at once "blacked" Duke Len, the consumerama, the individual fruit pie factory and the hospital. She thus involved the Union of Consumerama Operatives, the Amalgamated Association of Individual Fruit Pie Workers and the Union of Medical Workers in a multiple inter-union dispute which threatens to bring the economic life of the country, such as it is, to a standstill.

Ever Onwards

An important branch of the race relations industry, the Institute of Race Relations, recommends that "Asian communities" should form self-defence organisations capable of taking direct action in defence of life and property.

"The voices of reason in and out of the black (*sic*) community who counsel us to keep calm are mistaken," says a statement by the Institute.

It is no surprise to learn that some of the funds which support the Institute come from that esteemed body the British Council of Churches, a subsidiary of the World Council of Churches, one of whose spokesman has said that the "freedom fighters" of Africa "kill in a spirit of love."

Dr Spaceley-Trellis, the go-ahead Bishop of Bevindon, has given his full backing to the Institute's view. But he thinks it is too moderate. He is hoping to persuade churchgoers to contribute to a fund to buy arms for the "Asian communities" to defend themselves with.

"This is the only way," Dr Trellis declared vehemently in a sermon he preached in his cathedral the other day, "we can make sure that the predictions of evil men like Enoch Powell, who has said that arms will eventually be used in racial riots, are falsified and shown up for the deliberate attempts at trouble-making that they are."

At Mountwarlock

Mountwarlock Park, in Leicestershire, the "stately home" of the Earl of Mountwarlock, famous for its collection of fabulous monsters, is having a record season. Already, says a spokesman, more than 30,000 people have visited the estate, though it is open only on Fridays, and (another record) more than 5,000 have left in recognisably human shape after their visit.

The present Earl is profoundly conservative. Suggestions by his gifted major domo, Phantomsby, one of the few practising werewolves left in the Midlands, for new attractions to pull in more visitors are invariably turned down.

"Hang it all, Phantomsby," the Earl said the other day, "they've got the safari park, with griffins, basilisks, gorgons, chimerae and what have you; the Deadly Upas Tree; the Bottomless Abyss; Circe's Boutique and Souvenir Shop and the 'Shirt of Nessus' Men's Shop; they've got a good stretch of the Flamin' River Acheron flowin' through the park; what more do the beggars want?'"

Phantomsby, who had been reading reports in the *Morning Post* (supplied by supernatural newsagents) about the craze for hang-gliding, had suggested (with the greatest respect) that this sport might be a useful new feature for Mountwarlock.

"What I had in mind, was an 'Icarus-type' contraption made of some kind of wax or those miracle adhesives you hear of, which would take visitors up into the air, up to a point—" Phantomsby showed his long white incisors in what to anyone but his master would have been an infectious smile.

"I thought Mr Daedalus, the estate-carpenter, might do us a mock-up, my lord," Phantomsby went on persuasively. But the Earl had already turned on his heel with a dismissive gesture, leaving Phantomsby grumbling half-affectionately to himself and trying to work out other methods of solving his increasing worrying supply and nutritional problems on nights of the full-moon.

"Not as nippy on me pins as I used to be," he said as he loped off rather creakingly to his mist-enshrouded quarters.

Nature diary

by "Redshank"

Old ways linger on in our part of the country. There are some who think they linger too long. Where else, for instance, would you find not one but dozens of genuine old hostelries with so many inglenooks that each drinker—be he Shepherd Dick or Poacher Fred or Seth Gummer the Waspkeeper—has his own personal nook—and woe betide the stranger who trespasses thereanent?

But it is not just a matter of ancient hostelries and old customs whose origins are lost in the mists of antiquity, like Dough Tuesday, when all the young women of the neighbourhood present a piece of dough to the man of their fancy, or Shouting Friday, the first in February, when everybody in the village of Angstmans Ambo, from the babe in arms to the oldest inhabitant, goes into the main street and on the stroke of noon shouts as loudly as he can.

There are literally hundreds of ancient customs like these. It is curious, come to think of it, how we find time to attend to anything else, such as tilling the fields, getting in the harvest or carrying on all the other occupations which make up the immemorial procession of the changing seasons.

But stranger still, there is a part of our countryside where, according to legend, no man has ever been—and lived to tell the tale. Surrounded by well-nigh impenetrable thickets of gorse and whin, and stretches of marsh where bullrush and bittern rule unchallenged, the "Moor," as it is called, always in hushed voices, is said to be inhabited by a race, already immemorially old when the Roman came to Britain, of men and women whose sole occupation it is, and always has been, to write nature notes and tales of old times which, legend has it, make puny efforts like mine sound like Old Whitaker's Almanac.

Many are the dark and dreadful stories of these people—if people they be—who were established in their fastnesses before the Picts were even heard of. In four-ale bar and gunroom men still talk of the night of the Great Gale in 1926 when suddenly the heavy oaken door of the "Three Tuns" was flung open and a strange voice was heard above the howling of the wind: "Send a typewriter mechanic—and send one quickly."

We looked from face to face and vice versa. Who would be bold enough to obey the dread summons? We looked long and deep into our pewter pots of ale. Several of us, men of tried and tested courage who in their day had calmly faced angry bull or demented owl, pretended to fall asleep or obsessively counted their small change.

At last Young Fred the Typewriter Mechanic stood up, as we knew he must if we waited long enough. "I'll go." We watched as he opened the door and went out into the night.

He was, of course, never seen again. But years later, on another such night of tempest, a Remington Imperial Upright No. 6, with tell-tale blood-stains on the back-shift key, was found abandoned on Platform Two of Kingston Halibut Station, nigh on 50 miles away!

Fun-commonwealth

"We are a funny Commonwealth, the funniest ever seen...." You can easily supply the second line of this new version of an old song for yourself, and go on from there.

The British Commonwealth of Nations, we were constantly told at one time, and still are told occasionally, is one of the most remarkable and admirable political institutions ever known, an institution so enlightened that it cannot fail to secure us the Moral Leadership of the World, as well as full-hearted acclaim at the Bar of World Opinion.

Remarkable this Commonwealth of Nations certainly is. Two of its original members, India and Pakistan, have twice been at war with each other; on the second occasion, one member, Pakistan, resigned, but the number was kept up by the accession of a new member, Bangladesh. Another very important member, South Africa, had already been forced out.

From time to time various pseudo-States belonging to the Commonwealth, such as Tanzania, have broken off diplomatic relations with Great Britain. Now Great Britain has herself broken off diplomatic relations with the pseudo-State of Uganda, employing all the solemn and dignified procedures and verbal formulae which would be appropriate if, say, she broke off diplomatic relations with a genuine State like New Zealand (which, if agitators like Peter Hain had their way, she would).

What other feats can this remarkable Commonwealth achieve? At one time it was suggested that Great Britain herself should be expelled from it. Unfortunately this did not happen. But even if it had, be sure that the British Commonwealth of Nations would still have gone on shambling through the 20th century and to the end of time. An institution so uniquely and sublimely preposterous can surely never die.

The British Commonwealth is the degenerate heir of the British Empire, an heir whose least affliction is a kind of political delirium tremens. It was George Santayana who said of the British Empire that it would be a black day for the human race when that Empire was "supplanted by scientific blackguards, conspirators, churls and fanatics" (or words to that effect).

He did not foresee that the shadow of the Empire would persist, under a false name, as an idiotic pantomime.

Strange times

Sheikh Iblis Ez Zifti, an Arab sovereign of incalculable wealth, visited the Earl of Mountwarlock's "stately home" in Leicestershire not long ago and was so enraptured by the "wild life park" that he offered to buy the whole place for any sum the Earl cared to mention and transport it lock, stock and barrel to his own country.

Through Phantomsby, his factotum, one of the few practising werewolves still left in the Midlands, the Earl sent a polite refusal. The disappointed Sheikh then offered to buy Phantomsby. But the werewolf, shaking his head, bared his sharp gleaming white incisors in a smile which caused a man whose lightest word, in his own country, is law, to fall back with a cry of terror.

However the Sheikh did not give up hope. The other day a large packing-case arrived at Mountwarlock. When Phantomsby opened it he found an exquisitely engraved incubator of pure gold, with a single roc's egg in it. There was also a letter in Arabic and English in which the Sheikh said he hoped the gigantic bird, when hatched, would thrive at Mountwarlock and prove a useful addition to the fabulous attractions of the estate.

"If there be a paradise on earth," the Sheikh concluded, "it is there, it is there, it is there." He added a few hints on the best methods of rearing and conserving rocs, mainly drawn from passages in the "Arabian Nights."

Phantomsby was far from pleased. "Soft soap," he muttered to himself. "The wily old oriental so-and-so is still after the estate, and then what becomes of Yours Truly? You won't catch me passing my declining years in a Trackless Desert, thank you very much.

"And another thing. This roc, if all they say is true, will be about half a mile long from beak to tail when it's fully grown. The Harpies aren't going to like that." He looked at the enormous egg, in which a sound like a steam-hammer could already be heard.

"Least said, soonest mended." Catching a passing basilisk, Phantomsby ordered it to "do its stuff," and in a trice the largest omelette ever seen in Leicestershire appeared.

It was later served at one of the Dark Ages Banquets in the Great Hall of Phantoms. One visitor, Mrs A. Lemming, 56, a housewife, of Loughborough, complained of a "funny taste" and while walking in the park later on was incinerated by a wyvern's fiery breath.

"Serve the old besom right," was Phantomsby's comment. "Flaming cheek."

Shame on you!

No single sign of the docility and inertia of the people of England alarms and angers me more than their meek acceptance, with scarcely a murmur, however weak and vain, of the Heathian reforms of local government.

"Cursed be he that removeth his neighbour's landmark." By these reforms (and I say nothing here of their disastrous cost in terms of money wasted and the proliferation of superfluous officials) not merely were landmarks removed wholesale, but historic counties were wiped off the map or carved up into bogus new areas reflecting only the vacuity and rootlessness of statisticians and businessmen.

The object of this process, conscious or unconscious (and the mauling of the English counties is only part of it) can only be to unsettle the people and make them uncertain who they are and where they came from, to sever their links with the past and turn them into an inchoate crowd of zombies which officials can more easily hoodwink and control.

It is no accident that Yorkshire, the greatest of English counties, potentially, indeed, a self-sufficient State, should have suffered worst of all from this carving up process. *That* bastion, in itself a provocation to the planners, must fall. Yet here a doubt arises. It may be that the apparent docility of the people is only superficial, and is due to the fact that they are simply ignoring these senseless and abhorrent changes. What Yorkshireman, or any man in his senses for that matter, can really believe that Bowes and Mickle Fell are in County Durham or that Dent and Sedbergh are in "Cumbria?"

Will no English political party promise to restore the ancient counties when it comes to power? When is the Conservative party going to show the slightest sign of being genuinely conservative? Here is an opportunity.

"You can't put the clock back." At least you can try. There is a precedent. One of the plans proposed for France by that great and good man, Marshal Pétain, during the war was the abolition of the departments created by the illegal revolutionary regime at the end of the 18th century and the restoration of the ancient provinces, such as Gascony and Berry. It is true that for various reasons this plan was not put into effect.

Many people will not find this precedent to their liking. But after all, it's the principle that counts, isn't it?

Paradox

The Welsh Language Society is to begin a campaign of "direct action" in protest against the Government's delay in setting up a television channel in the Welsh language. Members may occupy Government property and that of broadcasting authorities, and cause "limited damage" to selected buildings and equipment.

Nobody on earth can wish more fervently than I to see the day when the ancient and noble language of Wales is spoken by every man and woman in that country. I have suggested before now that Welsh should be taught even in English schools, on the ground that without some knowledge of the history of Wales and of its language—are not the Welsh the true heirs of the Romans?—it is impossible to understand the history of Britain itself and what lies at its deepest roots.

But the proposed campaign of the Welsh Language Society is unlikely to help the cause to which it is so sincerely devoted. It will annoy many people in Wales and widen the gap—which some are only too anxious to exploit—which already exists between those who have the happiness of speaking Welsh and those who do not yet speak it or (incredibly) do not even want to speak it.

There is also an inherent paradox in the Language Society's campaign. The Welsh language is certainly being eroded by English television. But would not a Welsh language television service further erode that Welshness of which the Welsh language is an essential part?

Isn't television—a device at best superfluous and shallow, at worst positively evil—a profoundly *un-Welsh* thing in itself? Instead of campaigning for a Welsh language television channel, oughtn't the Welsh Language Movement to campaign for an all-Welsh jamming station which would make it impossible for anyone in Wales to watch any television programmes at all?

Autumn thoughts

In lovely, sex-maniac-haunted Sadcake Park the rain falls mournfully on the maze of paths around the lake, splashing on leaves, yellow, brown and hectic red, which are trodden by the just and the unjust alike and have brought not a few, mostly the former, squelching to the ground with curses as profuse as they are futile.

Only a few maniacs are about today, their grubby mackintoshes, treasured uniform of their profession, buttoned up against the rain. One, straggle-bearded but (strange contrast) with brilliantined hair parted in the middle, wheels a rusty bicycle by the lakeside; from his saddlebag of stained imitation leather protrudes a mouldering, greenish two-pound "family-size" pork pie; with his disengaged hand he shoulders his bicycle pump as if sloping arms.

In the rotting boathouse sits Mr Bloth, custodian of the leaking boats, reading a mildewed copy of volume one of Samuel Smiles's "Lives of the Engineers." He looks up irritably as a strange cry, half peacock scream, half booming, distorted station announcer, comes from the wooded island in the middle of the lake.

It is Mr R. D. Viswaswami, thought to be the only immigrant naked sadhu in this country, who is employed by the Stretchford Council to live in a specially-built hermit's cave of artificial stone and has the status of environmental amenity officer (grade three).

The holy man is angry today because Bloth, absorbed in his reading and deterred by the rain, has forgotten to row over to the island with the Sadhu's copies of the *Guardian* and a Hindi-language magazine full of pictures of Indian film-stars, and, more serious, with a fresh supply of pulse and of the spiritualised white ash he needs for rubbing on his naked body.

With a groan, Bloth rises creakingly to his feet. But the Sadhu, losing patience, has already begun to climb into his sacred inflatable nylon coracle, woven by the thin brown hands of devout women. Evidently he means to paddle over to the mainland to fetch his requirements himself—a rare occurrence which always leads to trouble: the fainting-fits of shop-assistants, major traffic pile ups on treacherous, "distinctly dicey" road-surfaces, or (on one occasion) an unscheduled partial eclipse of the sun which, though it drew a lot of correspondence in the local papers, has never been satisfactorily explained.

You have been warned

There will be no lack of Happenings this Christmas. The Marylou Ogreburg Multi-racial Bread and Marmite People's Dance Theatre Group will be out in force in South London again, concentrating on the Brassgrove Park area.

Marylou Ogreburg, a tall, gaunt, thirtyish woman with big round lenseless spectacles and an unforgettable laugh, comes, like most members of the group, from Dissentville, California. She was one of the famous "Grand Rapids Sixteen" and at one time worked with Ed Yadler.

She uses a combination of dance, mime, dustbin lids, lumps of solidified risotto and mobile "big character" wall-posters to create a uniquely impactful effect of protest and social awareness.

"I kinda want to bring some light and happiness into the awful, awful lives of these poor, underdeprived people in these awful neighbourhood suburbs of your South London who never have a chance of experiencing theatre," she says.

"I kinda want to bring real people's multi-racial theatre into these awful, awful streets and make these kinda dead middle-class British people really and fully aware of what's going on in their country—I mean in Occupied Ireland and spending cuts and this torture of journalists and trade unionists and all the crimes of your awful, awful Establishment."

When the Marylou Ogreburg Group brought street theatre to North London last winter, most people locked themselves into their houses, some reinforcing their doors with sheets of corrugated iron and hiding up the chimney. Those who were caught in the streets had to run for it but not all escaped.

Mystery intruder

Described as a haulage contractor and freelance counsellor on personal problems, Frank Canister, 44, of Prestonpans Road, Lampton-on-Hoke, was charged at Nerdley Magistrates' Court yesterday with failing to keep a dangerous creature, a pterodactyl, under proper control.

Det. Sgt. J. Mackenzie, 41, of Nerdley Special Branch, said that after receiving a number of complaints from Canister's neighbours, he went to investigate and found accused sitting in his

kitchen with the pterodactyl on his knee. The creature appeared to be asleep.

Told that several neighbours had complained of a "reign of terror," Canister said that the pterodactyl, Fred, was perfectly harmless. He was fond of children and often hovered over prams, occasionally snatching off babies' woollen bonnets in a playful sort of way but always returning them without fuss.

Fred also liked to frequent supermarkets. Told that Mrs Linda Wotan, 47, cake and biscuit superintendent at the Hanging Gardens of Babylón Supermarket, one of the Nadirco chain, in Victoria Road, had complained that the pterodactyl had on one occasion taken a packet of ginger nuts (5p off) and flown away without paying, causing panic among old age pensioners, Canister became abusive. Witness then arrested him and after a long struggle with the pterodactyl, in which he sustained contusions and minor damage to the notebook, took him to the station, leaving the creature behind.

The chairman, Dr Ellis Goth-Jones, 61, asked accused how he came to be in possession of a creature which was known to have become extinct several million years ago. Canister, claiming that he was a serving officer in the Veterinary Corps of the Provisional IRA, refused to recognise the court.

Dr F. Gestaltvogel, 55, a psychiatrist at Nerdley General Hospital, said he had examined Canister and found that apart from a morbid terror of telephone directories and a belief that he was a barometer, he was a perfectly normal member of society. He thought that the pterodactyl was a collective hallucination, caused by stress and sexual repression.

Binding Canister over, Dr Goth-Jones said there were several puzzling features in the case, but he could not make a destruction order on an extinct creature and would give accused, who was of previous good character, the benefit of the doubt. He added that much of the trouble was a failure to recognise the importance of higher education in our multi-racial society. But he did not think the introduction of turnstiles and spot checks for pornographic material in supermarkets was necessarily the answer.

Talking point

Every life is like a deck-chair: it may be set up with brisk efficiency; or unstably, its supporting rungs arranged on grooves not parallel; or it may collapse in utter confusion together with its would-be user. But to all at last comes, with his roll of tickets, the Great Deckchairman—Ralph Waldo Emerson.

1977

Correspondence

Sir—Scientists, I note, believe that the Round Table at Windsor, traditionally said to be the original of King Arthur's well-known article of furniture of that ilk, was in fact made in or about the year 1336.

Many people may not be aware that the genuine Round Table of King Arthur, as used by that much respected Monarch and his Knights for dining and conference facilities, is to be found in a house in Inkerman Road, Stretchford, where it is in the custody of those guardians of local tradition, the Men of Stretchford.

As present Secretary of the Men, I can assure you that the Table, which is strongly constructed of what experts have pronounced to be oak, with tasteful mahogany inlays and folding legs on bronze type hinges, making it convenient for packing and transport, is in safe hands.

It bears the names of King Arthur himself and of many of the most prominent Knights in fine gilt lettering. It is in good

condition except for some tureen-shaped stains, evidently caused
by the soup served at Camelot on festive occasions, and some signs
of gnawing at the edges, particularly at the place marked "Sir J. B.
Mordred, Bt."

For those who are interested, we also have several "nests" of
King Arthur's Round Coffee-Tables, whose origins are, of course,
lost in the mists of antiquity and which have always been
something of a "puzzle point" to furniture manufacturers, geom-
etricians and students of social life in the Dark Ages of that ilk.

J. PELMET
Stretchford

March of science

Did man originate in Soup Hales? This, at least, is the theory of
Prof. J. S. Goodbone, head of the Anthropology Department of
Soup Hales University.

He claims that a skull unearthed during a routine "dig" on a site
near the "Star of Bangladesh" Take-Away Curry Institute in
Sebastopol Road is over 1,000 million years old, predating the skull
discovered in Nerdley two years ago by "at least five years" and
making other anthropologists' claims for Africa, Central Asia,
China, Tierra del Fuego, Pateley Bridge and so on as the "cradle of
the human race" look, he says, "pretty silly."

Like Homo Nerdleiensis, Homo Souphaliensis, says Prof. Goodbone, "must have lived in an environment very different from that
of Soup Hales today. Most of it was under water and a modern
man, if he could be transported there, would immediately be struck
by the absence of supermarkets, traffic-lights, bingo halls and
other things we take for granted."

The skull, which is in excellent condition, has one thing in
common with the skull of Homo Nerdleiensis—there is no space in
it for a brain of any kind. Prof. Goodbone believes that "the brain
must have evolved through millions of years in response to
environmental factors, and to the gradual shrinking of Homo
Souphaliensis's unusually large teeth and blockage of the nasal
cavities as a diet of reeds gave way to a diet of giant dandelions
after the tilting of the Continental Shelf and the discovery of
curry, provisionally dated Feb. 14, 102,456 BC."

Protestological note

"Dutch police ousted three youths, allegedly professional demonstrators, from a peace rally for Northern Ireland in Amsterdam yesterday when they chanted 'British troops out of Ireland'" (*Sunday Times*).

The report does not say whether any policemen were electrocuted. But there will be some red faces this morning, as the saying is, at the Rentacrowd factory on the North Circular Road where semi-automated demonstrators are assembled, packed and despatched, at the ease with which the Dutch police were evidently able to identify and neutralise their products.

Rentacrowd's much-heralded "Troops Out of Ireland" model, the pride of the mammoth mob-supplying consortium's backroom boys, has proved nothing but a liability. Some of these models ordered for a recent demonstration in London started chanting "Boots Out!" and one short-circuited and caught fire.

There have also been some unfortunate errors in the invoicing department. The other day two hundred of these demonstrators (possibly ordered for Bangor, Co. Down) turned up in Bangui, capital of the Central African Republic (or Empire, as it now is), shouting "Troops Out of Thailand!" They were driven into the forest by the angry and alarmed inhabitants to be a puzzle, perhaps, for future anthropologists.

Others have been reported, singly or in small groups, at places as far apart as Bogota, Windhoek and Katmandu, and Australian railway passengers claim to have seen them vainly trying to board trains, shouting incoherently, on the Nullarbor Plain.

A spokesman at Crowd House, £145 million London headquarters of Rentacrowd, said that all "Troops Out" models were being called in for examination by experts, but it would be some time "before the headaches are all ironed out. There seems to be some sort of hoodoo at work," he added.

Provincial news

"Way of the World" Reporter

At a "Europe Day" rally Mr Edward Heath (former leader of the Conservative Party) said that if there were any further delay over direct elections to the European Assembly the consequence would be "a shameful humiliation for the British people in the eyes of the rest of the democratic world."

As the full impact of this statement smashed home to the people of the Stretchford Conurbation (and no doubt it was much the same in other parts of the country) many dropped whatever they were doing and, avoiding each others' eyes, hung their heads, sobbing uncontrollably.

Those who were indoors covered themselves with rugs or sacking, or crawled under beds or sofas. Of those who were caught out of doors as the stern message made its way from shamed mouth to humiliated ear, some began running round in circles or gathered in small knots at street corners, gibbering and wailing; some slumped weakly to the ground.

In Inkerman Road, a tall, middle-aged woman carrying an outsize iron handbag marked "Direct Elections to the European Assembly or Death!" rose to her full height like a prophetess of old.

"Shame on you! Shame on you and your children and your children's children! Are you men—or rusty old bicycles? Stand up and look, if you dare, into the reproachful eyes of the rest of the democratic world!"

A few, shamefaced, got up from where they had fallen, then, helpless with laughter, collapsed again.

Discuss

For many people, even those who have never been there, Venice is the most beautiful city in the world; the epitome of European civilisation; without rival and without price.

In the natural course of things, eroded by time, weather, tides, industrial pollution, this bride of the everlasting sea (what treasuries of language have been poured out in celebration of this single city!), must inevitably disappear.

The death of Venice, it is said, is now imminent: only a certain combination of high tides is needed, working together with all the natural and unnatural agencies of decay, and Venice, within a short time, is doomed, either gradually or in sudden disaster, to sink beneath the sea.

It is said that Venice may yet be saved. All that is needed to save this peerless city from collapse and drowning, is money—very large amounts of money—advanced technology and human determination.

Shored-up with hyper-concrete and metal, protected by breakwaters and devices yet unheard of, Venice might yet survive, as in a vast museum, within a bubble of infrangible glass, to delight those who delight in her until the end of time.

Would such a destiny be fitting? Might it not be better, more glorious, more Venetian even, if Venice, rather than become the world's first "international urban amenity park" (I spare you any more of this familiar environmental verbiage), should sink, when her hour comes at last, beneath the sea from which she rose?

No mortal thing can endure for ever. Even that arid, universal culture which deluded liberals dream about, that culture in which Venice preserved would be embedded as a jewel, to be goggled at by regimented multitudes—even that, if it should ever come about, is already doomed to die.

Action now!

No wonder that militant body Action on Smoking and Health (ASH) scorns the new campaign against smoking as a "weak package which makes almost every conceivable concession to the tobacco industry."

No pillories for people caught smoking in public places! No system of rewards for informers who pass on the names of suspected smokers to the health authorities! No ban on smoking in private with penalties up to life imprisonment! No force of uniformed anti-smoking wardens, under the new Ministry of Non-Smoking, with powers to enforce the law at all places and at all times and make summary arrests of evildoers!

"Though accused denied the offence, there was an unmistakable smell of tobacco-smoke in this old people's home. When I found an ashtray, which one of the accused had vainly tried to conceal, that clinched the matter and I arrested all the inmates." "Have you anything to say? Very well. You will all do 20 years hard labour in a smokers' re-education camp."

No, there is nothing of this in Mr Ennals's weak and pathetic statement of new "measures" to extirpate what Pill-frenzied, fluoride-crazed, abortion-conscious Dr Llewelyn Goth-Jones, Director of Community Medicine for Stretchford, has called "undoubtedly the most fearful scourge which has ever afflicted the human race—and that is, if anything, an understatement."

At the very least, Dr Goth-Jones said yesterday, all cigarette-packets should carry the warning "Smoking Kills." If, as he suggested, smoking carried the death penalty, the point could be made even more forcibly.

An old dream

"Electricity Generated by SNO in Mahler." This headline to an item in *The Daily Telegraph* about a performance of Mahler's Fifth Symphony by the Scottish National Orchestra will have reminded many electrical engineers, as it did me, of the old dream of generating electric power by the non-stop performance of Mahler's symphonies.

If this could be done successfully it would provide a comparatively cheap and inexhaustible supply of power which would still be available when our supplies of coal give out and there is no room in the country for any more nuclear power stations if (as some experts recommend) there are to be a few people in it as well.

There are, of course, some environmental objections to Mahlerian power stations (noise, danger to mental health). But with advanced techniques of "screening" and the use of thick concrete casing for the "concert halls," the advantages would far outweigh the objections.

The main technical problem (I cannot go into details in a column intended for laymen) is to devise new types of switchgear and transformers which can be used to feed the current generated by the conductor and orchestra into the grid system.

A small-scale experiment was carried out by the Central

Electricity Board Research Division at Stretchford five years ago. The Municipal Symphony Orchestra was instructed to play all Mahler's existing symphonies (as well as six new ones specially composed by electrical engineers) for 48 hours.

The result was disappointing. After four hours enough electrical current had been generated to provide lighting for the hall and to operate an experimental revolving ashtray in the manager's office.

Then, just as the technologists, eagerly monitoring the experiment, were beginning to shout "Breakthrough! Breakthrough!" and do a ritual dance of triumph, the tip of Sir Jim Gastropodi's baton accidentally came into contact with the rail of his podium, causing a 1,000-volt flash-over which plunged the hall into darkness and blew several 'cellos to pieces.

"Back to the drawing board" was the only too banal and joking comment of the technologists. For the musicians, who had been dreaming of improved status as members of the electricians' union, it was not so funny.

All clear now?

A keen student of columnar affairs writes to me about the "serious territorial reverses" which, he alleges, this column has suffered lately. He refers to a "spectacular" advance to the north at the beginning of this month, followed by a "headlong retreat" which only ended when, presumably in the face of pressure from the east, the column was driven temporarily to the very edge of the Dreaded Western Void before it could be stabilised in its normal position.

He asks whether there is an embargo on news of this "disastrous series of reverses." The answer, of course, is that his whole account of the matter is, as a Directive from the Ministry of Columnar Guidance explained the other day, "a mere chimera."

It springs from a misconception of the nature of the column itself, which has to be regarded as at the same time a territorial, verbal and metaphysical entity.

Thanks to excellent relations with such neighbouring powers as Forthcoming Marriages, Wills, Obituaries and others, the eastern and western frontiers of the column are inviolable. The southern frontier abuts on another part (if such a term is applicable) of the Dreaded Void.

On the other hand the northern frontier is not exactly defined. The wide plains of the north, part stony desert, part rolling grassland, are peopled, though sparsely, by tribes of nomad horsemen and shepherds who from time immemorial have had the right to graze their animals and pitch their *yurts*, or black tents, all over this area. They have a seasonal tendency to push towards the north in search of better grazing, though they may also be drawn by ancestral memories (there is a legend among them that the north was their original "homeland").

Our columnar policy is one of "live and let live." This sometimes has amusing results, as when not long ago a group of these wild horsemen, born in the saddle, suddenly burst into a "forthcoming marriage" party and promptly entertained the guests with an amazing display of equestrian skill. They were rewarded before they left with champagne cocktails, a change from their normal beverage, fermented mares' milk, which they did not exactly relish but accepted with the natural courtesy of their race.

So much for the question of the northern region, its apparent expansion and contraction. The occasional so-called "displacement" of the column to the edge of the Western Void is in fact an optical or "apparent" phenomenon, depending, as Copernicus proved long ago, on the relative position of the observer. It invariably coincides with transits of the satellites of Jupiter.

Discuss

That esteemed journal the *Literaturnaya Gazeta* of Moscow discusses the case of Rudolf Hess, Hitler's deputy, sick unto death and still held in prison at the age of 83.

Why, it asks, should we show mercy to "the man Hitler sent to Britain by plane in May 1941, to persuade the British people to make peace in order to give Hitler the opportunity one month later to attack the Soviet Union without fear of his Western front," a man, it says, among those directly responsible for the deaths of 50 million people?

Why indeed should the Russian Communists, themselves responsible for the death of at least as many people (some of them the same people), show mercy to anyone?

But after 36 years, during which the abominable Soviet régime has survived and flourished to the point where it now threatens to enslave the world, it may at last be allowable to ask whether, if only on the low grounds of expediency, it might not have been as reasonable for this country to make an arrangement with the Germans in 1941 as it was for the Soviet Union to make an arrangement with them in 1939.

We do not know what the consequences of doing so would have been. But we do know some of the consequences of not having done so. Look around you at the world of Now, with eyes for once unclouded; and think.

Bugged

Eavesdropping, whether by normal or electrical means, is disgraceful and dishonourable. However, after long consideration and in the interests of fair play, I gave orders that a "bugging device," as these things are called, I believe, be installed secretly in the panel-beating section of the Boggs Factory at Nerdley, which produces such famous cars as The Boggs Yobbo and the Boggs Super-oaf.

I think the taped results are quite interesting. Here is a short extract, evidently recorded during a "tea break." I have, of course, altered the real names of the speakers . . .

Jim: Good morning, Fred. I wonder whether you have heard the latest news?

Fred: No, Jim, I cannot say that I have. What can it be?

Jim: Well, Fred, our shop steward, Mr Harrison, God bless him, told me that we can expect a new hand to arrive today. It seems he is called Mr Rashid Patel and comes from Pakistan.

Fred: Good gracious, Jim, Pakistan! Mr Patel will be a coloured gentleman, then, I suppose. Not that I ever notice such things myself. It is a man's worth, not his complexion, that counts, I always say.

Jim: I am with you all the way. And so, I am sure, is every other panel-beater in this panel-beating shop.

(General murmur of agreement.)

Fred: Capital. However, it is possible that as Mr Patel has come here to help us from such a distant country, where I am told there are strange sights like lions and tigers and such-like, he may feel a little strange at first.

Jim: Yes, Fred. Mr Harrison says, and we all agree, that we

must make a special effort to make him feel at home. But hush! Here, unless I am very much mistaken, comes Mr Patel himself.

All: Welcome, Mr Patel, to our panel-beating shop. We hope you will be very happy here, and will find the work ineresting and instructive as well as profitable.

Patel: Thank you very much, lads, one and all.

Jim: Would you like a mug of tea, Mr Patel—or may I call you Rashid? These cheese and tomato sandwiches are very good too. My name, by the way, is Jim. And this is Fred, and this is . . .

Patel: Thank you, Jim, Fred, all of you . . . the tea and sandwiches are delicious. They remind me . . .

Jim: Well, now we have refreshed ourselves it is time to resume the panel-beating. I hope you will not mind, Rashid, if I give you a few hints. It is really quite easy, once you know how . . .

As I say, I have altered the names, but it is just possible (though very unlikely) that some of the individual ways of talking may be recognised. I do hope nobody gets the sack.

A strange argument

At the General Synod of the Church of England, during a discussion on sexual ethics, the melodiously named Canon Douglas Rhymes of Southwark asked for an investigation into the world's changed attitudes to sexuality (*sic*), so that a "Church of England viewpoint" could be formed, presumably one more in line with the world's.

He argued that the widespread use of the Pill and other birth control appliances meant that most married people—and, he might have added, unmarried people—"only secondarily regard sexuality as a matter of biological mating for procreation." He believes, presumably, that the Church will have to accept this.

This is an argument which is commonly put forward by progressive Christian verbalisers of all denominations, even the Roman Catholic. It is, of course, utterly baseless.

To argue that the Pill—a mass-produced factory-product—ought to "change" Christian or any other kind of sexual ethics is plainly absurd. What happens, for instance, if the factories which produce the Pill are unable—and such a thing is by no means unimaginable —to go on producing it? People cannot make the thing themselves.

Do Christian ethics immediately change back again? How can technology—and modern contraception is simply technology applied to sex—change sexual ethics in any way?

It is a matter for amazement that so many clerics should unthinkingly accept the idea that as the world changes, so ethics must change with it.

Literary engineering

Ever since "REDSHANK," the columnar Nature Diarist, mentioned that beavers in his neighbourhood had at one time begun trying to build hydro-electrical installations after studying Barstow's book on the subject, hundreds of readers, some claiming to be hydro-electrical engineers themselves, have been writing to inquire about Barstow and his work.

Paul Ohm, the well-known Edgbaston freelance technologist, has written quite an acid letter casting doubt on the existence not only of the book but of Barstow himself. In the intervals of building a nuclear accelerator in his bedroom and boring for oil and natural gas in his dining room, he says, he is constructing a hydro-electric power station in his garden—without, he adds nastily, any assistance from the "so-called Barstow," thank you very much.

I had better set the record straight. S. J. Barstow (1886-1929) was, as far as I know, the only hydro-electrical engineering member of the Bloomsbury Group. "Basil," as everybody called him at Garsington, though his real name was Stanley, was a contemporary of D. H. Lawrence at Nottingham University and later studied at the Slade before realising in a sudden flash of inspiration that his real métier was hydro-electrical engineering.

He had already written the book by which he is best remembered, "Hydro-electrical Engineering: a New Art Form," which anticipated some of the discoveries of Fender and Mactaggart, when Lawrence first introduced him to Lady Ottoline Morrell in 1925 at a combined poetry-reading and electrical engineering demonstration at the Modigliani Memorial Hall in Oxford, now, alas, no more.

An invitation to Garsington followed. Soon everybody was talking about the handsome young engineer who could make sparks of phenomenal voltage fly from his hair at will. Lytton Strachey fainted when he first met Barstow; Keynes declared he was an aesthetic consequence of the peace; Virginia Woolf, fascinated by his talk of coffer dams, wrote a long passage about him, subsequently deleted but now available in a limited edition (Viper and Bugloss, £265) in her novel "The Waves."

Vanessa Bell, at first repelled, also fell heavily for Barstow's "feline-engineering charm" (see "Aspects of Vanessa Bell" by James Crackenthorpe, Vol. 8, pp 2,071-89, Viper and Bugloss, £965·50); Mark Gertler "adored him" ("Collected Letters of Mark Gertler," Viper and Bugloss, £545).

Leonard Woolf was more guarded. His idea of publishing Barstow's book in a new, revised edition had to be abandoned when Barstow demanded, with threats of immediate electrocution, a royalty increase of ¼d per thousand copies. It was the beginning of the end.

Denounced by Lawrence as "a grey, maggot-like corruption of winds, waves and hydro-electrical soul forces," scorned by Carrington, derided even by Lytton Strachey, who had once loved him not wisely but too well, in 1929 Barstow took the only way out: self-hydro-electrocution.

1978

For the dog-lover

This is the week of Cruft's Dog Show. Once again Mrs Morag Ironheart, who breeds Clackmannanshire terriers at her kennels at Brig o' Dread in that county, will be excluded on the ground that the breed is not recognised by the Kennel Club. Once again she will be there outside Olympia demonstrating against this unjust discrimination.

Clackmannanshire terriers, though small, are, as Mrs Ironheart say, "game little chaps." They will bite anyone on sight, including herself, not once or twice, but all the time.

In former days they were mostly used by Scots landowners for evicting tenants. The method was to have the bailiff, or factor, or doer, as it might be, climb onto the tenant's roof and send one or more of these terriers down the chimney.

As the terrified tenant and his family rushed outside another couple of "Clackies," as the peasantry called them, would be waiting. The tenant would, if he was lucky, escape and hasten to secure a passage to Newfoundland (or anywhere else) as soon as possible.

Mrs Ironheart has lately been wondering whether these dogs would appeal to Glasgow football fans as an additional weapon for their armoury, perhaps the most terrifying of all.

But their inability to distinguish between friend and foe would count against them. Glasgow football fans, when bitten, would be more likely than most people to bite the dogs back and even take advantage of their own slightly larger size by eating them.

Talk about laugh!

When you are among Hampstead thinkers and upholders of the liberal consensus in general, there is no surer way of raising inextinguishable laughter than saying that most of the black people of Africa who were formerly ruled by Great Britain and other colonial powers would be only too glad to have their white rulers back again.

Tribal massacres, famine, ruthless dictatorships, Marxist and otherwise, and at the very least corruption and inefficiency have everywhere followed their departure. In a civil war in Nigeria two million people died to decide who should control the oil of Biafra.

Now all kinds of aboriginal terrors are creeping back into what used to be called the Dark Continent. While Hampstead thinkers denounce the White Rhodesians and South Africans for practising "slavery," genuine slavery is re-appearing in the form of forced labour, though of course it is officially described in other terms.

Pirates, once cleared from the seas by the White empires, are coming back, without the romantic trappings which made them popular in fiction but just as cruel and ruthless as their predecessors, and probably much better organised.

It would be laughable, in a nasty way, if one morning, just as a pair of Hampstead thinkers were having breakfast and discussing ways of persecuting the White Rhodesians, a gang of genuine African pirates were suddenly to appear at the window of their tasteful breakfast room.

Norman the Good

Mr Jack Jones, the recently retired leader of the Transport and General Workers' Union, went to Buckingham Palace the other day to be invested by the Queen, in private audience, with the Companionship of Honour. Mrs Evelyn Jones is reported to have said she would not be accompanying her husband, who, she explained, had managed to fit in the ceremony during a free half-hour.

How very accommodating of him! And how very different things will be in the coming days of our Socialist Monarch Norman the Good!

March 20, 2118
Mr Jim Potts, Supreme Chairman of the Turntable Underlookers' Union, was yesterday pleased to receive HSM King Norman and HSM Queen Doreen at Rotation House, London, to confer on them Honorary Membership (Class III) of the Union.

Their Socialist Majesties bowed low before the throne at a simple ceremony of investiture. Later Mr Potts, with high officials of the Union, chatted easily for a full minute with the King and Queen, who were accompanied by Sir Frank Tombs (Brass Stair-Rod-in-Waiting) and by HSM the Queen Gran and HRSH Duke Len of Erdington.

Then an unseemly series of occurrences somewhat marred the dignity of the occasion. Duke Len, who had been winking and smirking in an objectionable way for some time, suddenly beckoned to Miss Tracy Binns, the Canvey Island trainee coiffeuse who is his constant companion, to enter the throne-room.

As Miss Binns, giggling unsuitably, did so, HSM the Queen

Gran fetched her a clout with her outsize, iron-bound Great Handbag of State which, had it reached its target, might well have proved fatal. As it was the Duke, in an effort to shield his protégée, deflected the blow with a bottle of light ale he was carrying, which was smashed to fragments.

The subsequent altercation was cut short when Mr Potts, signalling to members of his Guard of Honour, had the Royal Socialist party hustled from the Audience Chamber and into the State Double-Decker Bus which was waiting outside the Union Headquarters.

The Royal Socialist party, still arguing loudly among themselves, piled in. But owing to a lightning strike of bus drivers, they were immobilised for over five hours.

Now it can be told

As the headmaster of a school in Sweden was discussing "racism" (what else?) with his staff he found that someone had hoisted a swastika flag on the school flag-pole. He reports that some of his older pupils have been distributing leaflets praising Hitler and calling on people to join in the struggle against the Turks, the Jews and the Yugoslavs.

While every schoolboy has heard of Swedish anti-semitism and of the Suedo-Turkish War in the 18th century—a misunderstanding due to anachronistic thinking by the Swedish General Staff and the inexplicable policy of the venerable, hallucinated Swedish Foreign Minister, Count Bengt Axelstierna (1699-1786)—the brief Suedo-Yugoslav War of 1935 is one of the more obscure episodes of modern history.

The purchase of a dud box of Swedish matches by a saddle-maker in Nish on Jan. 4 led to an outbreak of anti-Swedish rioting which spread through the whole country, though the Albanian minority, always pro-Swedish, held aloof.

Soon anti-Swedish rioting in Belgrade began to get out of hand. In March the Swedish Embassy was attacked; several tons of smörgasbord were seized and scattered over the main square of the city. A performance of Strindberg's play "Jerk Asplund" at a Belgrade theatre was broken up by a mob of women screaming feminist and anti-Swedish slogans.

The Swedish Government sent a note demanding reparations. In a stormy all-night session the Yugoslav Cabinet decided to reject it. From that moment war was inevitable. Both nations ordered general mobilisation. War was declared on April 27.

The war itself was one of the most remarkable of modern times. The logistical problems facing the Swedish General Staff, which had of course prepared contingency plans for an invasion of Yugoslavia, were immense, since it would have been necessary either to send an expeditionary force through Poland, Czechoslovakia and Hungary (or through Germany and Austria) or to send the Swedish Navy all the way round Western Europe into the Mediterranean.

None of the countries concerned would have allowed the Swedes passage through their territory, and either operation would have laid the Swedish forces open to a flank attack by the Helvetic Hordes, ever poised for aggression.

In the event the alarmed Powers decided that the best way to defuse the war was to mount a diversion. Mussolini was therefore secretly asked to invade Abyssinia and obliged. In the welter of sanctions, speeches by Sir Anthony Eden and other worries which followed, the Suedo-Yugoslav conflict simply dropped out of the headlines and only a small paragraph in the racing edition of the *News Chronicle* on Dec. 4 told the world that the war was over without a shot being fired.

Further reading: Dr Lars Gammerskjöld: *Sverige-Jugoslavien Kriget* 1935 (four vols., Uppsala University Press, 1963).

White-hot chips

Mr Callaghan's stirring announcement that the Government, encouraged by the fatuous-sounding yet sinister "Think Tank," would give £100 million in State aid to the microchip industry took some of us old folk back to the heroic days when Mr Harold Wilson (as he then was) had us all alternately sobbing hysterically and roaring in mindless frenzy like a dozen Nuremberg rallies with his talk of "the white-hot cutting edge of a technological revolution which will plant Britain's feet firmly on the precipice which leads to the sunlit vistas of eternal prosperity"—or words to that effect.

Mr Callaghan, disappointingly, did not use such colourful language as he spoke of these nasty little objects which are apparently going to change our lives once again. He has not got Wilson's mastery of meaningless verbiage. But he did his best.

He spoke of being on the "threshold of the most rapid industrial change in history." He said we must prepare for it. He spoke of "fear and excitement," of gain and loss, of "feeling our way into unexplored territory," knowing that "the mentality of the Maginot Line is no security," of a "major awareness campaign." The "Dunkirk spirit" was hovering about somewhere.

Well, we all know we have got to have these continual industrial revolutions whether we like them or not. At the moment we are still free to say we don't like them, and I for one am saying it. The next industrial revolution will probably enable the authorities to ensure, perhaps by some chemical agency, that we are not free to say we don't like it; and the next after that will probably remove our capacity to dislike anything we are not authorised to dislike.

In the meantime try repeating to yourself this ancient *mantra*: "In themselves science and technology are neutral. They place in Man's hands innumerable gifts which he (Man) can use either for ill or evil, for disaster or catastrophe."

Christmas at Boggs

I have ordered the "bugging" device I had installed in the panel-beating shop at the Boggs Car Factory at Nerdley to be switched off, or whatever one does to these things, at Christmas.

But if precedent is anything to go by the Christmas party organised by Mr Harrison, the popular shop steward, will be one of the most enjoyable in the country. Both the multi-racialness and the ecumenicalness will be terrific.

Last year Mr Harrison dressed up as Father Christmas, though in deference to Rashid Patel, the panel-beater from Bangladesh, he wore a snow-white dhoti over his robes and had garlands of plastic jasmine and other flowers hung round his neck which Rashid, Jim, Fred and all their workmates pronounced "exceedingly tasteful, if I may say so, Mr Harrison."

The saintly shop steward beamed as he handed out presents to all. By popular request they were of an improving nature: Jim, unwrapping gaily coloured paper, gave a cry of delight as he held up a copy of Samuel Smiles's "Self-Help" for the rest to admire.

"Be sure I shall study it with diligence and close attention, Mr

Harrison," he said. "I have always wished to possess a copy of my own, for it is generally unavailable at the local reference library, owing to the incessant demand."

Fred was equally delighted with his present, a volume of sermons and homilies, "Ecumenical Panel-Beating and its Lessons for the World Today" by the Rev. J. B. Sprout.

As for Rashid, he broke down and wept when Mr Harrison handed him a beautifully bound copy of the Charter of the United Nations Organisation. "Mr Harrison, I shall treasure this wonderful work all the days of my life, and peruse it constantly for the moral improvement it affords. Thank you, thank you, a thousand times! You are sun in my sky, Mr Harrison!"

Then, mastering his emotion, he began to beat some panels. All followed his example and soon the gaily decorated shop, with its glittering Christmas tree and coloured paper streamers, was working at full pressure—nay, the keenness and scrupulous attention to duty were even greater than on an ordinary working day!

1979

Twilight of the Gods

The Chancellor's threat to cut down jobs and spending in local government has been received in the newly built £2,000 million Stretchford Metropolitan County Headquarters with mingled panic and defiance. Some officials, particularly in the rapidly expanding Leisure and Amenities Department, say they will resist by force if necessary.

Work on the £1,200 million annex at Lampton-on-Hoke, designed to accommodate the thousands of officials in the new local Government Officials' Industrial Training Board, has been speeded up so as to present the Government with a fait accompli. Excavation of the underground motorway, with officials' multi-storey car park and "luxury service area," which is planned to link the two buildings, has been started ahead of time.

As the Chief Paper-Clip Controller, Mr Walter Goth-Jones, son-

in-law of the Chief Executive, Sir Herbert Nadir, said yesterday: "Even if the building falls down, burying everyone in the ruins, we shall have made our gesture of defiance against the Tories' wicked and cynical attack on the poor and underprivileged.

"Hopefully, if we go, we shall pull down the whole country with us, never to rise again," he added, as a hint of the closing scene from "The Twilight of the Gods" sounded on the £25 million Muzak circuit, tastelessly recalling a well-known precedent.

Elsewhere in the enormous building, which houses a unique five-tier local government structure, with sixth and seventh tiers projected, there were heart-rending scenes. In a corner of an office in the Public Relations Liaison Section of the Equal Environmental Opportunities Department one young Deputy Assistant Deputy Nature Trail Planning Liaison Officer, Kevin Goth-Jones, appointed only yesterday, was sobbing his heart out, not so much at his own plight as at the thought of man's inhumanity to man.

Days of rejoicing

Not since the Relief of Mafeking has London witnessed such scenes of mass rejoicing as during the last few epoch-making days. As soon as the news of Mr Jeremy Thorpe's acquittal was announced, Londoners poured onto the streets in their millions to give vent to their sheer delight.

For once all classes, their mutual feuds forgotten, were at one in a positive saturnalia of rejoicing—moleskin-trousered workmen from the factories of Hampstead, blazered clubmen and retired generals from the palatial ballrooms of Fitzrovia, many carrying bottles of champagne and traditional cricket bats, emaciated match-girls, portly dowagers still wearing the ostrich-feathers which denote their "debutante" status—all were at one.

Many shook hands, fervently embraced or danced the traditional "congereel" in tribute to the man who has been a popular hero for

Britons ever since he boldly urged, many years ago, that the Royal
Air Force should bomb the universally execrated Rhodesian fascist
rebels into submission.

Bells rang out; rockets exploded; "pearlie kings," as the inhabitants of the South-East End are called, excitedly fired their
"gasoliers" into the air; organ-grinders, hot chestnut dog men, girl
lavender-sellers, Beefeaters from historic Chatham House, sword-
swallowers—all the colourful "types" familiar in the Metropolis
showed their relief and delight in their own traditional fashion.

Ballad-singers and broadsheet men were doing a brisk trade and
here and there among the crowd blind harpists could be seen
playing folk-melodies or accompanying themselves in improvised
eulogies of the man of the hour. A single cornet pierced the din
with the stirring strains of "He's a Jolly Good Fellow."

Intermittent rumours that other popular idols—Lord Harold
Goodman and Baronet of the Garter Sir James Wilson, to name but
a few—had been seen passing through the streets in their
luxurious golden "taximeter cabriolets" roused the crowds to new
heights of frenzy. Indeed, had not a "mushy peasouper" fog,
endemic to the capital at the summer solstice, providentially
descended, reducing visibility to a few ems, they might have got
completely out of hand in an uncontrollable outburst of the well-
known "British phlegm."

Gradually the enormous crowds dispersed. But even four days
after the first outburst of joy, little knots of people can be seen here
and there at street corners, singing, dancing, cheering and playing
traditional games of ludo or dominoes on the pavement in honour
of their hero.

There is an irresistible popular demand that June 22, the day
when Jeremy, as everybody calls him, was acquitted, he made a
public holiday in perpetuity. The Thatcher Junta, already reeling
into difficulties, cannot but realise, in this instance at least, that
the people's will cannot be flouted with impunity.

(*Dutt-Pauker Azerbaijani News Agency*).

A problem solved?

Senator Patrick Flannely of East Carolina said at a Press conference at Grand Rapids, East Carolina, yesterday that he believed
pressure by Irish American leaders to force the British hordes to

withdraw from Northern Ireland would fail because it was on the wrong lines.

"We shall never get these hordes out of Ireland until we start looking at the problem in terms of the British dimension," the Senator said. "We have got to get the British not only out of Ireland but out of England, Scotland, Wales, the Isle of Man, the Channel Islands and other oppressed territories as well. Where they go to is their own affair. They have caused enough trouble already."

Senator Flannely, who has a fair number of Irish and black voters in his state, suggested that a conference be held in some neutral centre such as Dublin in which representatives of all the interested parties in the thousand-year-old problem of the British Isles—the American Irish National Caucus, the Provisional IRA, the African Front-line Presidents, the Zimbabwe Patriotic Front, the World Council of Churches and the International Year of the Child—would take part.

"When the Stars and Stripes, the Irish tricolour and the flag of the United Nations Organisation fly together over King George's infamous Buckingham Tower, where so many brave Irishmen and black slaves were and are immured in torture-chambers which defy description, we shall know this age-old problem is solved.

"Mind you, we should still have to find some other ground on which to carry on the struggle against British colonialism," he added.

Film notes

Piledriver Films' latest offering "Wittgenstein and the Quangos from Outer Space," directed by Brian Hohenzollern (Odium Cinema, Mile End Road, from next week) takes this gifted director's well-loved formula for blood-freezing, thumb-gripping horror a stage further.

This time Wittgenstein, the mad, banana-guzzling semiologist from Cambridge (played by Bruce Braganza) is up against a new and deadly threat to Britain—an invasion of millions of quangos from outer space which are telepathically guided by Wittgenstein's old enemy, the monocled, sabre-scarred Junker Baron Zeppelin von Zwergendorf (Barry Saxe-Coburg-Gotha) who is using laser-type emanations from a mummified Egyptian Pharaoh in the British Museum to direct the aliens to their goal.

Wittgenstein is helped by his blonde, violet-eyed girl assistant (Kay Wittelsbach) and by his old comrade, the bearded explorer and amateur astrophysicist Sir Henry Curtis-Bennett (Stan Bourbon Parma) who first glimpses the quangos, resembling a huge mass of chewed-up cardboard several light hours in diameter, through his telescope at the prestigious Fitzroy Tavern Institute in Cambridge, heading rapidly towards the earth from the neighbourhood of a black hole (Fred Abdul Hamid) at the extreme edge of our galaxy.

Wittgenstein and his friends disperse the threatening mass in the nick of time by neutralising the Pharaoh's mummy with a new type of ionised, mint-flavoured anti-matter the eccentric genius has synthetised in his laboratory. But a few of the deadly quangos manage to reach London and there is an exciting chase through Whitehall before they are finally rounded up and neutralised. The evil baron, escaping in his luxury U-boat, lives to fight another day.

Music by Ted Hapsburg and Bing Karageorgevitch. Fashion advice by Marylou Romanoff. Research by Wayne Porphyrogenitus.

Persecution

Campaigners for "Women's Rights" have been demonstrating against Mr Arthur Scargill, the Yorkshire miners' leader, who has declared himself in favour of the inclusion of what are, I believe, called "pin-ups" in *The Yorkshire Miner,* the esteemed journal which he himself edits.

During a speech he made in Birmingham the other night a group of these viragoes interrupted him continually with mindless slogans, stood on chairs and marched up and down with placards, shouting abuse. Afterwards Mr Scargill said it was the first time he had faced scenes like this but "I suppose from now on I shall face them wherever I speak."

It is impossible not to sympathise with him. Yet in a way it serves him right. Spectral creatures engendered by a special perversion of his own egalitarian beliefs rise gibbering before him, interrupting his speeches, abusing him, following him about and soon, perhaps, haunting his Marxist pillow in forms even more appalling than they can assume in waking life.

As a one-time contributor to *The Yorkshire Miner* under a former editor (I used to write the "City Notes" and hints on antique collecting, and occasionally lent a hand with the crossword), I would like to help this unfortunate man, but hardly know what to suggest.

He could try substituting photographs of some of his persecutors for the "pin-ups" they abhor. But this might mean a drop in circulation except among those few miners whose hobby is teratology.

In Sadcake Park

Lovely sex maniac-haunted Sadcake Park, Stretchford's "iron lung," is, as the Metropolitan Council Department of Tourism puts it in its official brochure, "never more lovely or haunted by so many sex maniacs as in early autumn, when on calm, mist-wreathed afternoons its romantic, tree-girt vistas seem to fall asleep, emitting an occasional melodious snore which only adds to the timeless charm of this unique environmental scene.

"The declining sun seems to catch every gleam and glint from the picturesque collection of discarded objects—bicycle wheels, gas-cookers, bedsteads, all the stuff of social history—which rise from the mirror-like surface of the boating-lake, turning all to sheer ecological magic."

However, things are not as calm as they may seem. The long-standing feud between Mr Bloth, custodian of the leaking boats (Metropolitan Environmental Amenity Officer Grade IV) and Mr R. D. Viswaswami (MEAO Grade III), the naked sadhu who is employed by the Council to live in a specially-built hermit's cave on the island in the middle of the lake, has at last come to a head.

Bloth recently complained to the Parks Superintendent that the hermit was not "doing his stuff." Instead of sitting cross-legged in meditation, occasionally producing "thought forms" for the entertainment of the public, Viswaswami had acquired a television set and seemed to spend a lot of his time watching it.

Bloth also complained that the hermit was in telepathic communication with a betting-shop in Inkerman Road. To judge from the amount of new furniture and fittings in his cave and the addition of a patio, sun-lounge and barbecue-area, he was "making a packet on the horses." Bloth admitted that he had himself intercepted one of these telepathic bets and rushed to the betting-shop to place a week's wages on the horse in question.

It came nowhere. Bloth maintained this was due to last-minute supernatural intervention by the sadhu. His apparent ability to rearrange time and space, the boatkeeper said, would one day "get him into serious trouble." If he were not dismissed for misusing council facilities and replaced by a more amenable hermit, prefer-ably of the mediaeval western type (no Irish) he (Bloth) would consider resigning.

Bloth's threat is, of course, idle. If the sadhu were dismissed he would at once appeal, and with a cast-iron case, to an Industrial Tribunal, alleging unfair dismissal. The fact that both the disput-ants are members of NALGO might cause a dispute which would disrupt local government over a wide area.

Lastly, Bloth's expressed preference for a "mediaeval western-type hermit (no Irish)" might well lead to a massive intervention by the Commission for Racial Equality.

Thought for today

Take the wild flowers which you can see on nature trails or in conservation areas. None of them are employed in the textile industry. Yet even King Solomon in his £1,500,000 luxury home was not nearly so well-dressed as they are in terms of colourful visual impact (from the Bevindon New Testament).

School and community

By the provisions of a new Education Bill a minimum number of parents are to be elected, through fellow-parents' secret ballot, to the governing bodies of schools. Teacher-governors will be elected similarly. This measure, the Education Secretary thinks, will bring parents and teachers together "in an effective forum, forging a closer link between a school and the community it serves."

Asked what he thought of this, Dr Kev Burst, headmaster of Stretchford Comprehensive School, which with 176,273 pupils (estimated) is the largest and therefore the best in the country, gave a loud, rasping laugh.

"If you ask me," he said, "it's just not on. I mean, at our school, which takes in all the former educational facilities of the area, like, a lot of the pupils *are* parents. Some of them—the Darby and Joan Sunset Home lot, for instance—are grandparents and great-grandparents, arn' they?

"What with the forward-looking outlook we have here, we can't tell which are pupils, parents or teachers, can we? I'm not worried, am I? I mean what we got is a real educational mix, with everybody mucking in together, like what it says here in this book I got, NEW SOCIETY.

"We don't need these effective forums and links with the community this geezer Carlisle, the Education Secretary, is on about, do we? Our school *is* the community. And the community is our ——ing school."

As though in proof of this claim Dr Burst pointed through the cracked, slogan-smeared window of his bottle-littered study to an educational amenity leisure area outside, where as night fell a strange kind of battle, swept with confused alarms of struggle and flight, seemed to be going on between groups of ballroom dancers wearing Nazi helmets, Pakistani old age pensioners in punk costume, with outsize safety-pins stuck through their necks, and hefty youths in football jerseys carrying placards marked "Lesbian Mothers' Supportive Unit."

Chaos mystery bid

"Way of the World" Reporter

Once more the black storm-clouds of tension, which threaten to make all that has gone before seem like a vicarage hot dinner, are hovering ineluctably, like Sophocles-type Furies, over the fate-doomed powder-barrel that is Stretchford today.

Once again rumours that Greek shipping millionairess Christina Onassis is contemplating divorce from her Russian-type husband, Sergei Kauzov, threaten to ignite the spark which may trigger off a nuclear-style holocaust among the various fan clubs of typical housewives which, as a police spokesman, obviously under stress, put it yesterday, "are not exactly making our job any easier."

"It was bad enough when our Christina bought that island off Scorpio, with its legendary oil-tankers, last year," says Mrs Dinette Harris, secretary of the Our Christina Fan Club. "Now comes this bombshell report in the big-circulation Athens daily, KATHIMERINI. I say this: I don't know what to think."

Meanwhile, as the destiny-laden seconds tick by, the rival fan clubs muster for the fray. Sawn-off umbrellas are oiled and made ready. Outsize, iron-reinforced handbags are filed and sharpened.

Who will win out? The Our Jackie Kennedy Fan Club, doyen of all these multifarious, colourful groups? The Anti-Our Jackie Onassis Fan Club? The Our Christina Fan Club? The Anti-Our Christina Fan Club, with its bewildering kaleidoscope of Our Sergei Kausov, Anti-Our Sergei Kausov, Revisionist Our Sergei Kausov and innumerable other factions?

Or will the relatively unknown forces which many observers see as the deadly twins behind this tottering façade of human drama—the Our Auntie Artemis Garoufalides Fan Club and the Anti-Our Auntie Artemis Fan Club—intervene with massive effect and, after eliminating all other contenders, reap the ultimate harvest of victory in this Battle Which Nobody Can Win?

A slight error

Owing to a simple mathematical error, it is reported, the size and consequently the age of the universe have been taken by astronomers to be twice what they actually—if the term is allowable—are.

Many astronomers will be upset and even embarrassed by this. But one astronomer who is delighted is Dr E. J. Multimer of Stretchford, leader of the "angry young astronomers" who emerged in the early Sixties to poke fun at what they called the "eternal silence of infinite spaces lark."

At his observatory yesterday Dr Multimer, now in his forties but still just as brash and irreverent about the universe and as much of a pest to girl assistants as ever, was falling about, laughing coarsely and occasionally lashing out with his fists at a wretched comet—possibly poor old Kohoutek—he captured not long ago.

"That'll cut the Cosmos down to size by a few billion light-years," he guffawed. "But this is only the start. Before I've finished with it—I've got some smashing computations on now, as it happens—I'll have the Cosmos reduced to the size of this observatory—in fact it'll be smaller. Then we'll really sort out the supernovas from the white dwarfs! I'll show the Cosmos who's master! Man! Me!"

Prodigy

I reported the other day that Harcourt Globes, 66, of Simferopol Road, Nerdley, had taught his parrot, Woyboy, 42, to repeat a long sentence about Britain's now being a multi-racial society.

Since then Mr Globes and Woyboy have gone on to further triumphs. This remarkable bird can now say "We are all Europeans now," "Government Health Department Warning. Cigarettes can seriously damage your health," "Science has placed in Man's hands immense powers which he can use either for good or ill" and "censorship is the ultimate obscenity."

There seem to be no limits to Woyboy's phatic abilities. But he sometimes gets his sentences mixed up. The other day, when a deputation from the Parrot and Mynah Bird Authority, including its chief psychiatric adviser, Dr Heinz Kiosk, called to see a display of his talents, the parrot screeched out: "European science, obscenity, and multi-racial society can seriously damage your health."

Taking advantage of a shocked silence, Woyboy added: "We are all guilty," infuriating Dr Kiosk who for once had not managed to get it in first.

1980

Memorial

It is proposed to set up a permanent memorial in Whitehall to millions of victims of the Nazis, both Jewish and Gentile. Precisely how the figure of 11 million—that is the figure given—has been calculated I cannot say.

But that is not the point. I do not think this memorial is a good idea. In the first place, whatever the intention, it will serve to perpetuate for ever the notion of collective German guilt. This is surely implanted deeply enough in the public mind already. If not, it is certainly not for want of effort. The notion serves to divert the public mind from other guilty parties.

In the second place, Whitehall is at the centre not of "World Government" but of British Government. It already has a memorial, the Cenotaph, which specifically commemorates the dead of the British Empire and the British Commonwealth in two world wars.

There is no reason why those who want to set up a memorial to the victims of the Nazis should not set one up elsewhere. They will not meet with the sort of elaborate obstruction the Poles met with when they wanted to set up a memorial to the thousands of Polish victims of the Russian Communists, murdered in Katyn Forest.

The Cenotaph in Whitehall should remain alone and apart, a symbol for the British nation. This is not narrow chauvinism; it springs from a feeling that the British nation, whose identity is already threatened on all sides and by innumerable agencies, should at least keep one monument at the centre of its capital which unambiguously asserts it.

Lunatic fringe

With a shock of surprise, President Carter seems to have suddenly realised that it is not a good or sensible thing to support, by selling grain and supplying technological skills and artefacts, often adaptable to military purposes, a government whose leaders have openly stated that they mean to subject all other governments, including the American, to their own odious and tyrannical system.

There are people who wonder why Mr Carter and those who rule the United States do not seem to have realised all this long before. There are people who wonder why (for instance) American grain and technology were supplied to the Soviet Union while it was fighting, by proxy, a war against the United States in Vietnam in which it was eventually victorious.

There are even people who, ranging further back in memory, wonder why the government of the United States should have so lavishly helped the Soviet Union with all kinds of resources in the Second World War and subscribed so whole-heartedly to the idea, obviously fallacious even then, that as well as being an enemy of Nazi Germany it was an ally of the West.

There are even people who, ranging even further back wonder why the government of the United States, at the end of the First World War, instead of helping to prevent the Bolshevik occupation of Russia along with its allies, threw in its hand, encouraged its allies to throw in theirs and thus allowed the Bolsheviks to establish the system which, enduring to this day, has become a fearsome threat to what remains of liberty throughout the world, including the United States itself.

There are people who ask whether all this could have happened by accident or because of the crass, self-defeating stupidity of successive governments of the United States, rather than by some sort of design.

That people who ask such questions must be cranks, neurotics and self-deluding addicts of "world-conspiracy theories" goes without saying.

Victory

Because of the Russian invasion of Afghanistan, thousands of Hampstead liberal thinkers have suddenly discovered that the Soviet Union, whose little faults they have so long forgiven ("after all, in spite of everything, it is a socialist country"), is in fact ruled by old-fashioned militaristic imperialists.

Even at Marxmount, Mrs Dutt-Pauker's fine white house whose tall drawing-room windows look out on the Heath, a chill of doubt runs through the handsome rooms. Fear breathes in the well-stocked Marxist bookshelves.

The greatest of all Hampstead thinkers has seen a nightmare vision: there are tanks on her own broad cedared lawns, wired and sandbagged emplacements among her flowerbeds; rough, alien hands clutch at her treasures, making no distinction between Ming vase, Barbara Hepworth maquette or silver-mounted upper set of Bukharin's false teeth, the gift of Stalin himself. And there are things almost as horrible as loss of property to come. . . .

But like the stalwart fighter and builder of socialism she is, the chairman of Housewives for Peace and innumerable other bodies once proscribed by the British Labour party puts the treacherous vision aside. Are 50 years of work for world peace and higher living standards to go for nothing?

Calm and composed, moment of weakness past, she joins her daughter Deirdre in the morning room. Deirdre, who is busy knitting thick woollen socks, hot water bottle covers and, oddly, Balaclava helmets for the Soviet freedom fighters in snow-bound reactionary Afghanistan, silently hands her mother some balls of wool and knitting-needles.

No need for words. Mother and daughter knit on in perfect misunderstanding. Could even the finest social realist painter do justice to such a scene?

Controversial

Neville Dreadberg, the brilliant novelist, actor, singer, sculptor, poet, multi-media activator and self-publicist, has been commissioned by the GPI Network to write a "documentary play" about the British police.

Due to be broadcast next month (Dreadberg has done several hours' research on newspaper files as well as photographing the outside of a police station). "Monsters in Blue" is sure to repeat the success of his classic documentary television plays "Serviettes of Death" and "Blood Orange," which dealt mainly with cannibalism among the White Rhodesians and Ulster Protestants respectively.

Although Dreadberg's new play touches on cannibalism among the police (there is a horrific scene in a police canteen in South London), the emphasis is on violence and corruption, which are shown to be universal.

The play shows how new recruits start their careers with instruction by police experts in picking pockets; then, as they rise in the force, proceed by way of mugging, handbag-snatching and small-scale breaking and entering to the organisation of major crime-rings. The levels of violence rises correspondingly from minor cases of unprovoked assault on the public to massacres involving thousands of victims on a near-Cambodian scale.

The play ends in a shattering climax: shots of Blair Peach, the Martyr of Southall, alternate rapidly with shots of a ruined, devastated city and of a bloated Superintendent sitting in a luxurious hall furnished entirely with stolen goods, occasionally rising with difficulty from his cushioned divan to beat some captured democrat about the head with the stolen silver presentation golf-club which Dreadberg uses throughout, with consummate skill, as a fascist symbol.

Anticipating controversy, Sir Paul Fobster, chairman of GPI, has already arranged a balanced 15-minute "Hear All Sides" discussion programme to go out at 12.15 a.m. after Dreadberg's three-hour play has been broadcast.

Those taking part include the playwright himself; eleven "broad left" representatives of the media, including Gillian Paste of the Anti-Nazi League, former producer of "Sneer with Mother," Dr Pixie Dutt-Pauker, head of the Social Protestology Department at Stretchford University, Dr Heinz Kiosk, the eminent psychopenologist, Mr Gastriq Ali, the revolutionary leader, and Mr James Thinweed, 79, a retired country police constable who has recently undergone a course of electro-convulsive therapy.

Correspondence

Sir—I see that the Greater London Council, opposing the Government's decision to make Stansted the third London airport, is reopening the case for Maplin Sands as an alternative.

Many of us, who remember that wonderful feeling of sheer joy when the shining vision of a great new airport-city on the barren flats of Essex seemed to beckon us on like a foretaste of heaven, may well applaud this new development.

But should the silly sentimentalists of Stansted, who are once again blindly rejecting the chance of making way for a bigger and better airport, be allowed to get away with it a second time? Will not this encourage all the luddites, neurotics and sinister perverts in this country to oppose essential progress in their own areas?

At the time of the previous controversy about the third London airport, I put forward my own solution—a third London airport at Stansted, a fourth at Maplin, a fifth at Gatwick, a sixth at, say, Exmoor and so on. In the course of time all these airports could be linked up to make one large London airport covering most of the southern half of Britain, adequate for expanding air traffic until the end of the century, when it would probably be necessary to extend northwards, covering the rest of the country.

My solution was not heeded then. Will it be heeded now? Or will the weak-kneed policy of truckling to reactionaries who seem to think so-called "people" are of more consequence than airports triumph again, making us the laughing stock of Europe and the world?

> PAUL OHM.
> Atomdene,
> Edgbaston.

Mystery intruder

What was described as "an ordinary petty squabble between neighbours" led to the appearance at Nerdley magistrates' court of Mrs Betty Tureen, 49, of 63 Kandahar Road, and Mrs Joan

Inkwell, 51, her neighbour, charged with behaviour liable to cause a breach of the peace. Neither asked for any similar charges to be taken into consideration, believed to be a record for the court.

In evidence, Det. Sgt J. Mackenzie, 41, of Nerdley Special Branch, said he was proceeding along Kandahar Road on the morning of Oct. 30 in a routine check for "certain substances" when he heard sounds of altercation.

Investigating, he found Mrs Inkwell shouting at Mrs Tureen over the fence separating their back gardens: "Yes, and another thing: I'll thank you to keep your astral body to yourself!"

He noticed that Mrs Tureen's astral body had "come loose," giving her a blurred appearance at the edges. Part of it was "impinging on Mrs Inkwell's side of the fence" and it was to this that she was objecting.

There were traces of ectoplasm in both gardens and on the roof of Mrs Tureen's house near the gas-vent. But the Kandahar Road area was noted for excess paranormal phenomena and in the ordinary way he (Sgt Mackenzie) would have thought little of it.

When the two ladies, after being warned, continued to shout, causing several horrific thought forms from neighbouring houses to manifest themselves and producing a major hazard to motorists he had no alternative but to prefer charges. Although he was in plain clothes his own astral body, which was of a dark blue colour, with prominent sergeant's stripes, "felt uncomfortable," he added.

Asked if they had anything to say, accused said they were willing to "shake hands and let bygones be bygones," if all entities concerned would do the same. Mrs Tureen added that she had been worried at the time about the loss of an ouija board and was under stress.

Dr F. Gestaltvogel, 61, psychiatric consultant at Nerdley General Hospital, said that although he was willing to treat the two accused in his clinic he thought in-depth counselling with a view to euthanasia might produce the best results.

Binding the accused over, Dr Ellis Goth-Jones, 62, the chairman, said there were puzzling features in the case but he would give them the benefit of the doubt. Growing interest in the Occult, due to a need to fill the gap caused by the decline of orthodox religion, was a feature of the times. But he did not think better facilities for séances in motorway service areas, even with a stricter curb on smoking and gambling, were necessarily the answer.

Writing on the Wall

A reader, who visits Venice quite often, reports that the graffiti on the walls of San Marco airport are, though constantly changing, always in English. The subject matter consists of messages about English football teams and advice on human reproductive processes. Other travellers, he says, confirm that English seems to be the sole language used by European graffito artists.

This is sad and bitter news for those who know the heights English artists scaled in days not long ago when a chosen few disdained the scrawlings of the unwashed too-many and made the graffito a medium both for exquisite graphic design and for the profoundest poetry.

The ultimate fate of the Master of Paddington's masterwork, "Far Away is Close at Hand in Images of Elsewhere"—though some think his lost "We are the Writing on Your Wall," once to be seen in Piccadilly, almost its equal—is still uncertain.

But it is good news that Dr Anita Maclean-Gropius, the chief authority on the Master, is preparing a new and sumptuous *catalogue dérangé* of all his works, both certified and attributed, which will supersede the once respected but now dubious catalogue of Sir Hubert Trout, formerly Keeper of Graffiti at the National Gallery.

Art historian that she is, Dr. Gropius will mercilessly shoot Sir Hubert's work full of holes. Her enemy Dr. J. S. Hate, Keeper of Graffiti at the Victoria and Albert Museum, will mercilessly shoot her own work full of holes in turn.

Whether, as some believe, the Master of Paddington still lives, or whether he is inscribing, on an eternal wall in the Elysian Fields, graffiti more profound and beautiful than any seen on earth, he must be smiling gently at the pygmy controversies of those who can catalogue graffiti but not create them.